THE EMBATTLED MOUNTAIN

F. W. D. DEAKIN

The Embattled Mountain

'Blood is my daylight, and my darkness too'
Ivan Goran-Kovačić
The Pit (Jama)

London
OXFORD UNIVERSITY PRESS
NEW YORK   TORONTO
1971

Oxford University Press, Ely House, London W.1

GLASGOW NEW YORK TORONTO MELBOURNE WELLINGTON
CAPE TOWN SALISBURY IBADAN NAIROBI DAR ES SALAAM LUSAKA ADDIS ABABA
BOMBAY CALCUTTA MADRAS KARACHI LAHORE DACCA
KUALA LUMPUR SINGAPORE HONG KONG TOKYO

ISBN 0 19 215175 4

Printed in Great Britain by
Richard Clay (The Chaucer Press), Ltd., Bungay, Suffolk

This book is dedicated to my wife

CONTENTS

PLATES

With three exceptions all these photographs are reproduced by courtesy of the Military Museum, Belgrade. Those facing page 61 are reproduced through the kindness of Mr. W. N. Armstrong, who took them at Žabljak in 1966; the photograph facing page 173 was lent to me by Walter Wroughton.

MAPS

PREFACE

THIS BOOK has been long in gestation, and has at times assumed elusive and protean shapes. It was my original intention to present a study of the battle on the Sutjeska river in Montenegro in early June 1943 between the main operational forces of the Yugoslav National Liberation Army and the encircling Axis divisions—an operation given the code name 'Schwarz' by the German planners and mounted for the final destruction of the partisan movement of Tito.

The scheme of the original work was drafted as a set piece, in the tradition of national epic, and I engaged in minute research of the events of the operation itself as a classical study in partisan warfare, erupting round the mountain stronghold of Durmitor and raging through the surrounding river valleys and barren crests. The account would be situated in the context of the Mediterranean theatre of the Second World War, and unfold the aims and attitudes of all belligerent parties.

But the quest as an historian in search of the realities and myths of this symbolic conflict, fought out in the isolation of one corner of enemy-occupied Europe, was soon bedevilled and blocked at every turn by the intruding personal memories of the commander of a British military mission, which had been dropped with unsuspecting innocence into the ring.

Every exertion to blend the mental images of a witness with the detached reconstruction of a scholar spent itself in a confusion of disordered riches.

Many such missions were sent into enemy-occupied Europe during the Second World War, and have been the subject of invaluable autobiographical record. It is not my purpose to add, in such a form, another account to a distinguished list.

But I have been driven to garner and harvest the essence of past recollections and impressions, aided by surviving companions, British and Yugoslav, before embarking, on a future occasion, on the professional study planned in the beginning. The present book has thus assumed the lineaments of a prelude to such a work.

The episodes here described took place a quarter of a century ago, and are presented in three deliberate stages.

Firstly, a prologue which evokes the embattled mountain of the story.

Secondly, unclouded by hindsight, our appreciation of the Yugoslav partisans and their daily lives, of the personalities of their leaders, the nature of their military and political structure as seen within the limits of the time of our witnessing and the contours of our wanderings: a simple account of a crisis of some import to a subsequent appreciation of the causes of the final victory of Tito and the National Liberation Movement of Yugoslavia. It is intended to be a fragment of history as seen in the mirror of the moment, an admission of personal involvement, and the evidence of a helpless witness with the sole responsibility of honest recording and without the assurance of prior and learned understanding.

It would be idle and improper to hint at the fiction of an olympian impartiality. We were engaged in an hourly fight for our lives, shielded by the protecting sacrifice of our companions. The core of this record is marked by such memories.

But the concluding and third stage of my account is intended as an exercise in reconstructing, in strictly historical terms, the broad military and political issues which determined our coming: the historian replacing the witness and seeking to set in perspective the decisions of the British authorities to send a mission officially to the headquarters of Tito in Montenegro in May 1943, as the culmination of a series of attempts to contact resistance elements in the country since the Axis occupation two years previously.

I have tried to throw new light on the frustrated vicissitudes of British policy towards Yugoslavia through the history of earlier British missions, piecing together early notes and drafts, and engaging in long hours of disputations and discussion with their surviving commanders. In the absence of official records, I have not burdened the narrative with the impedimenta of formal notes and bibliographies, but have sought a collective and provisional reconstruction of the historical record of these events, which in view of the known post-war destruction of part of the official British archives, may prove to stand in some measure the test of the release of the remaining evidence.

I can only hope to have snatched from oblivion some decisive aspects of British relations with Yugoslavia during those years.

The story is confused by the dilemma of contradictory intentions, by lack of vital and accurate British intelligence of events within Yugoslavia at critical moments. Many myths and mutual suspicions remain to be either dissipated or examined in the light of further evidence.

This book is intended to be an impressionistic prelude to such a study, to incite curiosity, and to serve as a gentle spur to wider controversies.

April 1971   *F.W.D.D.*

ACKNOWLEDGEMENTS

THIS BOOK could not have been written without recalling the history of 'Typical' mission in the company of its two radio operators: Sergeants Walter Wroughton and Peretz Rosenberg. But for their technical skills the mission would have failed and probably disappeared. The pocket diary which the former placed at my disposal made it possible to reconstruct our movements at the time and to recall scenes, and piece together drafts of messages. The latter, in long talks at his farm in Israel, enabled me to record details and bring to life episodes which had passed from my memory.

I owe much to the patient examination of the manuscript and pertinent comment of my friend General Vladimir Velebit, who shared with us the worst hardships of the time, and from whom I learnt more than any Yugoslav companion.

It has been my good fortune to discuss with Colonel S. W. Bailey the historical achievements of previous British missions to Yugoslavia and especially of his own. Our conversations started in 1942, and have continued up to the present. He generously allowed me to consult surviving drafts and personal notes which are vital to the story. I owe a similar debt to Colonel D. T. Hudson, whom I first met in my flat in Cairo after his return from Yugoslavia early in 1944—an occasion marked by a marathon and still unending dialogue.

During the last twenty years I have had occasion to consult many British officers who served on missions both to Tito and to Mihailović. Although we did not talk with the conscious purpose of writing this account, their impressions have broadened its frontiers. The interpretation of events is of course my own responsibility.

Many conversations, both professionally at the time and later as a friend, with my successor at Tito's headquarters, Brigadier Sir Fitzroy Maclean, have enriched the reconstruction of this narrative. I learned much from his second-in-command, Colonel Vivian Street, with his unobtrusive wisdom and invaluable military experience, during our all too short time together. His recent tragic and sudden death is a bitter loss to all those who had the good fortune to know him.

My warm thanks are due to Major Melvin O. Benson, United States Air Corps, Legion of Merit, who came in August 1943 to our mission as the first American officer to be parachuted to Yugoslavia. He has not only read parts of this manuscript, and added details of our experiences together, which bear witness to the unruffled harmony of our relations, but provided me with copies of his reports and material to his superiors at the time.

The Yugoslav witnesses whom I have consulted on the events described in this account are legion. Recollections of many talks with Marshal Tito are central to the narrative, beginning within an hour of our arrival in Montenegro, and ending with a recent interview on the island of Brioni. It would be invidious to mention the names of companions of these troubled times, with whom many debates and discussions have been held. They range from senior commanders, Generals Peko Dapčević, Koča Popović, and Kosta Nadj, to junior officers, commissars, and peasant soldiers; and include leading personalities of the staff of the National Liberation Army at the time: Edvard Kardelj; the late Moša Pijade; Alexander Ranković; the late Ivo Lola Ribar and his father; Milovan Djilas; Vladimir Dedijer, whose diary is still the most valuable single record of those days.

My gratitude is due to my friend General Gojko Nikoliš, the head of the Medical Services of the Supreme Staff with whom I was closely associated throughout the period of our mission, and who has advised me on the organization of the care of the Partisan wounded, which he built with skill and compassion.

During the preparation of this book I have had the unique advantage of receiving unstinting help and much unpublished evidence from the Institute of War History in Belgrade, and its successive Directors: Generals Petar Brajović, Branko Borojević, and Fabijan Trgo. To their subordinates, Colonels Konstantin Popović, Vojmir Kljaković, and Lieutenant-Colonel Vinko Branica I am indebted for their patient and thorough collaboration.

An invitation to a colloquium held by the Institute of Sarajevo in July 1968 on the history of the Neretva and Sutjeska battles gave me the opportunity to meet all those historical specialists, academic and military, working on an exclusive study of the epic of the National Liberation Army.

My appreciation is due to General Idriz Ćejvan, Director of the Military Museum, Belgrade, for his help in assembling many unpublished photographs and placing them at my disposal.

I have benefited from the thoughtful criticism of the text by patient friends: in particular, my former colleague at St. Antony's, David Footman; Alan Bullock, Master of St. Catherine's College, Oxford; John Bell of the Oxford University Press whose detailed comments on structure and style have borne me through moments of disenchantment; and from Peter Janson-Smith and Erich Linder. Miss Angela Raspin, the former head of the Enemy Documents Section of the Imperial War Museum, has been generous of time and effort in obtaining microfilms of hitherto unused documents.

My friend and university colleague Professor Jovan Marjanović has given me valuable advice on numerous occasions.

Miss Anne Abley, Librarian of St. Antony's College, has borne with patience my requests for rare books and documentary material and my debt to her is of long standing. Miss Caroline Bourne and Miss Eileen Dewhurst have brought order into the chaos of the manuscript; to them my sincere thanks.

The Leverhulme Trust has helped me with research assistance in the latter stages of this book, and I would express my appreciation to the Trustees.

On many recent visits to Belgrade I have received many kindnesses and the refuge of warm hospitality from Her Majesty's Ambassadors, Sir Duncan Wilson and Sir Terence Garvey. They submitted with courteous and friendly patience to interminable monologues.

My wife, a relentless critic, has never ceased to encourage me in times when I doubted that this book could ever be written. She shared with me its vicissitudes, and her comments and judgement have been decisive in its shaping.

B

NOTE

IN GENERAL I have used the Serbo-Croat version of personal and place names, with conventional diacritics, rather than an approximate transliteration into English phonetic spelling.

To avoid excessive pedantry, exceptions have been made: e.g. Belgrade not Beograd, Serbia not Srbija.

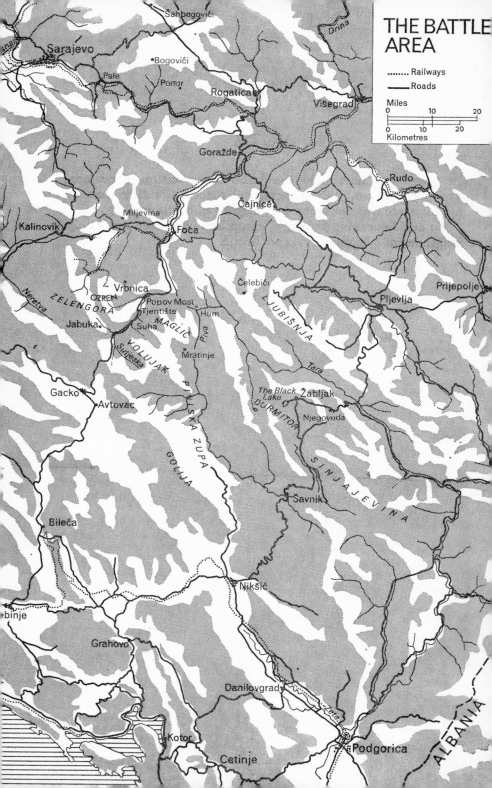

THE BATTLE AREA

.... Railways
——— Roads

Miles
0   10   20
0   10   20
Kilometres

Sahbegovići
Sarajevo
Bogovići
Pale
Portor
Rogatica
Drina
Višegrad
Goražde
Rudo
Čajniče
Miljevina
Foča
Kalinovik
Prijepolje
Vrbnica
Čelebići
ZELENGORA
OZREN
Popov Most
Tjentište
Hum
LJUBIŠNJA
Pljevlja
Jabuka
MAGLIĆ
Suha
Neretva
VOLUJAK
Mratinje
Sutjeska
Tara
The Black Lake
Žabljak
Gacko
Avtovac
DURMITOR
Njegovuda
PIŠKA ZUPA
GOLIJA
SINJAJEVINA
Savnik
Bileća
binje
Nikšić
Grahovo
Danilovgrad
Zeta
Kotor
Cetinje
Podgorica
ALBANIA

PROLOGUE

On 27 May 1943 a Halifax bomber of the Royal Air Force took off at dusk from an airfield at Derna in North Africa. On board were two British officers and four other ranks, embarked on one of many such special operations flown from secret bases into enemy-occupied Europe.

Their mission was deceptive in its simplicity. Operation 'Typical' was to parachute by night in the highlands of Montenegro as the official representative of the British General Headquarters in the Middle East accredited to the central command of the Yugoslav Partisans. The officers, Captain Stuart and myself, bore certain instructions from Cairo, which were committed to memory.

During the previous weeks, two advance parties had preceded us, dropped to points to the north, in Croatia and Bosnia. These men had been selected from Yugoslav emigrants to Canada, and chosen for their local knowledge of the regions where they were parachuted 'blind' after patient study by the Special Operations section in Cairo of all available intelligence, and with the task of finding a Partisan headquarters in an area through which it was known that fighting had passed on to the south. Radio contact with one mission was established within hours, and they reported their arrival at the main command of the Yugoslav Partisan movement in Croatia. The second group was dropped in Eastern Bosnia, but no immediate contact could be established with them. A third party led by two British officers followed on 19 May, and even before their arrival, Cairo had signalled a proposal that a further British mission should be received by the central headquarters of the Yugoslav Partisan command whose whereabouts were unknown.

On 17 May a message reached Cairo, through the mission in Croatia, from the Partisan central command. 'We regard co-operation with the Allies as logical. Let them send a liaison officer to our staff. He could parachute at once in Montenegro near Durmitor . . .'[1]

After a rapid briefing on 20 May our party left Egypt two days later without awaiting further operational details, which would be handled on their arrival by the mission now headed by British officers at the Croat Partisan headquarters. We were to decide on final technicalities at our air base at Derna in Tripolitania.

We merely knew that we were to go to Montenegro. The maps would be studied at our African airfield, which we reached on 23 May by train and lorry from Cairo. A number of messages from the central headquarters of the Partisans awaited us, hinting at heavy fighting in the dropping zone and the surrounding regions where the Germans had thrown in eight divisions. British air support was urgently requested, and a list of towns to be bombed was given, headed by Sarajevo, the Bosnian capital and the main German headquarters. 'We consider this to be in the interest of the Allies.' The Germans were planning to clean up the whole area and to organize the defence of Montenegro and Hercegovina 'against Allied invasion. Send quickly representatives and explosives.'

Although an essential part of our task was to arrange for joint sabotage of the main lines of communications running through areas in Partisan hands, a last-minute decision in London ordered the withholding of any such supplies until our party had made its first reports. A radio message, however, had already been sent from Cairo informing the Partisan command that we should be bringing medical stores.

On 24 May we received the decisive signal from Montenegro. A reception party would be waiting for us on a small plateau near Mount Durmitor on the following night. The British 'must not start later because the Germans are trying to advance with strong forces. In event of bad weather we will wait another night.'

That evening we made our final plans with the commander of the Royal Air Force bomber squadron assigned to such special operations.

Our air crew were young New Zealanders: all were under twenty-one; the captain was a sergeant-pilot. Their brisk and confident precision in our last-minute briefing was infectious.

As we made the final preparations, a signal from Cairo ordered us without explanation to remove from the aircraft the medical supplies, which had already been announced to Partisan headquarters. We were thus to fly into a dimly perceived battle against a common enemy bearing with us no form of aid and with the simple burden of our presence.

According to plan, our Halifax bomber took off the next evening on our plotted course northwards over the Mediterranean.
Weather reports had been favourable. As we crossed high over
the frontier between Greece and Yugoslavia we could see, looking
down from the bomb bay, the lights of enemy transport columns
moving on the roads, but our plane ran into electric storms which
tossed us in a swinging violent course away from our flight path,
over Salonika to the Aegean.

The members of the mission had no oxygen masks, and as the
bomber was forced higher by the weather, each of us lapsed imperceptibly into unconsciousness – unaware that we were being
driven to abandon the attempt to reach our rendezvous.

At dawn, we recovered abruptly. The plane was flying low over
the Mediterranean, all guns pointing upwards, speeding away
from the German fighter base at Heraklion on Crete, and braced
for an enemy air attack which never came. After nine hours in the
air, we landed, without further incident, at Derna.

Prisoners of the weather, we spent the next hours in our tents
on the rim of the airfield, aware of the tenseness of the watching
patrols with the unlit signal fires at the point of our destination.

The air crew received their new briefing. On the early evening
of 27 May we again boarded the same aircraft. In the darkness, as
the Halifax rose steadily in its northward flight, we sank back
among our bundles and equipment into the hum of the engines,
which cut us off from the desultory and disconnected small talk
which springs up in such moments, into a wordless and noisy isolation. Our second trip through the night hours passed without
incident.

We had already adjusted our harness and equipment when a
gap through the clouds and the darkness below revealed a cross
of fires – the prearranged signal on the ground. Our watches
showed that it was just three o'clock in the morning.

The engines of the bomber glided into a quieter note as the pilot
turned, throttling back for his run over the fires. He flashed the
green light over the exit from the aircraft, and with the sharp
downward cut of the dispatcher's hand, we dropped into space.

The whiteness of a parachute was floating level with me, a short
distance away. It was Stuart, and we shouted greetings. The night
was so thick that we could not distinguish the outline of the
ground below. Only bright flashes of gunfire lit the pervading
gloom.

There was a strong wind. Our party had dropped out about two thousand feet above the loftiest and wildest part of Montenegro. We were drifting rapidly down, away from the fires which were cut abruptly from our view by the formation of the hills. A wind current in the mountains took me upwards again. Then, falling rapidly, in complete blackness, I shut my eyes, pressed my legs tightly together, and relaxed, waiting. I hit the ground, gave a gasp, and rolled over in astonishment.

It was too dark to see where I was, or where the others had landed. A few moments of whistling brought the whole party together, each of us filled with surprise that no one had received a scratch. We signalled our position with torches and the aircraft overhead turned in a wide sweep to make its second run to drop our stores. Flashing us a friendly signal, the pilot turned away, heading back towards Africa. There was no sign of the fires and no sound.

Leaving the rest of the party grouped round the heaped parachutes, I set off in a direction in which we agreed the fires must lie, marching with a truculent air and holding a revolver in front of me. In a few moments I collided with a soft human object which emitted a sharp cry in Serbian. I replied suitably that I was a British officer. The figure embraced me with energy, and I could dimly see a tall youth in a worn greyish uniform. He was one of the Yugoslav patrols which had moved out from the fires to look for us. As I led him back the short distance to the spot where our party was waiting, he fired his rifle in the air. Within seconds there were sounds of scrambling feet behind me on the grass. My companions had heard the shot and feared the worst.

It was growing light. We found that we had dropped into a narrow upland meadow, less than a hundred yards broad, and bounded on either side by rocks and clusters of fir trees. We were now surrounded by a small group of young men, all shouting at once. Each was equipped and armed in a highly individual manner, some in a greyish uniform, others in worn civilian clothes of every variety. As we gathered our belongings and started to walk off, a burst of dialogues and questions started up simultaneously. Why hadn't we come before? Where had we come from? How old were we? What were our military ranks?

All this and more tumbled out of the straggling knot of youths scampering along beside us, eager and excited at this novel form of meeting.

Within a few minutes we came upon a broad upland plateau, the prearranged pinpoint for our landing. Stacks of the brushwood signal fires in the crude form of a cross were still smouldering in the sharp light of dawn.

Patrols were out searching for our stores. A tall officer in a smart grey uniform and black jackboots came forward to meet us, and introduced himself as 'Veljko'. He had been sent to bring the mission to the general headquarters about ten kilometres distant.

We paused in a small stone cabin amid a cluster of peasant houses. The only room, and the narrow doorway, were silently crowded with friendly, uncertain faces. In the tradition of Montenegrin hospitality, even at such a moment, bread and plum brandy awaited us on a rough bench.

An escort lined up. Our party set off on foot in single file, cheerfully refusing the offer of horses. We strode with an excess of energy after safe landing. It was still early. The air was clear and crisp. As we walked, 'Veljko' conveyed to us in simple words that the Partisan forces were under severe enemy pressure, at the end of their resources in weapons and munitions, and that the wounded lacked drugs and even bandages.

Our small column was walking along a track leading across woodless open country, with wide fields and clusters of grey rock. In the far distance in front of us spread a jagged range of mountains crowned in the centre by the giant peak of Durmitor – to us as yet a stark word in a recent radio signal – rising in proud domination of the landscape, tipped with snow, above a thick carpet of forest.

We were now approaching a straggling town. Houses lining the single street were gutted and silent. To the right, on a neat mound, was an Orthodox chapel, with its onion spire, standing alone – a symbol of a past victory over the Turks. This hamlet of Žabljak was the centre of the region, and as 'Veljko' told us, had changed hands many times during the fighting of the last two years, and had been intermittently the Partisan headquarters in Montenegro. On the last such occasion they had burnt the town to deprive the enemy of a base, and on the previous day it had been bombed by enemy planes and evacuated by the local garrison. Most of the population had taken refuge in the surrounding hills.

Small groups of peasants lined the street, staring quickly at the group of strangers in unfamiliar uniforms. Many such had passed that way, but it was rumoured that friends and allies were at last among them and there were brief sounds of clapping and mumbled words of greeting conveying to us a note of shy welcome.

We passed beyond the skeletons of buildings, and the path in front of us was suddenly bordered by rich glades of beech trees and bright green meadows. The woods fanned out on both sides, hiding from sight the edge of dark waters. This was the Black Lake, a peaceful splendour encircled by dense trees reaching round to a narrow path which traced a wide circle round the shore. Across the lake, in the translucent air, the mountain of Durmitor, flanked by descending slopes of lesser crests, commanded the scene.

Along the tracks which fringed the edge of the lake came a file of ponies bearing wounded – dummies with hollow faces, wrapped in worn blankets, swaying over the rough wooden saddles of the animals.

We turned sharply into the trees, and 'Veljko' led us steeply up until suddenly we stumbled upon a group of men and women camping in small tents. Girls were moving among them, passing round a meal, and by their dress and manner it seemed, for one unreal second, that we had encountered a skiing party in some mountain resort.

In the centre of the glade, seated on a rough-hewn ring of tree stumps and fallen boughs, we saw a group of armed men in uniform. They rose to greet us. One of them stepped forward, with an air of natural authority. Slim and neat in a grey uniform with no badges of rank, he was wearing an army side cap and black riding boots.

No names had been revealed in the radio signals which had been received from Montenegro before our departure, and the British had no firm evidence of the identity of the Partisan leadership. It was merely known that the commander of the military forces in Montenegro went under the pseudonym of Tito.

The British party halted at attention in front of him, and saluted. We then advanced in turn and shook hands with Tito and the officers surrounding him.

These were to be our companions during the coming months, but our first meeting above the Black Lake was conducted with a formal simplicity of strangers divided by a parachute descent and still poised between two separate worlds.

Bill Stuart and I presented our credentials in brief memorized sentences. Our mission had been sent under the direct orders of the British Commander in the Middle East at a moment when the war in the Mediterranean had reached a stage where the Allies would be taking the offensive. It was desirable to co-ordinate our joint efforts and in particular to enlist Partisan support in attacking the enemy lines of communication running through Yugoslav territory. We had instructions to report on the military situation in those regions held by the Partisans, and to send by radio the views of Tito to our own headquarters in Cairo.

Against a background of gunfire, which had already punctuated our descent, Tito replied in short practical sentences. He welcomed our presence at a grave moment. The Germans had launched an operation to encircle and destroy his main forces in these barren mountains, which lacked food and cover. All tactical dispositions for the passage of the main Partisan units to the north-west had been made before our landing, and the main forces were already on the move. The final orders had been given by Tito to his senior commanders that morning, just before our present encounter, and we had appeared through the trees as this conference was ending. The screen of Partisan units guarding the hills circling the landing ground of Negobudjo now withdrew. Enemy patrols were at close quarters.

Tito and his staff had stayed behind for us. The sense of urgency which had been conveyed to us in the signal which had reached us at Derna was now clear. The brief delay caused by the weather had stretched the tension of waiting as the nearest German units closed in on Žabljak.

The Partisan units ringing the airfield and the group of Tito and his staff were a 'rearguard and the worst fed'.*

Allied air support was urgently needed to blunt the enemy pressure, and with explosives we could concert attacks on the railways and roads bearing the Germans and their allies to the battle in progress, and to Greece and onwards to North Africa.

Together we would discuss such matters.

We then seated ourselves in the circle and each engaged in a casual dialogue with his neighbour, almost unaware of the drama of our encounter. A polite question as to the arrival, together with our party, of the medical supplies which had been signalled, could only be left without answer. We could but stress that other planes were to follow us.

* Tito to the author at an interview on Brioni on 5 August 1967. He also confirmed that it was not correct that the dispositions of the main body were thrown out of gear by the delay in our arrival as some Yugoslav historians have asserted.

In the talk which ensued during the meal which we shared among the tents, Tito asked, with directness and no touch of irony, why the British command had not until now sent a representative mission. Was it because an earlier party under a Major Atherton, which had reached the main Partisan headquarters early the previous year,* had been lost, and did we think that this disaster had been at Partisan hands? Stuart and I answered at once that in Cairo no such interpretation of this episode was held, and that there would be time for talking on all issues between us.

The preparations to receive our mission had been kept a tight secret, and the villagers in the area had been warned severely. Years later they remembered, with a wisp of disquiet, that one night strangers had landed from the sky in the dark. The bleak mountains of Durmitor have their mysteries, lakes where at appointed times devils rise and dance, and snakes appear. Perhaps we in our turn were added to such legends.

For the company awaiting our arrival the task was novel and weighted with grave responsibility. Some of them had spent many weeks nearby early in the previous year, with similar orders to receive a Soviet mission which never came.†

The men had been picked from the Escort Battalion of Tito's staff. They had been told that they were to expect the appearance of a British mission by parachute, and that the secret of their waiting presence and the circumstances of our coming must be preserved.

The reception party moved to the village of Negobudjo. They had received orders as to the construction of stacks of boughs in the form of a St. Andrew's cross which must be lit only when the aircraft, unknown in its silhouette to the watchers, would circle the area. If the fires were kindled prematurely, the Germans would pinpoint them and their fighters on night patrol might bomb them, or, unknown to the Partisans, might, according to previous experience of such British parties, imitate them and entice us to drop on to their positions.

The British plane was due between the hours of ten and two on the night of 24/25 May. The watchers waited in vain. At dawn the stacks were cleared and hidden in the surrounding woods. At

* See p. 156 ff.   † See p. 160.

dusk on the following evening the stacks were placed again on Negobudjo field, a soldier with matches beside each pile.

The men were exalted and impatient. To them the noise of planes had been always a signal of danger. For the first time they were to meet friends from the air.

In the night of 27/28 May, the waiting groups heard the beating sound of engines. Our bomber wheeled in a circle, and shapes of canisters and figures were seen dropping beyond the circle of fires.

The watchers were awaiting tensely the arrival of friends. 'The strangers', as one of the Partisan escort company wrote in retrospect, 'must have felt less sure. The descent alone on to this landing ground and at that hour was not a friendly thing and there was always the possibility that, by some chance, they would fall into German hands.'

Much was expected of us from the first moment. News of our landing spread to neighbouring units, and was discussed in the nightly gathering held by the commissars. We represented a symbolic link with the world outside and our physical presence was a token recognition, breaking the isolation, for the first time, of our new companions.

One of the Croat leaders, Vladimir Bakarić, wrote later: 'The news was heard in the battalions. At last we received what had been long awaited, a great moral recognition of our struggle. We were aware that it would have an enormous effect on the future development of the political situation and the course of the war.'[2]

A warm flood of emotion was released by our coming. As one of the witnesses to our first meeting with Tito put it: 'Amid the fir trees above the peaceful shores of the Black Lake, I had the impression that there emerged, and poured out from all sides, the great truth of the heroic fight of the Yugoslav Partisans.'[3]

Our party took leave of Tito towards noon that morning, and moved to a small hut on the side of the lake, where our stores and radio equipment had been brought from the landing ground.

The British mission was provided with a personal escort drawn from the battalion protecting the Staff.

These soldiers were to be our devoted guards during the coming days. They were the first Partisans to be in our close and daily company; a microcosm of the army units which we would be encountering.

There was the Commander 'Tomo': a young peasant whose

wife and children had been killed. He had no schooling and could not read or write. His stocky figure could be seen at all times, marshalling our ragged company, supervising the unloading of our radio sets at brief halts, and during rare pauses erecting our improvised tents made from parachutes.

'Tomo' was a young man of few words, sturdy, unruffled, and unsmiling. Like his fellow soldiers he was inured to the extremes of hardship and indifferent to danger.

He was killed in a later action.

Among the other members of our escort, there were two boys of fifteen; a teacher of music; and Jagodinac, a Serb carpenter by trade, literate and alert, certain that he was engaged in fighting for a new and better world.

Late that afternoon 'Veljko' came to us with a message from the Staff that we must move at nightfall. We were not surprised.

The woods around us began to come to life with armed men. We handed over our superfluous stores to be distributed by the Staff, and with our escort, and mules bearing the wireless sets and a minimum of personal kit, we joined the moving columns. A drizzle was falling. The forced march which began that night ended some two months later.

Mount Durmitor rises at its highest summit of Bobotov Kuk to over seven thousand feet. Precipitous cliffs in scattered clusters dominate the highland plateau, which towers above the sheer plunge of the river canyons of the Tara to the east and the Piva to the west, protecting on either flank this mountain fastness. There are no tracks leading across the higher slopes, and eternal snows crown the uplands. Save for rare stone sheepfolds and the wood cabins of shepherds on the bare pastures there are no signs of human settlement. But for generations the mountain has been a refuge and its caves and wooded gorges have been the hiding places in dangerous times of the Montenegrin tribes.

This region was now designed by the enemy as a field of destruction of the Yugoslav National Liberation Movement, whose main forces were to be pressed into the rugged barren triangle marked by the gorges of the Tara and Piva rivers and the mountain ranges.

The battle in progress was a race for the heights, and for the river crossings. The line of the Tara to the east, held in delaying actions by the Yugoslavs, was now sealed by German battle groups. The main Partisan forces, anticipating the constricting of the circle in the vital sectors to the west and northwards, were scrambling ahead to hold the Piva crossing and the heights of Vučevo and beyond. The column of the Staff was at the rear of the main body of the army, and the last group to follow the critical manoeuvre upon which Tito was now engaged – the thrusting search for a line of escape from the enveloping pressure of the Germans and their allies.

The crossing of the Durmitor range, during the night of 28 May, was, for the members of the British mission who had parachuted the previous dawn from Africa, an initiation, physical and mental, into another war. Although trained soldiers, we were men of the cities flung in the space of a few hours into the long march of an army inured by instinct and tradition to the strains of warfare without quarter, fought for survival in the cruelty of mountains which would yield respite and refuge only to those who could scale and dominate them with more secret knowledge than the foe.

We were dimly aware of the cold union between the mountain and the army as the column stumbled through a curtain of dense rain and slipped on the rocks and in the slush of melting snow. There are few scratches on the memory of those hours. My radio operator, Corporal Walter Wroughton, had, unknown by me at the time, been concussed on landing, and had no recollection of any incident until the following day. At times we were staggering, and moved only by a conscious effort of will.

The downpour of rain and dense mist concealed our movements from the enemy planes, and the next hours were without history in our column of march. We were heading, with brief halts, towards the right bank of the Piva canyon. In the early hours of 2 June we sought cover in a hillside cave at Barni Do, without food or water. The screen of mist and cloud had lifted, and the Germans were searching from the air throughout the day for the target of the one remaining bridge across the Piva below us.

In the early evening, by a single muddy track hewn in the sheer mountain side, we descended towards the river bank, where in the protecting darkness both sides of the swaying suspension bridge were marked with flares. In their flickering moved the shadows of our forward columns, bunched and sliding in chance groups. There were Italian prisoners among us, stunned with misery and touching in their mute anxiety to serve. Many carried the stretchers of the wounded; others with natural skill coaxed the laden

mules down the invisible track, seemingly as steep as the side of a
great wall. At times a cry and rattle of tumbling rocks sounded the
crashing and mortal descent of a mule or horse or a companion
over the edge of the mountain path leading to the river.

By midnight the Staff, together with a group of the Escort
Battalion and the British mission, had gathered in another and
more spacious cave on the path rising towards the small ruined
hamlet of Mratinje – a scene of hand-to-hand fights in the hours
before. This vantage point controlled the river crossing, over
which a whole army must pass or disperse.

During the day of 3 June, Tito called a meeting of the Supreme
Staff and his senior commanders in this cave. Here it was decided
to split the main operational group into two halves: the First and
Second Divisions together with the Staff to thrust westwards over
the tracks leading to the last river barrier of the Sutjeska, to seek
a breakthrough over the main Sarajevo road and to link up with
strong Partisan forces in East Bosnia; the second group, composed
of the Third and Seventh Divisions, with the prime task of protecting the central hospital with its burden of nearly three thousand wounded, were to struggle back on the paths behind us to
the gorges of the Tara, and fight their way to the east through the
enemy ring now sealed hard along the line of that river and into
the relative quiet of the Sandžak, the region lying between the
borders of Montenegro and the frontiers of Serbia.*

Stuart and myself, together with the other members of the mission, were encamped within the cave in our own allotted corner.
After the conference Tito crossed the floor to tell us the substance
of his decisions.

The nature of the country – at the base of the canyon – the
moves by night and enemy air activity by day made any regular
radio link with Cairo beyond our powers. In snatched moments
our two operators would strive to mount an aerial, often in vain
as when we were on a steep hillside which would form a barrier, or
among trees. But an abrupt order to move, or a sweep of aircraft,
would intervene, and no signals had been dispatched.

At four o'clock on the morning of 4 June the task of scaling the
precipice of the right bank of the Piva confronted our columns.

High above the gorges of the Piva river, which we had crossed

* Together with this group were also some of the political leadership of
the movement elected as the provisional assembly at Bihać in November
1942 (AVNOJ). See p. 36.

Tito and members of his staff

A Partisan detachment: Vicko Krstulović, Commander of the Fourth Dalmatian Zone, in the centre

by the single causeway the previous night, we lay in heaps, dark figures against the white mountain, among the unsheltering boulders and tufts of thorn scrub. Deep below us, in the winding path of the river, the enemy Stukas were diving on the last remaining bridge, which was hanging limply as the only link with those of us, and they were many, still massing on the other side. This rickety construction, vanishing at moments in the spray of exploding bombs, appeared as a symbol hanging between life and death. The Piva was the Styx for the brief hours of that day. On our side, we were pinned in the open. The bare mountain stretching in front of us to the west was no refuge; and behind us, eastwards, to the far side of the canyon, were gathering our comrades on the tracks leading down to the edge where they must cross or be lost.

Through the hours of daylight, above our heads, the enemy planes wove in circles, searching to strike at any sign of movement on the naked and waterless heights.

It was a stage in a sinister race. Beyond the ranges of the mountains, the enemy were constricting a ring of forward units, searching to close the circle around the main body of Partisan forces, lamed by their wounded and the columns of their field hospitals.

It was a race against both time and light. The day belonged to the enemy. The planes, backed by mountain artillery, had the task of trapping our fighting units, blunting their military cohesion, curtailing their mobility, machine-gunning the last herds of cattle and mule trains, tearing at the morale which bound the soldiers to their own wounded by mowing down and pounding the long columns on the narrow tracks.

We lived for the night when the mountain was ours. Each day gained was one step forward. We came alive in the dark, and groped ahead.

On the morning after we had crossed the river, a messenger from the Staff brought us a captured German order. It was a radio instruction from the German commander of the whole operation in course to local units. 'After the successful and complete closing of the ring, the Communists will attempt a partial break-out through the front. Order: no man capable of bearing arms must leave the circle alive. Women to be searched in case they are men in disguise.'

A few hours before the signature of this directive, we had been lying on the sands of Africa, below the airfield of Derna, waiting to board the Halifax bomber which had dropped us two nights before above the mountains which lay to the south of us. The theatre of desert war, with its touch of chivalry between regular armies, was now beyond the grasp of our imagination. During one of the brief halts of the columns, invisible in the darkness, I muttered aloud to myself, 'To think that only a few hours ago we were in North Africa', and a clear female voice answered in French, 'A few days ago I was in a concentration camp.' But this unbridged gap between our experiences meant little in the moment.

In a small space of days we had been buffeted, protected by an evaporating innocence, into an epic now being fought out within a cauldron.* There was no front and no quarter. We had been pulled into a closed and simple world. We had no past and the future would be counted out by minutes.

The pattern of our lives was reduced to a narrow screen of sights, sounds, and sensations. Except in the air, the enemy was as yet invisible to those of us in the column of the Staff. We seemed to be moving across the landscape of the moon, lit fitfully at night by flashes of gunfire and signal rockets. The mountain was hostile and cold, pitted with the craters of steep gorges and trackless rock-strewn wastes, devoid of human habitation except for the rare clusters of the abandoned ghosts of *katuni* – the stone shelters of the shepherds in summer.

This was our stumbling route and our moving battlefield. The troops ahead of us, and on the flanks, were striving for each height and ridge. Each peak must be dominated, and secured in advance of the enemy. Every step was a grimly contested race to the next summit, lost and won in sharp clashes.

Moving at night in silent files, one was withdrawn and empty of thought, but also part of a human company, invisible in the dark, emitting at intervals familiar sounds which broke the loneliness and quickened the vital instinct of the herd. The whispered commands and brief messages passing down each column were the tokens by which we lived. *'Pokret'* (move). *'Odmor'* (rest). *'Nema veze'* (we have lost touch). We moved as the blind, and survival depended on keeping touch. Fear was latent and subtle: its most conscious and pervading image in the mind was the thought of being lost and left behind alone.

---

* The word in the German order, *Kessel*, means literally cauldron and in a second sense a circle of mountains.

At dawn on 5 June the Supreme Staff halted at a group of deserted wooden cabins on the edge of the small grove of Mrkalj klade.

We paused among the trees and set up headquarters throughout the next two days. The commanders of the First and Second proletarian divisions, whose forward troops were pressing against the enemy barrier ahead of us, came to confer with the Staff. The dispositions now taken were the last central orders to be issued for the breakthrough of the main Operational Group of the army. Tactical decisions would henceforth be made by the commanders of each unit.

There would be a grim scramble for the initiative on both sides, seeking to hold the narrowing gap between the enemy ring and the advance Yugoslav units, which lay along the line of the Sutjeska river to the west. Here the final crossing must be forced, the main track leading over the wooded heights of Zelengora on the far bank held, and the German positions, now being hourly strengthened, stormed by frontal attacks.

In the woods near by were now buried the main archives of the Supreme Staff, and those of the Central Committee of the Communist Party.* This symbolic act marked the critical hour.

A further decision was now taken: the order to all units of the Partisan forces to bury or destroy all heavy weapons and equipment. In such a manner all troops were faced with the dimension of the battle now engaged for the Sutjeska crossing and the hills beyond. Only in mobile and isolated groups could the army break out and survive.

At dusk on 6 June the Staff moved to the edge of the mountains dominating the Sutjeska valley. We halted in a forest glade at Dragoš Sedlo, a cluster of wooden huts just below shining white cliffs towering above us to the sky.

At first light, the panorama of the last encounter lay at our feet. Green meadows swept down in front of our encampment, and then fell steeply to the river banks far below. Away to the left, rising almost vertically to seven thousand feet, gleamed the razor-edge of Maglić. At first sight this mountain guarding the southern approaches seemed impregnable and deserted but, as we searched through our field glasses, we saw tiny figures in German uniform crouched round the summit, and soundless puffs of smoke, like a

---

* They were later recovered, and transported to the island of Vis in 1944.

signal gun, revealed to us the menace of this commanding position at the entrance to the valley across which we must force our
final exit.

Along the line of the river far below and on the paths and slopes
of the hills beyond, our advanced battalions and brigades were
dotted in tight pockets cut off one from the other, smashing out as
the more cumbrous Germans pressed in from the south, the west,
and the north dragging in reinforcements along the outer lines
of the fringe of the ring barring the way into the sheltering forests
of Bosnia.

Directly across the Sutjeska in front of us some six hundred
Dalmatians were making a stand to hold the deserted settlements
of Bare against nearly four times their number. If this group broke,
the southern approaches to the Sutjeska would be closed and the
only crossing still open, a small stone bridge near a ruined police
post at Suha, would be lost. The Germans at one moment were
within a few yards of this point.

A message from the Dalmatians reached the Supreme Staff
column as it moved on the path leading sharply into the valley.
They had held a political meeting, and the following numbers
were present. The scribbled pencil figures were a laconic calcula-
tion of the dead.

During the late afternoon hours of 7 June our column halted in
dense woods above the steep descent to the river. The British
mission was able to establish one of the rare radio links with Cairo
since landing. There was time to send our bearings and a brief
hint of Tito's intention to strike out into Bosnia and link up with
strong Partisan forces there. We managed to tap out one message
in haste: we were near Suha and leaving that night for Krekovi
and Vrbnica, two villages in the hills across the river, on the sole
track along which those units of the First and Second Divisions
still grouped close to the Staff could move to the north-west.

It seems that, on 8 June, we received a garbled message from
the commander of the British forces in the Middle East during this
wireless contact and a deciphered fragment was handed to Tito.
'Hold on . . . the Second Front is not a dream . . . Your struggle
will be of even greater importance in the coming months.'[4]

This reached us as an encouraging but distant whisper from
another world.

In the early hours of that day we crossed the river at Suha without incident, and the column skirted the open meadows on the

right bank in the direction of the small hamlet of Tjentište, where the Germans held two ruined Turkish forts in which they were entrenched.

Our column divided and dispersed in the woods in the direction of the main and only path along which we could move as a cohesive body, and which was the scene of grim and swaying clashes ahead of us.

Columns of a Hercegovinan brigade had arrived alongside us, linking up with the main group and strengthening the defence of our left flank, in confused and fierce fighting launched by the Germans from strongpoints marking the closing ring of encirclement.

Among these men was an old peasant who held the highest Serbian decoration – the Karageorge Star – which he had earned on the Salonika front in the First World War. In this present conflict, he had joined a Partisan brigade from Hercegovina, together with his three sons. Two had been lost in earlier actions. In one of the woodland clashes now raging over the whole battlefield, the last of the sons was killed, and the brigade commander bore the news to the father.

Each unit was on the move through the woods, and there was no halt to bury the dead. The body of the son lay covered with branches. As the brigade commander told me later, the old man insisted on addressing his comrades, with the enemy invisible but at hand. He spoke almost gently, and the sense of his words was: 'My son, let the leaves lie lightly on you, I will not weep. That will be for the widows of those whom we are about to kill.'

We reassembled, together with the covering units of the main group, in the thick woods covering the vantage point of Ozren, a steep hill just to the north-west of the Sutjeska, encircled by the sounds of fighting hidden in the woods and on the meadows of the neighbouring hills. The slopes above us were rough, and we clambered upwards with linked hands. As we felt our way, the German patrols could be heard talking.

But they were not the only enemy. Hunger had now gripped the army and the wounded, draining their failing strength and bringing death to the weak and exhausted. The last rations were distributed to the fighting brigades and battalions forming the spearhead of the last assault now being launched against the encircling German positions in their strongpoints on the hills rising to the west of the Sutjeska.

The British mission had arrived with basic food supplies, most of which had been distributed at the Black Lake. Each of us carried what we could, and we also shared the meagre rations of Tito and his staff. These were now a brew of nettles, and our first introduction to this dish was from Bill Stuart: 'Not bad, but needs some salt.'*

Our party itself could muster at this moment a last tin of sardines. It represented a symbol of our mood and circumstances. I was in favour of keeping the tin, determined to believe, in spite of marked signs at hand to the contrary, that we should be alive to consume it on the following day. Stuart disagreed, and prevailed. 'It is better to open it and die with a full stomach.'

The jest proved to be a premonition.

The enemy planes, a motley circus of Dorniers, Henschels, Stukas, and weird flying machines, caught us at dawn in the glades of birch trees just below the summit of Ozren.

In low continuous sweeps along the Sutjeska valley they sought to close the crossing to the second group of the Yugoslav force now trapped between the Piva and the river line just behind us. But the aircraft had also spotted and identified our concentration of figures among the trees on the crests of the surrounding hills to the west of the German strongpoint at the village of Tjentište.

A sinister game was imposed upon those of us caught on the heights. The planes, in low dives, criss-crossed the wood in straight patterns, leaving in each run a neat path of bombs and, at times, the smaller fry tossing grenades from their cockpits.

One could only dodge among the birch trees, seeking cover in an instinctive variety of postures: now rigid against a tree trunk; now crouched among the shattered branches.

On such a bombing run, a group of us was cornered. I had just time to shout to Stuart: 'Take cover; they are using explosive bullets.' † As the explosions darted through the trees, we scattered in the tight space around us: Bill Stuart and a group of officers in one direction; Tito, the commander of his Escort Battalion, and myself in another. The remaining members of the British mission and the Yugoslav Staff dispersed amid the trees. As the last bomb of one stick blew up a few feet from us, Tito, several of his men, and myself found ourselves heaped in a shallow depression in the

* The recollections of Sergeant 'Rose', his radio operator.
† Ibid.

ground. We pulled ourselves out and sought fresh cover from the following wave, but we were not unscathed. One of the commanders of the Escort Battalion and several of his men lay dead; Tito, wounded by a bomb splinter in the shoulder, lay under the body of his Alsatian dog 'Tiger', who had thrown himself across his master at the second of the explosion; and I hobbled out, my left boot blown away, and limping with a slight leg wound.

Stuart was out of sight. He had sought, standing upright, the protection of a stout beech tree, but had been killed by a bomb splinter or bullet in the head. The rest of our immediate party were unhurt. Stuart's radio operator was dazed by the impact of a splinter, which had been embedded in a pack of cards in his breast pocket.

Senior officers swiftly took charge of Tito and with the Staff and members of the Escort Battalion found a cavernous lair roofed with rock. Here, as the air attack mounted in intensity throughout the day, a command post was improvised. At a short distance the British mission, except for Stuart whose body lay on the opposite slopes of Ozren, was trapped on a narrow ledge of rock on an outlying spur. Below was a steep drop into the valley and, just above, the crest of the hill.

The planes, at times flying below our eagles' nest, seemed to gather like vultures awaiting the kill, and the stuttering note of their machine guns was punctuated by the crump of artillery and mortar shells from German positions on the neighbouring heights. For the remaining daylight hours we were pinned down, motionless.

Above our narrow foothold was a line of overhanging rock which shielded us from the bombs and grenades tossed at us from the enemy planes, so that they bounced monotonously past us into the valley below. We had built a shield of stones along the ledge where we crouched, while, in line with us on the far hillside, a German company kept up a fusillade. We watched them sullenly as they moved like brisk dolls in their tidy uniforms.

At dusk Partisan patrols crossed the valley bed and stormed these German positions. A few moments later we passed, and there remained but the stripped bodies of their dead, and a broken pennant of 'The Devil's Division'.

The dark brought respite, and silence. Bill Stuart and others were accorded burial. Over a hundred dead had fallen among these trees and rocks. The air was damp. Clambering for the first time since our arrival on to the mere skeleton of a horse, I rode into the line of march as the darkness engulfed the path which led northwards to the German lines.

Late that night we found ourselves on the jagged edge of the enemy ring. Our column was reduced to some thirty people moving with two scouts in front. A clearing opened suddenly, and a camp fire was burning. German soldiers were pacing round the flames.

One of our scouts knifed the sentry, and we slipped noiselessly and unperceived along the fringe of beech trees.

In another move, the two British radio operators were separated from our party and pinned down by air bombing while attempting to transmit to Cairo. One lay concussed; the other sought to protect him with stones dragged around the wireless set in a thin circle.

A narrow gap had been blasted in suicide actions by men belonging to the First and Second Divisions. The last message from one company has survived. 'We shall do all in our power to hold the Germans. As long as you hear the firing of our rifles, the Germans will not pass. But when there is no more sound then you will know that there are no more communist "proletarians" * alive.'

It was in silence from all sides that, in a column in single file, we moved between the German strongpoints. There were few surviving horses. They were covered with branches and their bridles muffled. Under strict orders not a sound was heard along the line of march. The Germans seemed unaware of our presence. The night had always been ours, and so it was at this hushed moment. But the safety of darkness had been bought at a savage price. Near us, still watching in tight groups, were our troops facing the Germans in their bunkers, and at first light they would, and they knew it, be overwhelmed. At one point two hundred yards separated us from the German positions. We shared with the enemy the limits of exhaustion, and arrived in silence beyond the main encircling barrier upon which the whole enemy operation mounted against us depended. The gap was closed behind the rear of our column by a sudden German reaction, and the last defenders on either side were overrun. Sergeant Wroughton noted in his diary a few days later: 'Passed through the German lines at night, about one kilometre on one side and five hundred yards on the other. The ring closed fifteen minutes after we passed through.'

* The word here has no ideological content. The 'proletarian' brigades and divisions were *élite* troops, and the term is used in this connotation.

Most of the fighters of the First Group of the army, together with the Staff, had crashed the German circle, followed by knots of walking wounded, and leaderless battered companies, separated from their battalions which had been crushed in the last hours.

Behind the columns of the fighting troops and the wounded, or often in furtive and separate groups, were small bands of civilian refugees. They were on the edge of human survival. Many had followed the columns of the army on the long march from the borders of Croatia during the enemy offensive in the winter and spring of the previous year. Some were Jews from the cities who had fled to escape from internment in concentration camps. One old man comes to mind: in a ragged suit clutching an Italian pistol.

These shadows were not bound to us. They were just out of range of our immediate pressures, and in concentrating on our own survival they appeared almost alien; a symbol of chaos from which we were not far removed.

The army itself and the hospitals had already run out of food and water. These huddled groups of civilians were seeking to survive on the scattered entrails of the horses and mules which had been our last resources. At times these figures were a threat to us. At night they lit fires for warmth and would have to be dispersed by force.

The forward troops of the First and Second Divisions were the victorious standard bearers of our survival: Serbs and Montenegrins whose homes were in enemy hands and their comrades from the Sandžak; men of the Bosnian mountains and forests, and from the old Croat military frontier; Dalmatians, whose sacrifice at the settlements of Bare had protected the Sutjeska crossing; Hercegovinans whose villages and families were being exposed to the passage of enemy reinforcements on the outskirts of the conflict.

Ahead, in the plains, lay hamlets and villages, roads and railways, leading to centres of habitation.

Spreading as a stain on the landscape, the surviving Yugoslav brigades fanned out. By a thin and deadly edge they had broken clear of the mountain. The hunted were now the hunters, and they stormed in avenging waves into the villages where new German battle groups from fresh divisions were engulfed in this torrent from the hills.

Our column rode at dusk among the burning peasant crofts and outhouses into the hamlet of Jeleč, pressed together and moving slowly between the fences which bounded the farms and orchards of the village. Along the alleys lay enemy dead and wounded. Their crying revealed them to be of the same race as our men, soldiers of a Croat division under German leadership, thrown into the last stage of the battle to stay the impetus of our rush.

Pity had long drained out of us. Edging my horse among the bodies, a flick of the rein would have avoided the trampling of the imploring shadows. But in our triumphant wrath and the explosion of our release, we crushed them.

Surprise came in retrospect, but with an understanding that, as a stranger, I had taken on by stages a binding and absolute identity with those around me. The cruelty of exaltation was isolated and personal. The memory would fade without trace in the mind. Its cleansing intensity was measureless. The hallucination of riding in a Mongol horde was momentary.

The last move to the roads and railway was but fitfully contested. These were the lateral communications of the enemy divisions, which had been lumbering back and forth during the previous weeks to bar the northern exits from the designated theatre of our destruction. These lines marked a frontier beyond which lay those regions of Bosnia out of the immediate range of the German formations, and held protectively by units of the Partisan Bosnian Corps, refreshed from recent conflicts. Air bombing and at times mortar and gunfire still marked the pervading pressure of the enemy, but also the limit of their mastery.

The column of the Staff and its Escort Battalion assembled in early morning light amid the undergrowth bordering on a stretch of the road from Foča to Kalinovik, already cleared and patrolled in each direction to ensure our safe passage.

At the point of crossing, three light German tanks were slewed motionless and smashed across our path. A few minutes earlier they had fallen victims in an episode which brought laughing relief to our subsiding tension. One young Partisan soldier, not bearing to obey the general order of the Staff to bury or destroy all guns and heavy equipment after the Piva crossing, had nursed throughout the battle a captured Italian anti-tank rifle, unobserved save by the escort company of his battalion who abetted him. He was in the ditch of the roadway at the moment of the passing of a German tank patrol. This Partisan gunner and his companions carried only three shells. Each hit its target in succession, and, as we emerged on to the road, we witnessed the consequences of a rare indiscipline.

Rolling country, patched with woods, swept northwards from the road to the Sarajevo–Višegrad railway, which marked the last barrier across our path. The enemy were again invisible, but their presence manifest throughout the daylight hours by mortar shelling, and bombing and machine-gunning from the air. By night we crouched in pockets, unaware of time, quenching our thirst from the dew on the fir cones, and boiling clover and wild spinach in our mess tins.

In a brief snatch of talk, Tito had urged me to keep the British party within call of his Staff and Escort, but at moments we were lost and scattered by the sudden intrusion of enemy planes flying at ground level along the slopes of the hills and over the trees.

A no-man's-land stretched from those German positions now behind us and, in front, lay the lines of communication along which the enemy were lumbering reinforcements to hold the last exits. The battle had dissolved into a rush of small parties on both sides, undirected and unco-ordinated by any central control or communication.

It was only sixteen days since our arrival and just a month since the opening of the German attack. Cairo knew of our safe landing and had received terse signals from our two sets just before and after the Piva crossing. We had reported on the early evening of 28 May that 'party all safe after lucky drop in dark, and high wind. Excellent reception arrangements by armed and uniformed patrols. Three hours' march to headquarters.' Two days later, a laconic message read: 'Heavy enemy pressure.' On 5 June Cairo was told that we were running hard before the German attack and were abandoning all cattle and horses. The members of the mission were tired and lacked food and water, but all was well. Contact was lost during the next days except for a message from one set: 'Stuart killed by bomb on 9 June. Contact impossible. Air raids all day and walk all night.'

On 13 June scouting patrols had moved up to the main Foča–Kalinovik road, and two Montenegrin battalions blocked any threatened enemy movement to allow the crossing of the main forces. By the following night the main body, with groups of wounded, was safely across to the north.

On that day, after four days of silence, this signal was received in Cairo: 'Have broken through the German ring north across

Foča–Kalinovik road near Jeleč last night. Tito has extricated over ten thousand men. One division left in Montenegro in Piva area. Bitterest fighting witnessed.'

On the afternoon of 16 June, Tito ordered the advance units to hold a narrow sector of the railway line and two nights later our column crossed the tracks, as a German armoured train shelled the railway station at Pale, held by Partisan troops to protect our passage. As my radio operator Corporal Walter Wroughton noted down in his pocket diary: 'Things definitely seem to be improving.'

On 20 June we reported to Cairo that the railway had been crossed, and that some units of the Third Division, which had been left in Montenegro, had escaped and joined us. 'General Headquarters is moving on tonight.'

On the early morning of 22 June, our party halted above the Bosnian village of Medojevići, and at daylight we took up our quarters in the deserted houses.

The time and setting for reflection and analysis, the express purpose of our mission, was near. But, in the moment, hunger and exhaustion engulfed us all.

Walter Wroughton had scribbled after the passing of the German lines: 'No food today. Our main topic is beautiful food. I dream of boiled apple pudding and custard.'

The march which began on the tracks of Durmitor had ended. Across the inner lines of the enemy encirclement, the sector of the ring masking the highway to Sarajevo, where the German Commander of the operation was hourly expecting reports of the successful destruction of the main forces of Tito, had been breached. The cost was as yet to be assessed. One division and the mass of the wounded forming the second group of the army were cut off and were trapped within the closing ring to the east of the Sutjeska. News of their fate and sacrifice trickled out into Bosnia in the coming weeks, borne singly by fugitives and by weary parties.

Faulty German intelligence during the fighting led their command headquarters to believe that those scattered Yugoslav units and columns which had broken out to the north-west did not contain the central command of Tito nor the leading divisions. The Germans were convinced that he and his main forces were trapped to the east of the Sutjeska river.

On 10 June, the commander of the operation, General Lüters, radioed to the staff of the German Mountain Division in that area: 'Strong enemy forces hemmed into very narrow area in Sutjeska-Piva, among them the presence of Tito is for certain confirmed. Last phase of the battle, and with it the hour of the complete destruction of the Tito army has come . . . Tito and staff probably in German uniform, check all paybooks.'[5]

Another German report, two days later, noted: 'Enemy forces, which have broken out, have succeeded in advancing farther northwards.' A marginal note by an Italian liaison officer was more pointed. 'It seems that Tito is in the middle.'

The Yugoslav forces trapped behind us and between the Sutjeska and the Piva rivers were mainly troops of the Third Division, dedicated to the protection of the wounded of the Central Hospital.

The territory between the two rivers was dominated by the mountain stronghold of Vučevo. Here the wounded and fighting units were collected in preparation for a desperate sortie across the Sutjeska. All contact with Tito and the First Group had been lost after a last message on 11/12 June that no help could be expected. Smoke and flames spreading in the villages along the Piva plateau on the far side of the canyon revealed the presence of strong enemy forces. There was no hope of breaking eastwards.

In front, the whole line of the Sutjeska river had been sealed tight by reinforced German units, and the crossing would have to be contested in a savage frontal assault. The Third Division was under two thousand men in battle strength, surrounded by twenty times their number. The Yugoslav commander, Sava Kovačević, a Montenegrin hero in the epic tradition of centuries, conferred with his commanders on the night of 12 June. There was no choice of plan. There could be no direction on a divisional level. Each of the three brigades would fight independently, dividing among them the walking wounded with their own commanders and commissars in military formation, and would strike on their own against the Germans waiting for them in prepared strongpoints and trenches in the woods set back from the river bank, dominating both the heights and the valley.

Small isolated Partisan units were about to attempt a forlorn action, bound in each group to their wounded. Every man able to bear a rifle was armed. The last cattle were slaughtered and rations handed out.

The columns moved down to the right bank of the Sutjeska. The first parties crossed without a shot being fired from the German positions. The enemy were awaiting the kill after the crossing of the river.

Sava Kovačević led his Montenegrins across the Sutjeska, in each group the commanders and commissars in front. The storming of the German bunkers sited between the trees on the narrow woodland paths began. Exhausted men followed their leaders by instinct, but at times slowly, with dragging feet.

The main German positions were dug on the height of Krekovi, and this key position must be overrun if any control at all of the battlefield was to be wrested from the enemy.

Kovačević sensed that the assault must be led in person. Drawing his revolver, he advanced up the steep narrow track between the trees, and turning to shout the battle cry 'Forward, proletarians', he quickened his pace. The German trenches were visible twenty yards ahead.

Suddenly, from the shelter of a bunker, a figure stood up. It was the German commander. He advanced, also alone, with pistol in hand, towards Kovačević, as in a symbolic tournament. Both men fired in the same flash, and both fell dead.

The nearest Partisan officers, close behind, hastily covered the body of their commander with branches to conceal his death from his men, and the troops swept on.*

During the three ensuing days, the remnants of the Third Division, the surviving wounded of the hospitals, held out in iso-

---

* The author has studied this episode on the ground, and talked to eye witnesses. The above version was told to him by one of the Yugoslav officers in the group round their commander. There are others, but they all insist that the body of Kovačević was at once covered by his staff. The Germans were holding a disconnected line of dug-outs and manning machine guns, whose field of fire was out by the trunks of sturdy trees.

According to the recently published memoirs of Vlada Zečević, delegate of the Staff with this division, who was present, Kovačević was leading men drawn from his Escort Battalion and as the column came under machine-gun and mortar fire from the German positions, at some distance on the sole track which led up the hill, he shouted: 'Escort company forward and follow me.' He was almost at once, and some distance from the Germans, cut down by machine gun fire. 'We covered his body with a greatcoat so that the soldiers should not see him.'

The death of Sava Kovačević has passed into legend, and perhaps the precise details are of little account.

lated pockets. At moments they overran the smaller German posts in the woods; clubbing with rifles, ammunition exhausted, hurling rocks, and stabbing with knives, they prolonged the agony. But, combing with precision, the Germans set out on a merciless annihilation.

The badly wounded had been hidden earlier in caves and clefts in the gorges of the Piva, in the first days of June, at the time of the decision to divide the Yugoslav main group into two formations.

The only hope of these men and women was to remain concealed until the Partisans returned to the area or until friendly peasants found them. Almost every small band was left with some weapons and ammunition, and at times, with larger groups, a doctor, or at least nurses, stayed with them.

The Germans, Italians, and Bulgars, advancing from the east, took Žabljak and scaled Durmitor after fierce rearguard actions with units of the Third Division covering their vain final move to the Sutjeska. Cleaning-up operations were ordered, in particular as the task of the Italians. The first search was for the Partisan wounded remaining in the battle area.

The last stand of pockets of the disabled disconcerted the enemy patrols, causing them unexpected casualties. But, one by one, using police dogs and local scouts native to the trackless uplands and canyons, almost every hidden group was discovered and done to death.

One group of fifty wounded from the Central Hospital lay alone and cut off some two miles west of the Piva bridge, which had now been destroyed by the sappers of the Third Sandžak brigade to hinder a further enemy infiltration to the west. Most of the cases were legless, many without arms. Only one man was able both to walk and use his hands. He had been blinded by a bullet.

A party of nurses stayed with their patients, gathering wild clover and nettles, birch bark and roots, for food. These girls carried water daily from the Piva bank, until one morning they did not return. After two days, with mounting hunger and thirst, one legless soldier, crawling from the group, came upon the bodies of the nurses. The rock was too savage, and no grave could be scratched.

A horse was observed straying along the edge of the Piva, and shot with the only rifle remaining within this circle of the wounded. The carcass was dragged up the hillside and dissected. During the next hours, this putrefying flesh was attacked by vultures by day, and wolves by night. The wounded sought to drive them away with stones.

With the killing of the nurses, there were no carriers of water. It was the blind man who now bore on his shoulders one of his legless companions daily to the Piva with a goatskin.

The days trickled slowly. Towards the end of June, two weeks had passed. One morning a rabble enemy band appeared, looting tents and clothing, and leaving the wounded barefoot and many naked. They were followed in the next days by silent scouring patrols on their mission of extermination. One of these halted on the edge of the group, and with the tossing of grenades and bursts of submachine gun fire yet another cleaning-up operation, as listed in the daily reports, was ended. Those wounded who still moved were battered with rifle-butts and sticks.

The blind man lay at a short distance, undetected. He stood up with deliberation. There was no sound save the creaking of heavy boots moving towards him and then a blow and a pistol shot in the head.

The patrol marched off, leaving this group for dead.

For the next two days the blind man lay still but conscious. The rain poured and, as the birds were silent, he thought that a long night was passing. Three badly wounded also survived the massacre. It was the last day of June 1943. In mid-July peasants found them. Only the blind man was alive, and he was taken to safe shelter below the cliffs of Mount Durmitor.*

The killing of the wounded was only part of a comprehensive plan of destruction. The previous pattern of anti-Partisan offensives by the Germans had revealed one major flaw. The military forces of the Yugoslav Partisans would resist in fierce delaying actions, drawing into new regions the pursuing divisions of the Germans and their allies. In due time, the Partisans would filter back into the area from which they had been evicted, and where they had left behind the elements of a political and military organization.

Operation 'Schwarz' was called off on 16 June. During its progress, the effect of the previous Axis offensive in West Bosnia had been effaced by the Yugoslav command in Croatia, who had

* This soldier is now living in an Institute for the Blind in Belgrade. He has dictated an account of this episode, which is published in *Sutjeska* Volume I, pp. 512 ff.

'*Pokret*' : on the march

'*Odmor*' : a pause

Carrying the wounded: December 1942

Typhus: at the Piva crossing

organized the infiltration of units and political and military
leadership back into the 'free territory' traversed by superior
enemy forces. The Partisan troops had been met by a welcoming
population, whose link with the Partisan forces had not been
broken, and by an underground structure of local administration
which had survived the passing storm.

This must not happen again.

The 'free territory' of Durmitor, and the region above which
the mountain towered, must be ground to dust and ashes. It
was not enough to inflict casualties on the military units of the
Partisans and strike at their morale by the slaughter of the
wounded.

The civilians must be hunted; killed if resisting, cowed if passive.
All settlements must be burned, and livestock seized. From the
mountain and its 'free territory' all trace of life must be expelled,
save for scattered settlements of families, terrified into submission.
The Partisans, as an organized force, must not return.

The records of the German First Mountain Division convey
these intentions of the German command. Special orders issued
on 3 June read: 'The whole population in the divisional area capable of bearing arms are to be regarded as communists, and treated
as such. Those in possession of weapons are to be shot . . . All
houses inhabited by communists to be destroyed.'

In the divisional War Diary an entry on 13 June reads: 'Thirteen civilians shot this evening. Two hundred houses destroyed.
Otherwise nothing new.' And on 16 June: 'The Division will ensure that whatever bands eventually return to this area will be deprived of every possibility of survival.'[6]

Moving from the Tara canyon to the east, and through Žabljak
to the Piva plateau, and from Šavnik on the southern fringe of the
circle, German, Italian, and Bulgar patrols and military police
began the search for civilian refugees in these zones. Many villages
were deserted, others burnt in the fighting, some haunted by the
typhus dead.

Secret hiding places, known for generations, housed whole
families and their kindred. Cattle and livestock, the last depleted
herds, were driven to trackless pastures high in the ranges of
Durmitor.

But the work of the patrols was thorough, and precise. Police
dogs or local informers would ferret out the refugees in their caves
and gullies. If identified as Partisan sympathizers, men, women,

D

and children would be shot in batches. Four hundred inhabitants, from four villages, were dispatched in such a manner, and the bodies thrown into a pit. Two hundred and forty in another.

Five hundred were buried by the enemy in the mass graves at Šćepan Polje: workers, students, and peasants from all corners of Yugoslavia – a symbol of the unity for which they had been fighting. Others were scattered in separate places.

In some villages, the aged stayed in their houses. The Turks in past raids were more sparing. The presence of the old men and women seemed to provoke an atavistic savagery in the enemy hunters, and the atrocities spread through many settlements.

Ancient family clans were extinguished. One leader of *Komitadji* * bands from former generations met the Germans as they entered his deserted village below the summit of Durmitor.

'Where are the Partisan houses?' he was asked. 'There are none except mine,' was the reply. 'I have sons and five grandsons; they are all with the Partisans, and two of them killed fighting against you.' The Germans then asked: 'Where are the people from this village?' and the old man answered, 'On the heights.' The German officer leading the patrol ordered the burning of the houses, but, in a gesture of chivalry, placed a sentry to guard this one cottage. [7]

Such acts were rare.

As each terrified group was unearthed, some returned to their homes, but as the Intelligence Officer of the German First Mountain Division phrased it: 'Only a small section of the population wants peace at any price.'

The choice of horrors was wide. In one cave, where ninety men, women, and children huddled together, a German patrol approached within ten yards, without perceiving the entrance. At that moment a new-born baby began crying, and the mother sought to calm the child. The wailing continued, and panic seized hold of the people. A voice whispered to kill the baby, and the mother held out the infant in silent resignation. Even in terror no one had the will to commit the act. The mother strangled the infant. The Germans appeared at the mouth of the cave, shot down some of the aged occupants, and moved on their way.

A child's cradle has remained in the cave since that day.

---

* A general Balkan word denoting irregular bands formed to raid the Turkish garrisons and ambush their military convoys.

But before the last enemy patrols had done their cleansing, small groups of fighters and local leaders were stealing back into the folds of the mountain, to the silence of the Piva heights between the peaks of Maglić and Volujak now held by German Alpine units perched above them.

A group of the Central Committee and Staff for Montenegro, about fifteen men under the Party secretary, Blažo Jovanović, had remained with the last units on Vučevo. Some of the hospital staff were still with them, and members of the Durmitor district committee. Ivan Milutinović had remained as the Supreme Staff delegate.

A meeting of the Regional Committee was held, and those surviving members of the Montenegrin General Staff were picked to set out on the task of keeping alive the decimated structure of the movement in the surrounding districts of Montenegro.

On the Piva plateau German camps could be discerned and captured herds of cattle, the livelihood of the local peasantry. The villages were in flames and the remnants of the population had fled to the secret fastnesses, the refuge for generations, of Golija and Pivska Župa.

Jovanović toured the hideouts urging the villagers not to return to their homes, and ordered his political workers to stay in the district and maintain the presence of the Communist Party.

Milutinović collected isolated fighters from the disintegrating units, and a band of some seventy men was formed in the semblance of a battalion as the core of future detachments to be formed on the Piva highlands.

Vain attempts were made to locate and succour the abandoned wounded in the caves and gorges along the river, and on the ranges of Durmitor.

Precise figures of the murdered, wounded, and typhus cases are not known. But across the battlefield from Durmitor to the paths leading to the Foča road, from the Tara across the Piva and beyond the valley of the Sutjeska to the north-west frontier of Operation 'Schwarz', the Germans counted, with fine precision, 5,697 Partisan dead.

There were few prisoners; they were in the majority shot: in the case of the First Mountain Division, 411 out of 498.

In the district of Durmitor 1,437 civilians were killed: 1,100 in the villages on the plateau above the Piva gorges. The population of the area had been about 11,000 souls. Fifty villages were burnt after the battle.

The mountain was wreathed in the flames and ashes of villages and settlements. The scattered dead lay, spilt in heaps, as if by a giant hand, across this landscape of the moon.

PART ONE

The crossing of the railway marked a frontier in our fortunes. The troops had smashed a corridor through the enemy circle, which now closed behind us with impeccable but belated military precision.

The column of the Supreme Staff had been severed into isolated parties during the previous hours. Tito and his close advisers, together with the Escort Battalion and the members of the British mission, moved in one group, halting briefly in empty wooden peasant houses clustered at ragged intervals on our path. German columns, invisible, their presence marked by sporadic gunfire and searching aircraft, were in pursuit. Their main headquarters at Sarajevo lay twenty miles to the west.

Our brief mood of exhilaration had seeped away. Insecurity dulled our senses, blunted by hunger and isolation. Lack of news of the fate of those behind us deprived the Staff, reduced to a handful, of any awareness of the cost of the fighting.

The main Yugoslav forces in the northern sector of the battle were across the railway by the night of 18 June. On the following evening we halted in an empty cottage in the village of Bogovići, ahead of the pockets of the rear columns and cut off from them.

The silence of the deserted place was broken as a courier ran into the room. He blurted out that the mule train carrying the Staff and Party archives * and the radio set of the British mission,† together with unnamed senior members of the leadership, had been ambushed behind us, and overrun.

Tito put his head between his hands and leant forward on the table. No one moved or spoke. Each figure was shut in a private circle of disquiet.

Noises, muffled but human, punctuated by trampling of hooves, broke the silence round the rough-hewn table where our party sat transfixed.

As we crowded to the doorway, searching in the gloom of the village street, the outline of a strange company in an untidy file appeared before us: a weary escort of soldiers lining a drooping

* The bulk of these documents had been buried on the heights of Vučevo. See p. 15.
† One W/T set had been lost when the mule carrying its burden crashed exhausted over the edge of a steep path.

column of animals. In the centre, a spare form was perched on a horse. Dimly perceived in the dark, one could glimpse a face, crowned by a narrow peaked cap like a medieval archer, fringed by a sharply pointed and defiant beard, whose whiteness shone like a beacon.

The effect of this apparition was startling. Members of the Staff group with us shouted excited greetings; Tito ran forward to embrace the old man, who descended with agility from his horse. I stood aside, puzzled and unaware of the significance of the scene, until a whispered remark beside me revealed the identity of the traveller. He was Vladimir Nazor, one of the leading poets of Croatia, who had left his villa in Zagreb and taken to the woods to join the Partisans.

He seemed to have walked out of the world of Cervantes. Behind his emaciated mount was roped a protesting cow. This, as Nazor told us gaily, was his milk supply. Holding the horse was his Sancho Panza, a devoted body servant, 'Mario' – an Italian prisoner. He had accompanied his master on the long march of the previous year from Croatia to Montenegro and through the odyssey of the mountain battle.

This column had arrived with the archives and our radio equipment. The ambush had failed. Our disastrous mood evaporated as abruptly as it had clouded our company.

Nazor was a member of the 'war parliament', the anti-Fascist Council of the National Liberation Movement of Yugoslavia* which had been set up in November 1942 at the town of Bihać, on the borders of Croatia and Bosnia, as the provisional civilian arm of the Partisan movement.

The British were aware, from radio broadcasts, of the existence of this body. Some of the representatives had met us in pauses of the battle, but the snatches of talk revealed little of their personalities or the background of their fleeting presence amid the clashes with the enemy, and in the columns pressing across the mountains.

Some now arrived with Nazor, and others, in scattered parties, reached Tito and his Staff during the ensuing days, bringing news of their own casualties. Two members had been cut off during the Sutjeska crossing: Sima Milošević, Professor of Biology in Belgrade and a leading personality in the Montenegrin leadership; and

* Known as AVNOJ (Antifašističko Vijeće Narodnog Oslobodjenja Jugoslavije).

Ivan Goran-Kovačić, the Croat poet,* who had joined Vladimir Nazor in leaving Zagreb for the woods.

Milošević had been wounded earlier and hidden near the village of Vrbnica on the western edge of the Sutjeska, and Kovačić stayed with him. Both men had been discovered, and killed by local Četniks.

Nurija Pozderac, the leading Partisan personality among the Moslems of Bosnia, had died of wounds near Dragoš Sedlo, in the glades where we had halted before crossing the Sutjeska.

The reconstruction of the 'naked army',† the surviving units of Tito's main forces, called for every improvised resource to be mobilized: arms and ammunition, clothing and food. Discipline must be restored with ruthlessness. A 'free territory' must be formed, and defended against hostile penetration and a new encirclement.

The first step was to maintain a striking force on its feet.

The arrival of our mission had aroused expectations of British aid at a moment of supreme crisis. Before our descent the Partisan command had been informed by radio that the British sought their co-operation in attacking the enemy lines of communications. The requests made by Tito for explosives for such actions, and for the air bombing of enemy garrisons and bases, were considered premature in view of British official support and recognition of Milhailović and were countered by a more neutral offer to send medical supplies, which were withheld at the last minute.‡ 'Typical' mission parachuted from a single aircraft, bearing no gifts.

Within two days of our landing, on 30 May, a signal had been sent by us, in restrained terms. Partisan strategy was hampered by the wounded and by the lack of food, equipment, and clothing. 'Not much progress with detailed planning can be made until at least one medical sortie can be sent.'

The care and protection of the wounded in guerrilla warfare has always been conditioned by the human reactions of the enemy to the conduct of war. The very nature of Partisan fighting reduces

---

* The author of the poem 'The Pit' quoted on the title-page of this work.
† A phrase of Mladen Iveković, a leading Croat member of AVNOJ, whose memoirs *The Unruly Land* present a moving image of these days. See p. 55.
‡ See p. 221.

the antagonists to the primitive elements of human behaviour, beyond the range of formal conventions of military discipline or rules of war. The instincts of the hunter and the hunted are bared, creating a tense and instinctive climate of human relations which in turn reflects on the general conduct of guerrilla war itself, and the strategy of its repression.

In the long tradition of warfare between the Montenegrins and Turks, the notion of the brotherhood of warriors, and the call to supreme sacrifice in the defence of the wounded, was deeply rooted in the national epic.[1]

The bond between the fighter and his stricken brother lay at the heart of the fighting morale of resistance, forming a political and moral unity. The Partisan rising against the German and Italian occupation armies in the autumn of 1941 marked a total rupture of this implicit code of Balkan guerrilla war. From the outset the enemy embarked on a policy of deliberate extermination of the wounded and sick as an effective weapon against the fighting morale of the rebel bands, striking at its roots. In the daily bulletins of the German and Italian units the killing of the wounded is reported as a military success.*

The traditional cult of 'the care of the wounded' was thus intensified and narrowed by German action. The concept of humanity, rooted deeply in the Montenegrin epic, was obliterated by the enemy. The fate of the wounded and sick now became a pervading and often decisive element in the planning of the Yugoslav Partisan leadership. Their protection impinged upon the direction of resistance at every phase, and in every region.

The conduct of Partisan warfare, by its nature, was dependent on mobility and concealment, and this in turn created the shape and nature of the medical organization of the movement. There was no static front and no rear area where base hospitals could be set up. Temporary 'free territories' were held and organized, but the military need for sudden moves, and often long marches, imposed a correspondingly special and novel medical structure to succour and protect the wounded.

The first medical staff was formed in Serbia in early September 1941, on the territory briefly held by the 'Užice Republic'. Tito placed at the head of this infant service a young thirty-year-old doctor serving with a local Partisan detachment, Gojko Nikoliš.

---

* For example, Bulletin of the Italian Fourteenth Army Corps 16 June 1943: '150 wounded (and sick) partisans killed, who could not be removed.'

He was the son of an Orthodox priest from Croatia. He had graduated from the Belgrade Medical School in 1936 where he had been closely associated with the local Communist party. The following year, he joined the International Brigade in Spain, and took part in the Ebro battles as a medical officer. After internment in a French camp he had found his way back to Yugoslavia at the end of 1940. Quiet in manner, iron in will, and with outstanding gifts of improvisation and imaginative resource, Gojko Nikoliš, backed by a devoted team of doctors from the enemy-occupied cities, mobilized a novel construction – the medical services of the National Liberation Army.

'The care of the wounded' became a branch of Partisan war and an operational factor. Wherever regional units formed, small hospitals were set up, and the wounded dispersed in them in remote places. In Montenegro, the first centre was organized in the tourist hotel at Žabljak by the Black Lake at the foot of Mount Durmitor.

By February 1942 members of this medical staff joined the Supreme Staff in Foča in Bosnia. In the forests of Slovenia hidden camps were constructed with ingenious skill, in deep glades away from roads and tracks. In mid-1942 a model hospital was set up, and never discovered, at Kočevski Rog, where ten thousand wounded and sick were treated during the course of the war.[2]

In the Srem, along the Danube, where the country was open and exposed to main lines of communication, hideouts were dug underground to serve as local hospitals: the first in May 1942.

As the rebellion spread throughout Yugoslav territory, and the mobile operational group of Tito with its *élite* divisions expanded, so the tasks of the medical staff widened.

The establishment of the 'Tito State' in West Bosnia and Croatia, with its mountain strongholds of Grmeč, Šamarica, and Petrova Gora firmly held and fortified against the enemy across the lines of approach around the circumference, produced an embryo political and military administration on a territorial base. It also created a certain illusion of stability and a temptation to static organization. There was no alternative base, and a dangerous over-concentration.

A network of hospitals was constructed in the mountains and at the end of winding forest paths, drawing on the experience of neighbouring regions in Croatia and Slovenia, and improvised with inventive imagination. This protection against hostile patrols, especially those formed by Četniks and Ustaša with local knowledge of the terrain and by tradition familiar with guerrilla tactics, and against the routine menace of air reconnaissance, became an essential branch of warfare.

The sites of the hospitals and the approaches to them were deftly camouflaged, often defended by specialist units trained in counter-intelligence, on permanent alert, and by now a special target of the enemy and their auxiliaries. These created special units with trackers and dogs to penetrate within the 'free territory'. The danger was all-pervading and constant. Shepherds were a peculiar risk with their wandering flocks in remote places, who might report on suspect traces. Approaches to hospitals were blocked at intervals by barriers of logs and brushwood. Footprints were obliterated daily, and, in winter, covered with fresh snow. Sentinels were posted, and patrols moved, through the surrounding areas. Self-defence groups were formed and armed within the hospital camps, often from the lightly wounded themselves.

One scene is described by a New Zealand military doctor, Lindsay Rogers, who was later parachuted into Western Bosnia:

We started out for the hospitals, and within ten minutes were in the shade of the great pine trees, the tallest pines I had ever seen. The track seemed to be an old unused road, and along the sides the moss grew green and thick, like a silent carpet, covering the huge stones which lined the road and formed the forest floor. After walking the forest road for almost an hour our guide stopped as though searching for something among the small trees on the roadside. We pushed our way through the low undergrowth, covering our tracks with dead branches, and then found, leading off at right angles on the stony forest floor, a series of stepping stones. He carefully turned each stone over, exposing its bare side for us to step on, and so we crossed from one to the next. Then, as we passed, the mossy surface would be turned back again so that no sign was left. Thus we went for fifty yards until we were well screened from the main route, and our track started again. This method of conspiration was repeated several times, and then another method adopted. After a moment's searching, we stepped into a clump of weed and found two parallel tree trunks, long and thin, leading through the hidden greenery. We walked along these and then stepped up on to an above-ground ladder. This was a series of tree trunks either sus-penced from the lower branches of trees or else supported on built-up rocks. My eyes were now well opened to the absolute secrecy which surrounded their hospitals. For over a hundred yards we crossed this

overhead bridge and then came down to *terra firma* again. Here we met
a lonely 'tovarish' standing, rifle at his shoulder. When we had crossed
he greeted us and then set to work to take down the bridge. When he
had finished the tree trunks were completely hidden by moss and
leaves; no sign nor noise nor track would lead the way to where the
wounded lay hidden. It was all very elaborate, and they told me that
since they had adopted this system of conspiracy not one hospital in this
forest had been found.[3]

The recent wounded themselves were often led blindfolded
along the secret trails.

At the beginning of 1943, the Germans and the Italians mounted
a series of large-scale joint operations to destroy this central
enclave of the Partisan movement, and as the encircling pressure
developed, Tito and his Staff were faced with the gravest decision
of the war. For the first time, and henceforth, the fate of the
wounded became a strategic and operational factor.

They were dispersed in hidden settlements over a wide area,
with supply depots in inaccessible places, at times over-concen-
trated in an ideal site, and now present in the middle of a territory
threatened by military operations, and implanted in the midst of
their own units.

Their security, in face of the operations of the enemy in January
1943 against the whole territory of the 'Bihać Republic', was a
central subject of sharp debate between Tito and his Staff. The
main body of the wounded would either have to be left in the forest
hospitals of Bosanska Krajina, the areas of Western Bosnia, along
the historic Croat military frontier, or transformed into mobile
groups which would encumber and impede the long march of the
main forces to the regions to the south-east of the 'Tito State'.

It proved to be the hardest and most fateful decision taken by
Tito during the whole war. For several days, 21 to 30 January
1943, Tito and his main advisers hesitated. The northern areas of
the 'liberated territory' of the old Croat military frontier where the
hospitals were scattered was not a 'safe' region if the Partisan
forces withdrew.

The only solution was to move all the wounded together with
the army. The shape of the battle ahead would now be conditioned, and at moments dictated, by the protection of the long
columns of the hospitals. There was no alternative safe territory
where their main body could be hidden.

As Tito put it, in an interview after the war: 'We were sur-rounded by the enemy and it was clear to me that the care of the wounded constituted a heavy moral factor for the army and the movement as a whole. The order sounded out: to save the wounded at all costs.'[4]

The main body of the sick and wounded were collected from the hospitals scattered throughout the territory of the 'Tito State', and protected along the fiercely contested route of the long march of the army from Bosanska Krajina to the borders of Montenegro: an odyssey of suffering over five hundred kilometres in ninety days.

Each hospital was a separate world, organized on military lines with its commander and political commissar, under the direction of the medical section of the Supreme Staff, headed by Nikoliš, exposed at every stage to the vagaries of tactical moves and the encompassing menace from abruptly changing angles of hostile assault.

The barometer of danger was erratic. Brief halts of relative calm, as between 6 and 12 February on the high plateau round the small town of Glamoč, were followed by crowded columns blocked on narrow snow-covered tracks at the mercy of the enemy planes and artillery, awaiting the storming of German and Italian garrisons as at Prozor and Gornji Vakuf, and the final nightmare of the crawling slipping haul over the trackless and precipitous wastes of Mount Prenj.

At this moment of crisis Tito considered the desperate step of detaching the wounded under escort north-westwards to the abandoned region of the Lika where local Croat Partisan units had infiltrated back and might form a thin protection.

But the frontal assault on the bridge and crossings on the river Neretva in the last phase of the whole operation released the imprisoned tension of the crowded groups of wounded on the eastern slopes of Mount Prenj and the plains of Hercegovina lay open before them.

Three thousand wounded had been brought from the forests and mountains of Bosnia out of reach of the pursuit of the German and Italian divisions, with their Četnik auxiliaries, and the specialized assassins of the Ustaša brigades, to the territories in Hercegovina and on the borders of Montenegro, thinly held by demoralized local Četnik bands, and Italian garrisons crouched in small towns on the main roads.

Most survived, but the cost was grim: the simple agony of the long march convulsed by typhus, breaking in infectious misery the fighting structure of the whole Seventh Banija* division and one Dalmatian Brigade.

But a revolution had been achieved. The morale of the army was shown to be dependent, in an intimate and mutual bond between the fighting Partisan and his wounded or sick comrade, on its ability to protect the defenceless and to preserve the unity and order of the whole main body under operational conditions. A large group of wounded as an integral element of an army on the march had been transported long distances under unfavourable battle conditions without affecting thereby the tactical ability of its units. During the first phase of the operations the wounded had not been a direct physical burden, nor had their presence affected the conduct of the battle, but, as the routes narrowed to the Neretva crossing over the mountain wall of Prenj, the increasing numbers of sick and wounded, the breakdown of transport, slowed the whole rhythm of the move.

This experience gained in the Fourth Offensive was noted by the Germans.

After the Neretva crossing in April 1943, the main body of the wounded forming the Central Hospital moved unmolested eastwards across Hercegovina to concentration points on the heights above the Drina, astride the borders of Montenegro and the Sandžak.

At the beginning of May, they were disposed in three hospitals: Number One was housed around the villages of Šćepan Polje and Rudine where five hundred badly wounded cases were brought, some on stretchers and others on horseback; Number Two settled near the hamlet of Hum where four hundred sick and severe typhus cases were isolated; and Number Three, containing the main group of the convalescent wounded and the more fortunate survivors of the typhus epidemic – about 2,500 cases – was concentrated in the area between the Drina and Ćeotina rivers, and on the heights of Ljubišnja.

Each division and brigade had also formed its own medical service averaging one hundred and fifty cases in the former, and

---

* Banija, one of the areas of the old Croat military frontier, lying between the districts of Kordun and Posavina and the lower reaches of the Una and Kupa rivers.

fifty in the latter, unit, and caring for about another thousand unattached sick and wounded.

The following weeks were spent in meticulous organization, drawing on the experience of the recent operations, and in preparation for inevitable movement in the days ahead.

The scant medical supplies evacuated from the 'free territory' of Bihać had been exhausted during the long march from Bosanska Krajina.

During the previous winter, a special organization had been created and a central dispensary set up at the town of Bosanski Petrovac, in the 'free territory' of Bihać.[5] Bandages and drugs had been collected at great risk by party workers in occupied towns such as Zagreb, in collusion with local chemists. Ambushes on enemy convoys and raids on isolated garrisons provided another intermittent source. But no stocks could be built up.

The suddenness of the enemy launching of the first 'Weiss' operation in Bosanska Krajina in January disrupted the whole medical structure of the 'free territory'. The main hospital on Grmeč mountain lacked transport to move even their meagre supplies which, with the exception of bandages, were buried. The central dispensary was evacuated from Bosanski Petrovac as the German tanks entered the town, and joined the main columns.

The brief halt of the wounded at Glamočko Polje had revealed the complete dearth of medical equipment. Tito intervened personally. Stocks of linen were captured and cut into bandages. Valuable medical stores, including surgical material, were found in the Italian depots after the storming of Prozor, but this was lost in the air bombing of the transporting lorries. The remaining stores were carried by soldiers and peasants on their backs – only three horses were available to the hospital columns at this stage – in the march over the grim obstacle of Prenj mountain, but this lack of transport prevented any further move of these remnants across the Neretva, and the last stocks were buried on the left bank.

Some medical supplies were captured in the Hercegovinan towns of Kalinovik and Nevesinje, and 'illegal' stores in small quantities were filtered out of Sarajevo. Italian medical equipment had also been captured but, in all, there was a perilous shortage during the brief pause of April and early May in the three hospitals which had been set up.

The Central Hospital, under the control of the medical section of the Supreme Staff commanded by Nikoliš, was quartered in the villages on the Piva plateau under two doctors: Dr. Herbert Kraus and Dr. Miroslav Slezinger, both of whom were recovering from typhus.

Each of the three hospitals was now an organized and completely independent unit, with its own command and supply columns, divided into companies and battalions ready to move at short notice.

Special attention was directed to party work among the wounded, and a special team was headed by Vladimir Dedijer, a former journalist from the Belgrade newspaper *Politika*.* His wife, Olga, was in charge of one of the surgical units in the Second Proletarian Division.

The team moved ceaselessly through the villages where the sick and wounded were grouped, holding meetings and enrolling Party members. These would strengthen the Party cells as they returned to their units, tightening existing human bonds.

A Medical Bulletin was issued in four roneoed sheets, the first number appearing on 12 May. Food supplies were organized, drawing on the wheat and cattle from the rich farming enclaves of Northern Montenegro and the Sandžak. Basic courses in hygiene were held, especially for protection against typhus.

By the beginning of May, the main hospital, Number Three, housed some two thousand wounded in the villages round the small town of Čelebić which had been destroyed in previous fighting.

The hospital consisted of thirteen battalions organized on a military basis. Each unit bore a name: 'light', 'convalescent', 'typhus', each with its own staff. Party workers were active, and political meetings were held, where readings and lectures were given. Apart from propaganda, these workers formed a link with the supply staffs of the army and were responsible for the feeding and clothing of the hospital.

Fighting commanders paid frequent visits to their own wounded, making them feel part of their unit, to which they would return. General Koča Popović of the first Proletarian Division came to one such battalion of wounded, and rebuked the staff for the inadequate protection of the approaches to the area. Even in deep forest there was no security.

The three hospitals were dispersed over a wide upland area

* See p. 60.

E

divided by the River Drina, which as it formed the frontier between Montenegro, the Sandžak, and Serbia was a line of strategic
importance and inevitably an early target for enemy activity.

Special precautions were taken for the defence of the region of
the hospitals, entrusted in the first instance to the experienced
troops of the Seventh Banija Division, who had fulfilled a similar
task during the recent enemy offensive.

The interlude of calm was closing. The enemy garrisons along
the Drina at Foča and Goražde were being reinforced, and probing to the south along the paths dominating the river valleys.

On 16 May the Supreme Staff issued urgent orders: all the
badly wounded were to be concentrated on the plateau of
the Piva or Number One hospital at Rudine. The lighter cases
were to be assembled on the high country around Čelebić to
the south-east in villages along the right bank of the Tara.

The medical staff assumed that this directive was issued in order
to protect the wounded in case of a firm enemy threat from
Foča. In fact the order formed part of the plan evolved by Tito
to break through with his main forces across the river Lim into
Serbia. Contact with Tito's headquarters was maintained only by
courier, and it took twelve hours to send a message from the
Central Hospital to the Supreme Staff, who themselves were as
yet unaware of the German preparations for the 'Schwarz'
operation to encircle the whole army and repeat, with improve-
ments, the plans of annihilation which had failed to achieve their
aim in the recent cycle of 'Weiss'.

The medical staffs were as yet unaware of the trials ahead. On
17 May troops of the Seventh Division, by forced marches, arrived
on the heights round Čelebić and picked up seven hundred
convalescent typhus cases. On the same day began the general
evacuation of the remaining sick and wounded to the south-east.

Enemy activity flared up abruptly, first in the shape of local
attacks. The medical staffs and the wounded could hear the noise
of bombing and see planes flying overhead. But they did not
know the full significance of these sounds.

On 21 May the Germans attacked the hospital at Hum, and the
wounded there were moved under fire across the sheer cliffs down
to the Tara, and beyond to the appointed refuge of Šćepan Polje.
Unaware of the general pattern of the spreading menace, confused
in mind by lack of news, in low physical condition, many of
these men and women died on the perilous tracks across the Tara

gorges. It was a prelude in miniature to the fate awaiting them all.

By 22 May, the whole of the Čelebić base had been emptied, and come under direct enemy assault. This was the first intimation of the offensive, which was confirmed by the journey of the commander of the Central Hospital, Dr. Kraus, on the same day in search of the whereabouts of the Staff in the direction of the bridge at Djurdjevića Tara. He met the staff of the First Division moving northwards towards Foča. They had been the first unit to assess the extent of the enemy plans, discerning to the east the presence of the German First Mountain Division in direct clashes with these troops.

It was now apparent that the main body of the wounded could no longer be moved to the south-east, and a return across the Tara to the Piva highlands would be unavoidable. This plateau, between the two rivers, was bare and narrow, exposed to air bombing and artillery fire, and barren.

The First Proletarian Division was withdrawing from the Sandžak and the immediate plan of the Staff was to probe in force towards Foča in the hope of breaking through at this point before the enemy could strengthen this sector of the general encircling ring.

On 29 May, Dr. Kraus reported: 'We know nothing of the general situation, but we gather that we are on the verge of a major move, and we need a clear picture. Here, in the district of Žabljak, we now have about one thousand wounded.' [6]

The headquarters of the Central Hospital was at a small village a few miles to the north, without food or transport. On the same day the last groups of wounded had crossed into the area from the right bank of the Tara.

On the afternoon of 28 May, Tito and his Staff had reached the Black Lake at the foot of Mount Durmitor on the northern edge of Žabljak. Here the decisive operational plan was worked out—to attempt a main break out westwards across the heights of Vučevo which guarded the southern approaches to the region, across the Sutjeska valley to the wooded slopes of Zelengora.

The Central Hospital was ordered to follow the same route, and no alternative proposal was discussed that evening. The only transport available for about two thousand wounded was about one hundred horses, and between two and three hundred Italian prisoners as stretcher-bearers.

One thousand wounded had already been returned to their units. Further casualties in the latest clashes increased the numbers in the hospitals to 2,200, who were now roughly classified as 1,088 capable of walking, 575 who should be 'horsed', and 137 stretcher cases. These were divided into groups, each with a political commissar in charge.

In spite of the devoted efforts of the medical staff to prepare for an organized evacuation in event of a new enemy offensive, arrangements were dwarfed into impotent fragments by the savage nature of the terrain. The Piva plateau had been already the scene of fighting against Četniks and Italians in the previous year. No food could be collected from the half-deserted villages. Local Partisan committees were no longer able to buy any supplies, as firmly instructed, on a voluntary basis from the peasants. The region had been a Četnik stronghold and, smelling disaster, many of the villagers who had stayed on their farms turned hostile to the Partisan authorities and obstructed the attempts at forced requisitioning. The essential link between the local population and the main body of the army, drawn for the most part from other territories, did not exist.

In human isolation, the troops and the wounded were encased in a grim and closed world of their own, haunted by a new and demoralizing enemy – 'the ghost of total hunger'. The last herd of cattle, which in April had been driven up to the plateau from the Sandžak, had been slaughtered. The last remaining rations were distributed to the fighting units, and the groups of wounded. During the first days of June, fifteen to twenty deaths were recorded daily in the hospital columns.

By 3 June the plan for a central evacuation of the wounded had to be abandoned. Only three surviving doctors were working with the medical section of the Supreme Staff. The silent column of the disbanded hospitals stretched, in dumb anticipation, for fifty miles across the naked heights between the rivers.

A brutal decision was taken. The serious casualties were to be hidden in caves and undergrowth on the steep slopes of the Piva: the lightly wounded were to be escorted by the Seventh Division to the north-west, and the remainder, who formed the main group, were to be protected by the Third Division, who were ordered to force a passage to the south-east back across the Tara to the Sandžak.

Movement began on the night of 4–5 June, and in the succeeding fateful days all central direction evaporated. The road to the Sandžak was closed. New wounded from the units were reaching the Central Hospital daily. The orders of the Supreme Staff could not be carried out, especially in hiding the badly wounded in the Piva caves. There was neither time nor the essential contact with the local population. In a phrase of Nikoliš, 'there were only the convulsions which precede death'.

Within hours it was clear that the Third Division group could not storm the Tara crossings now firmly held in superior strength by the enemy. On 6 June the divisional command received orders to turn back and join the first group now engaged in a battle for survival along the Sutjeska and the heights beyond.

Under air and artillery bombardment, the Third Division stumbled back to the mountain base of Vučevo with one thousand wounded. About the same number had been abandoned in clusters among the gorges of the Piva. Many of the nurses stayed with them; a few were armed to fight a last stand.

The night of 8 June was the worst of the war. The tracks were blocked by stretchers and these cases were abandoned to their fate. In one unit the numbers of troops and wounded could be counted only by the sections of bark torn from the beech trees for food along the mountain trail.

To the north, and still waiting on the eastern slopes sweeping down to the river Sutjeska, the Seventh Division, together with seven hundred walking wounded and its own field hospital, prepared its own assault on the river crossings. At dawn on the following day, in hand-to-hand fighting, these units forced their passage. The divisional hospital and one group of the wounded were cut off. Another section was captured and slaughtered, and few crawled to the temporary shelter of the positions of the Third Division on Vučevo.

Just as at the Tara, the Germans now sealed the last crossings over the Sutjeska and only scattered units of the Third Division, with a tiny band of surviving wounded, forded the river on 13 June. The bulk of this group dispersed in isolated bands to fight it out with the enemy columns closing in from the east and south. Small parties reached East Bosnia, Hercegovina, and Montenegro in the following weeks.

Of the wounded hidden in the Piva caves and gorges, a few were rescued by local peasants, the others killed by enemy patrols and Četnik bands. The Germans inflicted the main slaughter on the Sutjeska and in the woods to the east. Here also the badly wounded of the Third Division were killed.*

Of the original column of the Central Hospital of over two thousand sick and wounded, about nine hundred to one thousand survived and reached East Bosnia. They were protected by troops of the First and Second Divisions, who had carried through the final break out, together with the Supreme Staff and those who had escaped massacre in the rearguard action of the Seventh Division.

Of the medical staffs, thirty doctors were killed – half of the total cadres – and two hundred nurses who had stayed with the abandoned wounded and suffered their fate.

The structure of the Central Hospital, assembled with devoted care between the two enemy offensives, had crumbled away. During the savagery of the fight, the medical staff and Tito's headquarters were linked only by couriers, each journey taking six to ten hours. The hospital groups were trapped in aimless moves on rock-strewn trails, obsessed by the fear of losing touch, one with another, in the swaying columns, unaware of the changes in orders from the Supreme Staff with its agonizing dilemma of preserving tactical mobility which inevitably implied the progressive sacrifice of the wounded. The order to leave behind the serious cases came too late, and the desperate moves on the spot had but a symbolic value. The tracks were filled with evidence of movement and led the enemy patrols with ease to their victims.

But the tradition of sacrifice by the fighting units to preserve their stricken comrades held throughout the battle. The brigades of the proletarian divisions, most of whom were far from their home territories, carried their own wounded to the end. The sorely tried Seventh and Third divisions, to whom the columns of the Central Hospital had been entrusted, were decimated in their task.

But the interval between the two enemy offensives since January 1943 had been too short to enable the medical section of the Supreme Staff to create a firm local structure for the Central Hospital in Montenegro and the Sandžak, regions which had been areas of Četnik influence over a long period and not as yet effectively cleared by the Partisan forces.

* See p. 27.

After the battle the surviving wounded, without food or medical supplies, were huddled into the forest glades of East Bosnia, where the British mission encountered them.

The dispatch of medical supplies from North Africa was, as we were deeply aware, a desperate and urgent priority. The needs were all embracing: medical stores, arms, food, and explosives. Our signals listed them.

No immediate point of reception for supplies could be fixed. In the daily scramble our radio contacts were intermittent, and merely reported our movements. There were intervals of silence. In the offices of the British headquarters in Cairo little impression could have been conveyed of the scenes which we were witnessing. A summary of signals would barely indicate that Tito's forces, under air bombardment, encircled by a superior enemy, were striking north-westwards from the mountains in the direction of Bosnia, lacking food and water, and burdened by wounded. By 14 June it was known, from a laconic signal, that some ten thousand Partisan troops had broken out, and had reached the edge of Bosnian territory. The death of Bill Stuart on 9 June had been reported through the courage and technical brilliance of his W/T operator Sergeant 'Rose', under conditions of peril.

On 17 June the following signal from 'Typical' was picked up in Cairo. 'Chance of wrecking Sarajevo–Višegrad: Sarajevo–Brod railway. Immediate request for explosives.'

At that moment we were bunched along the southern edge of those tracks which we crossed the following evening. The significance of this signal had some impact in Cairo and London. Behind the bald phrases lay the essence of the Partisan tactics. The momentum of their rush must be propelled. Survival depended on preserving mobility and superior speed, and striking at the enemy concentrations. If the Germans could move re-inforcements along the concentric lines of the railways, and build a second trap, the remainder of Tito's forces would not survive. The cutting of these communications was the only chance of avoiding disaster, and of gaining time to re-form the shattered and exhausted units now grouping in the Bosnian forests.

The request for explosives was also a hint of unbroken morale. We could not convey the harsh reality of our plight.

I discussed these matters with Tito and his staff. We were still in the area of the village of Bogovići, and having recovered our radio equipment, contact with Cairo was steadied.

In our dulled weariness, I sought to convey to Tito and his Staff an optimism that aid was on its way. The members of the British mission were bent on this sole purpose.

As one of our Yugoslav companions described a conversation with me, I told him that 'the first consignment will be drugs and medical supplies, condensed food, explosives to mine the railways, and, if possible, clothing'.

In an exchange of radio signals with Cairo, the planning of the first air sortie was fixed.

Our party was moving daily. The surrounding villages of Eastern Bosnia were in the main Moslem and hostile. The small towns in the area were held by Ustaša units and local Moslem militia. Troops of the Croat army of Pavelić, together with German elements, garrisoned the main centres. Part of the Serb minority had rallied to Četnik bands. The German command was reinforcing its bases immediately to the west and based on Sarajevo, mounting a fresh assault.

In the confusion, we moved in seemingly aimless circles, pursued and bombed by enemy planes and seeking safe harbours for a few hours.

The British party was busied with the technicalities of air sorties. We had only two sets, upon which the execution of operations depended.

On 23 June a pinpoint had been fixed for that night near the village of Medojevići, where the Staff and the mission halted, as Wroughton noted, 'in great expectation'.

But, as with our own arrival, the first sortie was a failure, and we sensed a latent feeling of disbelief on the part of our Yugoslav companions that the British had any serious intention of ever producing material support to their cause. We were linked by a tenuous human bond of mutual confidence, by our sharing in the dangers and trials of the recent weeks, but undefined suspicions on their part were to obtrude from time to time. This was such an occasion.

There could be no waiting, and no explanation of the erratic moves of our column. Another dropping zone was signalled to Cairo, ten hours' march to the north.

On the night of 25 June a Halifax bomber made the first successful supply drop of explosives. We lit the signal fires and the aircraft dipped low overhead discharging its cargo of containers with their parachutes.

The consignment represented the full load of an aircraft—seven containers and six packages. These consisted of a small supply of explosives, a much needed spare W/T set, and some bandages, but still no food or other medical equipment.

The atmosphere among our party was polite but restrained. That evening our column marched into the small town of Olovo. The garrison of local Moslem militia had fled, and we found a pleasant settlement of empty and undamaged houses. The area was a centre of timber mills, and the deserted villas of the engineers and managers created a momentary illusion of a peaceful world.

Tito moved into the well-stocked house of the local *hodja* (Moslem priest). We dined in an appropriate manner. The arrival of one plane was a signal at least of our good intentions, and the evening was relaxed.

Ahead of us lay a larger town – Kladanj – with a strong Ustaša and militia garrison, encircled by Partisan units of the Second Division.

That night we left Olovo, moving northwards, and during our march the assault on Kladanj had been launched in fierce hand-to-hand fighting.

A new pinpoint in the area had been signalled to Cairo. We halted on the outskirts of the town, and were joined by the mission of Canadian Croats, led by Stevan Serdar, which had been parachuted 'blind' into Bosnia in the previous April.* They had witnessed the confused events in these regions during the past two months, and were bearing valuable information. But there was no time for conference or to celebrate our reunion.

The second sortie was due the following night. Radio contact with Cairo was clear, and our concentration keyed.

In the evening, the Partisan Staff and the British party moved into Kladanj. The town had just been cleared after sharp resistance, and was scarred by the action. The streets were lit by burning saw mills, and strewn with the dead: broken dolls with red fezzes.

An enemy counter-attack hastened our departure in the morning, and forced us to withdraw to the surrounding hills just out of range of a squadron of tanks emerging on the southern outskirts of the town. The daylight hours passed in the beech forests, which surrounded an empty cluster of houses marked on the map as Plahovići.

* See p. 1.

Our radio links were strengthened by the addition of Serdar's mission. This warmed the professional instincts of our operators – Wroughton and 'Rose' – and the cheerful and confident company of the three members of this early group relieved some of the strain and anxiety which we shared. Wroughton noted:

'This show will soon be a pretty big concern. Will have three W/T sets and 16 batteries. There will be lots of work to do.'

That night a Halifax bomber dropped one load with the first consignment of medical stores and some rations.

The supplies were meagre, but the sortie indicated that an air ferry service could function with elementary regularity in spite of the abrupt and – to us – inscrutable meanderings of Tito and his Staff.

The technical difficulties of holding a safe clearing in the broad belt of forests between exchanges of signals with Cairo, which then had to be relayed to the British air base at Derna, interrupted the rhythm of these operations. But we were in the midst of a battle to master the region of Eastern Bosnia in cruel clashes of rival formations. The territory was nominally part of the Independent State of Croatia, and held despairingly by its armed forces with the Germans massing on the western edges.

It was a sinister game of hide and seek, in which regular W/T listening and schedules must be kept. This task could not be improvised. Crouching in deserted villages at night, and hiding in woods from Dornier bombers by day, every chance was snatched to bring in an air sortie.

At times Wroughton and myself would have to stay behind on our own to maintain the radio links with the Middle East at the appointed schedules. On one occasion a battle of wits with a solitary German Fieseler Storch lasted throughout a morning, the pilot seeking for signs of movement in the abandoned houses of the village street mounting steeply up a hillside into the woods above. As we lay face down on the floor of the upper room of a Moslem house, we could glimpse the tiny German aircraft flashing past the windows, or below them.

Spread-eagled on the floor, Wroughton was in radio contact with Cairo. During one pause the enemy pilot flew over the hill, and I decided to make a cautious reconnaissance. Before I could emerge from the orchard of the cottage, the plane was skimming the trees in a straight path at ground level back down the narrow street. I fell, unobserved and headlong into a wooden Moslem privy in the garden, and crawled, malodorous and shaken, back into the house. Wroughton was still lying by his set, bent on his task. He was not unaware of my presence for long.

Having completed the planning of the next sortie, the two of us walked at dusk to join the main party near by in the woods above the village.

The following night a British aircraft dropped one load of stores.

One waited at times in vain; alone, in a forest clearing or meadow, with a small Yugoslav patrol as escort and reception party. On occasions we would hear, even see, our aircraft, which would miss our signal torches and fail to pinpoint us. On other nights the Germans would imitate our fires. These were visible to us across the neighbouring hills. We could only hope that our pilots would fail to locate them.

On an evening in early July, the main party of the Staff and the mission were concealed in the woods about a settlement of houses—the village of Brateljevići, a few miles to the west of Kladanj, which had been recovered by the enemy.

A tight untidy pattern of sudden moves, between the protecting trees and the empty hamlets, constricted our daily lives in a confined space, mental and physical. Lying among the trees our operators picked up a B.B.C. broadcast. The Allies had landed in Sicily. A ripple of excitement among the weary company roused our spirits and invaded our introspective meditations. Tito sent a bottle of plum brandy to the mission across the narrow clearing which separated the two 'headquarters'. The implications of great events and speculations on the Second Front, subjects of daily conjecture, were still beyond the range of our immediate anxieties.

I spent the enforced idleness of these hours in conversation with Mladen Iveković. He was a Zagreb intellectual and an early member of the Party organization of the Croat capital during the 1930s. Recently he had been exchanged, in negotiations with the Pavelić authorities, and released from a concentration camp.

We spoke together in French in friendly and easy discourse. I was troubled and impatient. The daily and to us aimless marches made our task of fixing dropping points a precarious gamble. I told Iveković of this.

We seemed to be moving towards the strategic point of Vlasenica, the small town which commanded the approaches eastwards to the river Drina and the frontiers of Serbia. Our column stumbled at night, in a weaving trajectory, north of Kladanj in this direction.

In a series of sorties, on the nights of 12, 15, and 17 July, assorted bundles of containers were parachuted at appointed places. The first operation near the village of Turalići brought in a significant load of medical supplies. These had been awaited since our landing. It was on 2 June that Gojko Nikoliš, the head of the medical section of the Supreme Staff, had first handed to me the list of essential needs.

The surviving groups of wounded were by now dispersed in the Bosnian woodlands, in the last stages of deprivation. Bandages were being taken from the dying, washed in the streams, and applied to those who had a chance of living. Drugs and equipment had long been expended.

On 19 July we were expecting reinforcements to the mission. Two planes were due that night, just to the west of Vlasenica, in an area controlled by the Seventh Banija Division, whose present task was the protection of the Staff.

Just before midnight three parachutists and containers of food dropped into the circle of the fires. The newcomers were a young Lieutenant, 'Tommy' Thompson, twenty-two years old, whose father had been the Vacuum Oil Company representative in Zagreb before 1939; he had been at school there, and spoke adequate Serbo-Croat; Lieutenant Mackay as an explosives expert; and Sergeant Robert Crozier as a relief W/T operator.

The nearby hills of Milan Planina provided us with temporary shelter. We had received a portion of a massive food drop which we were urging to supply the units now intended to head the march to the west across the river Bosna.

In the early hours of 25 July, one more drop of food supplies was successfully carried out. Empty tins were scattered to mark our passage, and to leave a defiant token of our presence for the enemy.

Tito had concentrated a strong operational group for the advance into Central Bosnia and on to the borders of Croatia. A new 'free territory' would be organized. The march to the Bosna river marked the first stage of this manoeuvre, heartened by the radio news of the fall of Mussolini.

The columns moved at partisan speed, and the air sorties would be suspended for a space.

In a signal of 17 June, before crossing the Sarajevo–Višegrad railway, the British mission had signalled a request for explosives for rail sabotage.

Packages of plastic charges and fuses were dropped in the first sorties, starting on 25 June, and swift use was made of them. There was a demolitions expert in charge of the technical section of the Supreme Staff, Vladimir Smirnov. He had arrived in Yugoslavia as a young refugee from Russia at the time of the Revolution. He graduated from the Technical Faculty in Belgrade, and worked as an engineer until the events following the invasion of April 1941. He joined the Partisans in Serbia during the rising, and was elected a member of the Communist Party the following year. I met him often during the battle in Montenegro in the company of the Supreme Staff.

Smirnov had built up a special military company of sappers and technical specialists from their peace-time trades: trained to blow bridges and to mend them, as across the Tara and Piva gorges, set up telephone lines and wreck them. He was now in overall charge of the present operations. In addition, several brigades had their own such companies, miners from Serbia, and from the coalfields of the Bosnian Marches and the Lika.

The railway system of the country, outside Serbia, had been reorganized after the Austrian–Hungarian occupation of Bosnia and Hercegovina in 1878 to provide secure communications between the military garrisons, for future extension to the coast, and as part of a future network to the south-east, following the stages of Vienna's policy of penetration into the Balkans.

The nodal junction of the system was based on Sarajevo, and railway yards were situated at Slavonski Brod where one line branched south to the town of Zenica, the largest steel works in the country, and the other due eastwards to Višegrad and on to the Serb border.

The minerals and timber of these regions were transported on these lines, coal from the Tuzla basin to the south of Brod, and the products of the Zenica complex of steel mills, which had been erected by Krupp before the war and were important to the economy of Croatia.

But the immediate significance of this network of single track railways was the dependence of the enemy upon the maintenance of their command headquarters at Sarajevo, the swift movements of their divisions in a concentric ring to supply the forward garrisons and bases to trap the Partisan forces under Tito in further offensive operations.

The coal to keep the railways functioning was drawn mainly from the mines of the Tuzla basin, in particular Kakanj and Husinja. These were now on our list of special targets.

Encouraged by the first supplies of explosives from British air sorties, the Partisan brigades in Bosnia were ordered to undertake special actions in every direction. Members of our mission in Bosnia took a direct part in these operations.

On 7 July the Serdar party left on such an enterprise carrying some of the plastic explosive recently dropped, together with the young sapper officer, Lieutenant Mackay, who had been parachuted to us in Bosnia, and went off with a Partisan Division, bent on the same purpose of sabotaging German troop concentrations, and the lines carrying coal to Brod.

Throughout the month of July, I reported progress. The Brod–Sarajevo line had been blown in forty places and the single track Brod–Zenica had been cut in seventeen places, and twelve bridges destroyed in the area around Doboj–Tuzla, bringing the coal mines to a temporary standstill.

Confirmatory reports had also reached Cairo direct from Serdar and the British sub-mission with the Partisan Bosnian Command.*

Our mission was now with the troops of the First Division approaching the Bosna river, and the railway leading south from Brod to Zenica.

We decided to stage a ceremonial event. I wished to be able to report to Cairo a direct eye-witness summary of railway sabotage. The main coal mines at Kakanj in the Tuzla basin were already isolated by previous actions, and the German Command Headquarters was temporarily cut off from all sides.

Just before dusk on 30 July, in the company of Koča Popović, the Commander of the First Proletarian Division, and his Staff, I reached a forward position in the woods dominating the railway line above the small station of Bijela Voda near Zepče.†

---

* On 18 July a sector of the Sarajevo–Višegrad line, just to the south of Rogatica, was destroyed in the presence of Serdar, and six kilometres of track in the rear sector on 29 July.

† This small town lay just to the east of the Sarajevo–Brod railway, built by the Austrian army in 1878–9, on the sector between Zenica and the Tuzla coal basin. The lines were repaired in the ensuing days, but the purpose of the disruptive operation had been achieved.

Through our field glasses we could see a small station below, and patrols in Četnik uniform moving along in trucks.

After dark, Popović and his staff moved down to a point near the railway halt. Over a stretch of six kilometres charges in generous quantities were laid to mark the first occasion.

Within seconds of lighting the fuses, an enemy armoured train appeared abruptly round the bend. Our party lining the track were taken by complete surprise at this apparition, a locomotive roughly protected by iron plates, a headlight projecting from the boiler and a wagon attached carrying a mortar crew.

The silence was broken by a Yugoslav soldier firing his rifle at the train lumbering past us at a distance of a few feet. At the same moment, in a deafening roar, the track behind disintegrated in a series of explosions lighting up the landscape.

Some of us scrambled up the bank of scrub behind us. Koča stood motionless and calm beside the track. The train bolted into a small tunnel twenty yards ahead, and halted just within the entrance. Their mortar opened up aimlessly in the general direction of the bursting explosions along the line behind them. Groups of Yugoslav soldiers scrambled over the mound which rose above the tunnel, racing to seal the far exit. But they were too late. It was all over in minutes, and the armoured convoy discreetly puffed on before any charges could be laid to cut its path ahead.

The demolition party and Popović's staff, together with the stunned British mission, rallied in ordered array.

On the following day a signal reached Cairo reporting this action: 'Fourteen kilometres of railway destroyed south-west of Zepče.' The same night other Yugoslav demolition parties attacked the railways to the north and south of Sarajevo. The German garrisons and the towns in the region held by the Croat troops of Pavelić were isolated, as was Tito's intention, to enable the safe crossing of the Bosna by the main Partisan operational group.

That night we forded the broad river, waist deep in its swift waters, and moved into the thick parklands of Central Bosnia; the massive beech trees, rich in foliage, stretching like the vaulted aisles of a vast cathedral, surrounded us with a giant protecting roof.

In forced marches we penetrated into the secret glades of these forests. As Walter Wroughton noted: 'Now just a matter of marching to Croatia.'

On 4 August 1943, in the early hours, we reached the broad plateau of Petrovo Polje above the town of Travnik, with an Ustaša garrison lying near us to the south.

The following weeks passed in relative and static calm at our new base. Amid the upland meadows and fields of Petrovo Polje, Tito and his staff established their headquarters, and the British mission was housed near by in a cramped stone-walled hut, used by peasants for storing winter fodder.

The plateau of Petrovo Polje had been selected as a halt and safe harbour on our progress to Jajce, a small town a day's march to the north where it was planned, as soon as the enemy garrison had been evicted, to establish the centre of a new 'free territory', based on Central Bosnia and on the lines of communications stretching to Croatia, and on to Slovenia and southwards to Dalmatia.

For the first time since the landing of the mission we had a thin roof over our heads, and a pause in which to sort out the images of our experiences and to consider the essential tasks assigned to 'Typical' in Cairo.

Our constant companion, apart from our escort, had been our first liaison officer 'Veljko' – Pavle Ilić – who had returned to his duties at the Staff, and since the arrival of the main Partisan group had been succeeded by Vladimir Dedijer.

The latter was a hulky giant Serb, of immense physical resistance and tireless converse, with whom the British mission had come into early contact as the representative of the Supreme Staff with the central Partisan hospitals.*

In the final hours of the breaching of the enemy ring, and on the same day as the death of Bill Stuart, Vlada Dedijer was smitten by personal tragedy. Already suffering from a severe and dangerous head wound in a previous action, he received the news that his wife Olga, a brilliant young surgeon, had been mortally struck down in the air attack which had engulfed us in the previous hours, and she lay wounded some distance behind our struggling line of advance.

'Vlada' returned alone to reach his wife as she was dying, and after simple burial, marched back to join the Staff group. His anguish was private and solitary.

He came from a family of Belgrade intelligentsia, in origin from Hercegovina. His father had been killed in the First World War

* See p. 45.

The British Mission and escort

Transporting the Mission radio set

The dropping zone at Njegobudjo

The Embattled Mountain from the ancient tombs near Žabljak

as a Serbian officer, and he had been brought as a child refugee to England. He spoke English fluently, and had made his early career as a foreign correspondent of the independent Belgrade newspaper *Politika*, after studying law at the university in the Yugoslav capital, where he had come into contact with the Communist student organization and its leaders – among them Lola Ribar and Milovan Djilas.

In the villages of Central Bosnia and briefly at Petrovo Polje, Vlada was constantly in our company. He and I would spend hours in talking, lying in the grass, and discussing passages in his diary, which he kept strapped to his waist in a large leather pouch. An inveterate and dedicated journalist, he continued his profession as a scribe of daily events, unperturbed by tiresome interruptions by the enemy. The diary survived the vicissitudes of war, and remains an invaluable record, open in places perhaps to friendly dispute in its references to the British.

In early August he left on a mission for Croatia, and I did not meet him again until the late autumn.

The business of the mission and my relations with Tito and his advisers increased and took on a more orderly shape during our sojourn on Petrovo Polje.

As a member of the Supreme Staff, Colonel Vladimir Velebit was now attached to us more formally as liaison officer to the British mission.

We quickly established a special and lasting personal relationship. Vlatko was of a Serb family from Croatia. His father had been a General in the Austro-Hungarian army in the First World War. The son had studied law at Zagreb University and become a provincial court judge. He was reticent about the past, and I was not inquisitive. During these days I merely knew that he had been engaged on dangerous illegal party work in Zagreb, and had been ordered to join Tito at his headquarters at Foča in Eastern Bosnia in March 1942. Later that year Velebit had been assigned the task of setting up the Military Legal section of the Supreme Staff – in approximate British terminology, as Judge Advocate-General. His attachment to the British mission was an addition to his normal duties, and our good fortune.

A man of wide education, which included remarkable linguistic gifts, Vlatko was a rewarding companion. We conversed in German, and our conduct of business was effortless, and in a steady

F

climate of mutual confidence. From our first meeting at Petrovo Polje, we were to be associated closely to the end of 'Typical' mission, and in the closing months of the war.

By camp fires at night on Petrovo Polje members and delegates of the Staff and visiting military commanders would gather with the British mission. At times, in the half light beyond the circle, stood mute and motionless onlookers. These figures were peasants from the scattered villages of the Polje.

Their presence was encouraged by the Partisan authorities, whose realistic scepticism about imminent British material aid on a significant scale was tempered by a marked appreciation of the propaganda value of our presence.

The appearance of the local population seemed to me to betray a marked lack of security.

On the occasion of one air sortie, the Command organized a ceremonial feast.

As the sound of aircraft reached us, the prepared signal fires were lit, illuminating the brightly coloured costumes of the peasants gathered round the circle of the landing ground. The two British bombers flew in at less than a hundred feet, by pilot error, and the dark cylinders of the containers plummeted down with unopened parachutes. Everyone scattered in panic in all directions, and mercifully without incident.

The celebration was not repeated.

Our camp fire dialogues followed an obsessive and constant pattern: impatience at the opening of a Second Front by the Western Allies; continued British support of the Royal Yugoslav government in London and of Mihailović, in spite of the clear evidence of the collaboration of his commanders with the Axis; and the delay in the recognition by the British of the National Liberation Movement as the dominating military and political organization in the country.

Underlying these frequent discussions was, latent and unexpressed, the conviction that the British and Americans would land in the Balkans, beginning on the Adriatic coast, before they had recognized the Partisans as their formal allies and broken with the Četnik movement. The prospect of such a landing was thus regarded with sceptical and jumpy anticipation of limited but not decisive military aid to Tito, and deeply graven suspicions

of the ultimate political intentions of the Western Allies, possibly
in secret accord with the Soviet government.

During our short talk with Tito and his staff on the morning of
28 May, at his headquarters in the woods bordering the Black
Lake below Mount Durmitor, Stuart and I had explained that
we had come as liaison officers under the direct orders of the
British General Headquarters, Middle East, and that the main
purpose of our mission was to inform the 'Partisan General
Headquarters' that the war in the Mediterranean had reached a
stage 'in which Allied offensives may be considered imminent',
and that it was desirable that these should be co-ordinated with
the efforts of the Partisans themselves. We were also to consult
with them on attacking specific targets on the enemy lines of
communication with supplies and if necessary British military
experts to be provided by us. We were to discuss the selection of
these targets with the Partisan Staff and report generally on the
military situation in the country as seen from their headquarters.

Our directive, which we had committed to memory in the office
of the Yugoslav Section in our headquarters in Cairo on 20 May,
also included general guidance regarding British relations with
General Mihailović which we were to convey to the Partisan
headquarters 'in a suitable form'.

At our first meeting this subject was not raised on either side. I
also had specific instructions not to regard myself in any way as
under the orders of Colonel Bailey, the head of the British Military
Mission at Mihailović's headquarters, nor would I, during the
course of my present mission, be in any contact, direct or indirect,
with him.

We had both been at our General Headquarters in Cairo since
the end of 1942, and had therefore been aware of the military and
political discussions at government level which had preceded the
decision to send exploratory British groups into territories, starting
with Croatia, in which the British had assumed that their formal
ally, Mihailović, had no control, and in regions from which we
had been able to piece together only an approximate picture of
conditions, primarily from German military intercepts. At a later
stage, if these early parachute operations proved successful and
working relations were established with the Partisan command,
the British intended to send similar missions to study the situation
in Slovenia and offer military collaboration in those regions.

The British Special Operations Executive, whose function it was to organize and aid resistance in occupied Europe and to collect intelligence regarding the enemy wherever contact with resistance elements could be made, had however only limited experience of operating with British military missions in uniform behind the enemy lines.

Conditions in Western Europe were such that S.O.E. had to rely either on parties composed of the nationals of the countries concerned or on individual British agents with special experience working underground and in civilian clothes. Although plans existed and parties were trained for ultimate operations in Poland in support of the Polish Home Army, operational conditions and aircraft resources were such that no missions had as yet been sent. Only in the Balkans and South-Eastern Europe with their mountain refuges and sparse communications could military missions operate in uniform. The first experiences had been gained by sending Captain Hudson to Yugoslavia in September 1941, followed by Colonel Bailey in December 1942.*

Similar missions had been dispatched to occupied Greece, but the structure of these experiments in irregular warfare was to bear little resemblance to the conditions which the present mission of Stuart and myself to Yugoslav Partisan headquarters was to face. The British missions to Mihailović, and to the Nationalist and Communist bands in Greece, were sent with the knowledge of the respective Yugoslav and Greek governments in exile, and in general co-ordination with them. The British officers commanding these missions were expected, and indeed instructed, to organize local resistance as far as possible under their direct command. They would be the channel of communication and orders sent to them by the British Headquarters in Cairo on main operational and political issues, after consultation between the British Foreign Office on the one hand and the Yugoslav and Greek governments in exile on the other. The British officers in Serbia included sabotage experts and it was intended that they should carry out independent operations, such as had been the model British attack on the Gorgopotamos bridge in Greece in November 1942. Mihailović, however, had refused to allow such operations in Serbia. This attitude had played a decisive part in the authorization by London of missions to be sent to Yugoslav territories obviously outside his control. But, although Stuart and I received

* See Part 2, passim.

no precise directives on the subject, we were in principle to be expected to take direct command of 'guerrilla bands' if local conditions permitted.

In addition to the written directives which Stuart and I had committed to memory on 20 May before leaving Cairo, we had received certain verbal instructions, which suggested from the outset that our party, if successful in the establishment of contact, was a precursory experiment to be followed up by a mission on the Greek model.

On 31 May a signal on our set was picked up which stated that Tito agreed in principle to the arrival of a senior officer and the sabotage of targets, and on 3 June Lord Selborne, who as Minister of Economic Warfare was responsible for Special Operations, was informed that I had seen Tito 'who has agreed to S.O.E. terms'.

The sudden appearance, after a long interval of isolation, of a British mission at Tito's headquarters must have aroused cautious speculation, exaggerated hopes, and marked suspicion. It was for us to explain the timing of our appearance and the intentions of our superiors, for Tito's immediate reactions were based on the fragments of past experience and present calculations as to the course of events outside Yugoslavia.

In his first words to us he revealed the basis of his suspicions. He had supposed that the British would not come again to his headquarters since the disappearance of Major Atherton from the temporary Partisan capital at the Bosnian town of Foča in the previous year.* Tito assumed that the British thought that he was responsible for the abrupt disappearance of this officer and for his murder. Atherton had left Foča in the night without giving any explanation of his abrupt departure. Tito could only assume that this had been on superior orders and that Atherton had probably reported adversely on the Partisan movement. Previous to Atherton's unheralded arrival, Captain Hudson had made contact with the Partisan command in the confusion of the early days of the rising in the autumn of 1941 during the First German Offensive against resistance bands in Serbia and at the time of Tito's negotiations with Mihailović and final break with him. Tito had a marked personal respect for Hudson, and this British officer who, unknown to him, had reported favourably on the military virtues of the Partisans, had left his headquarters openly in order to study the position in Mihailović-controlled territory in Serbia. Never-

* See p. 166.

theless, since the departure of Hudson and the disappearance of Atherton, the British had given no sign of sending emissaries to those regions held by the Partisans. We had given open recognition and support both in the form of military supplies and propaganda over the B.B.C. to Mihailović as the sole representative of Yugoslav resistance. Was our mission merely a repetition of these earlier contacts, and were we just engaged on a thinly disguised task of espionage to assess the aims and military strength of the Partisan movement, which we had never recognized, simply to make a comparison with what Tito assumed we must be aware of, with that of the Četniks and possibly in particular in those regions in which the Partisans were operating and where the extent of Četnik presence and the nature of their activities was unknown?

The unheralded arrival of a group of Communist Croats from Canada, by pure chance of planning, on top of the Partisan headquarters in Croatia, provoked a sharp reaction of suspicion.

To Tito's surprise and puzzlement the report which reached him on their arrival was followed by another which announced the parachuting of a British mission to the same spot with a request that he should receive a further group at his own headquarters.

It was with a noticeable and urgent curiosity that we were received.

When, at our first meeting, we summarized our instructions, this could only mean to Tito a confirmation of his own analysis of the general situation, namely that the Allies were planning in the near future a major landing in the Balkans, and that our arrival marked, in symbolic terms, the organization in enemy-occupied territory of auxiliary support from resistance elements, cooperation or possibly independent action against the enemy lines of communication, and general intelligence tasks. Indeed, unknown to us at the time, Tito had moved into the hinterland of the Adriatic coast and conducted a series of operations to liquidate the main Četnik groups of Mihailović in those regions of Hercegovina and Montenegro in preparation for just such an Allied strategic plan. It was also on precisely the same assumption that Mihailović himself had fought desperately and unsuccessfully for control of the same areas, and that the Germans and Italians had mounted a large-scale military encirclement of the whole region to destroy both movements. This aspect of the situation was only to be made clear to us in the days and months which followed.

Many other doubts must have been present in Tito's mind at

the time of our arrival. Why had the British made the first contact in Croatia?* Were we intending to organize, independently of his movement, our own 'diversionary groups' in this region, possibly with the help of neighbouring Četnik bands? Were we as a mission in direct contact with and under the orders of the British group attached to Mihailović's headquarters in Serbia?

Behind our ostensibly military tasks was there a sinister and long-term political plan? Did the British intend the ultimate division of Yugoslavia, supporting the return of the King and the exiled government to Serbia, and thinking up some undisclosed solution for the political future of other Yugoslav territories? Did we even intend, by first contacting the Partisans in Croatia, to seek to split the whole movement itself, over which Tito's central control had not been so easily established? Did the Russians know of British intentions, and was our arrival perhaps the result of some secret understanding between the British and the Russians in regard to the future of Yugoslavia and the conduct of resistance in that country? It was a strange and ironical coincidence that at the very spot where we had landed in Montenegro the Partisans had awaited in vain for several weeks in the previous year the arrival of a Soviet mission. Tito and his staff had never understood why the Russians had not come. Perhaps the Allied landing in the Balkans, which Tito was convinced was about to take place, and at which we had hinted, without being fully aware of the impact of our words, was in some way co-ordinated with Soviet strategic plans and related to an ultimate partition of South-Eastern Europe.

There was thus the conjured and pervading menace of a royalist restoration of the Serb kingdom, to include Montenegro, to be mounted by British landing operations on the Montenegrin and Albanian coasts. Alarming rumours had reached Tito's head-quarters of the activities of British missions with Albanian nationalist groups, who were known to be in league with the Montenegrin Četnik leaders—a point rarely but occasionally raised in conversation.

There was also speculation of rival plans for a Balkan Federa-tion: on the British side, based on Mihailovič in Serbia and to

---

* Starčević had arrived with our mission formally as my interpreter, which was his real status, but his presence was a source of some natural puzzlement to Tito and his staff as indeed was our whole concept, which was in fact purely operational, of using this group of Canadian Croats, who were all members of the Canadian Communist Party, in such a rôle.

embrace a post-war association with Bulgaria and Greece; on the other, from Comintern experience, a similar grouping under Soviet influence.

There were also more immediate fears in regard to British intentions in Croatia, and in Slovenia, where parties of British-recruited Slovenes had been parachuted without any prior warning to us as the British mission ostensibly accredited to Tito.

The problem of Croatia, which included Bosnia and Hercegovina, was central to the future of the National Liberation Movement. The structure of the Partisan military and political organization was firmly implanted, as other British missions were reporting direct to Cairo, and the recruiting of new divisions was steadily expanding.

But these were facing not only the German units stationed in those regions, and the armed forces of Pavelić; the ultimate and decisive predominance of Partisan control here, as elsewhere, though in a special form, depended on winning over the loyalties of the mass of the Croat peasantry from their traditional allegiance to the Peasant Party of Maček,* the most effective political organization in pre-war Yugoslavia, and alien to Communist influence.

The passive neutrality of the supporters of Maček, on his instructions given in April 1941 and unvaried by his house arrest by Pavelić, was equal in its threat to the ultimate primacy of Tito to the repeatedly alleged and in cases proven collaboration of Mihailović with the occupying forces, and the instructions of the Royal Yugoslav government, tacitly encouraged by the British for their own reasons, not to organize resistance against the enemy until the advent of an Allied invasion of the Balkans.

Tito discussed with me on more than one occasion † the 'legend' of Maček, who as he was fully aware was regarded with respect in British circles where Maček's reputation as the leading democratic politician in pre-war Yugoslavia had not been dimmed by his present obstinate neutrality.

Conspiratorial suspicions were rooted in the mentality of our companions, in their precarious isolation from the main stream of the outside war, and it was normal that I should be, however subtly, made aware of them.

The British Foreign Office never considered at any time a post-

---

* The HSS (Hrvatska Seljačka Stranka).
† In particular, according to my pocket diary, on 13 August 'for three hours'.

war partition of the Yugoslav State. The British government, in these months of 1943, was still totally committed to a legitimist restoration. As a junior liaison officer of one mission into enemy-occupied territory, I was naturally unaware of high policy, but as the direct witness of an isolated, outlawed, and hitherto ignored resistance movement on which I was instructed to report, the extent of the gap in mutual understanding which could not be bridged by one adventure of an experimental mission was not unperceived.

The political implications of recommending military aid to the Yugoslav Partisans, on evidence beyond dispute, and acquired in simple shared experience of war, had to be considered on another level.

In the Cairo directive of 20 May, I was instructed, in dealing with the Partisan headquarters, to be guided by certain general considerations. The British government had been only recently aware that certain of Mihailović's commanders outside Serbia had been collaborating with the enemy, and had informed Mihailović that they disagreed completely with his continued maintenance of relations with these men. Meanwhile, the British General Head-quarters, Middle East, considered that certain of Mihailović's units in Eastern and Southern Serbia were in a position to serve the Allied cause by attacking the enemy lines of communication, and wished that nothing should be done to interfere with these plans.

In simple terms, I was to assume that Mihailović would continue to be supported by the British in East and South Serbia;* that I was to recommend, subject to whatever evidence I might find after our arrival, support by air to all elements 'who offer resistance to the Axis': in the first instance, explosives for railway sabotage.

I had no instructions as to what attitude to adopt if the mission were faced with the presence of local Četnik units, which might, according to recent information, be collaborating with the enemy, or even fighting alongside the so far undefined 'Croat and Slovene guerrillas'.

It was implicitly left to my own judgement, in consultation with Stuart, to act as I saw fit, and presumably, should the occasion arise, to attempt to dissuade the Partisan Command either from

* See p. 217.

moving east of the Ibar river into Western Serbia or from conduct-
ing local operations beyond that line.

As the nature of our mission was experimental, and framed to
study on the ground evidence which was lacking in Cairo, it was
not surprising, although our orders seemed clear, that they bore
alarmingly little resemblance to the climate of warfare at the
moment of our arrival.

The presence of local Četniks in the area of the battle, into
which we had been dropped, was confined to an ambush in the
dark, after the crossing of Durmitor, on 1 June near the village of
Podmilogora.* Shots were fired in the direction of Tito and the
British mission, which were received imperturbably by the former,
and with some surprise by the latter. We sent a laconic signal:
'Ambushed by Četniks. One man killed; one wounded.'

During the ensuing nights we were at times engulfed at close
quarters by the encircling Germans in sudden clashes on forest
tracks and woodland slopes, and by day flattened on the bare
uplands and along the edges of the valleys by low-level attacks
from the air. Of the Četniks there was no sign. Unknown to us at
that time, Tito's forces had beaten through the whole surrounding
region before the opening of the present enemy offensive, dispersing the troops of the Montenegrin and Hercegovinan Četniks into
scattered bands. These sought refuge with the Italian garrisons to
the east and south of us. Mihailović and his staff were on the
run eastwards into Serbia.

Only in the last stages of the present fighting were some of these
Četnik bands from Hercegovina operating with the Italians as
scouting patrols, moving northwards on to the battlefield, and
killing those Partisan wounded and stragglers who were cut off.

Reports of these activities filtered to us in Bosnia after the break-
out of the main Partisan group with Tito and his staff through the
encircling lines of the Germans.

Tito and his staff were now in Central Bosnia. We were to
observe at close quarters the strategy of a pause; the erection of a
political and military base as the next stage for an operational
move from a new 'free territory'.

This opportunity was to reveal to us a different landscape, and
to heighten our perception of the nature and aims of the society in

* Launched by a band of Četniks from nearby villages on the Piva plateau
under a certain Anton Jokanović.

which we lived and moved and its struggle for internal supremacy, not only against the conventional military threat of the Germans and Italians, but faced with enclaves of bitterness formed by the isolated outposts of rival movements for the ultimate control of the country: the nationalist Četniks; and the extremist Croat formations of Pavelić, constructed in desperate imitation of a Fascist challenge to a disintegrating world, and created in the image of their Axis masters.

The land of Bosnia, to us as yet alien and unexplored, was to appear as the battleground of rival myths, and the microcosm of a savage and triangular civil war.

The fight between Yugoslavs for the control of this key strategic area, marked by atavistic hates which erupted in the first days of occupation and rebellion, revealed the true nature of these rivalries.

To the Partisans, Bosnia was the base of communications with their operational zones in Croatia, in Slovenia, and in Dalmatia. It was also from here that, skirting the abandoned fastnesses of Montenegro, the march back to Serbia must be launched.

To the troops of Pavelić, the region was geographically and economically an integral part of the Independent State and the border marches of a Greater Croatia, a crusading frontier between Catholic and Orthodox.

To the Četniks it was the symbolic refuge of Serb Orthodoxy beyond the historic frontiers of their state, for centuries under alien rule, and destined to be united in a Greater Serbia.

From the scant evidence which had been available to us in Cairo, we were aware of the presence of isolated Četnik groups in Bosnia, but little or nothing was known of their local activities, or to what extent they were an integral part of the organization of Mihailović.

The first direct intelligence which reached our mission came from one of two Canadian Croat groups which the British had parachuted 'blind' into Bosnia on 21 April, the same night as the parallel experiment in Croatia, and as a supplementary party to make the first contact with a Partisan command.*

On our arrival in Bosnia after the Fifth Offensive, I sent instructions for this group to report to us, and they arrived at Supreme Staff headquarters near Kladanj on the evening of 28 June. They had spent nearly two months in the midst of constant

* See p. 1.

fighting between the Partisans, the Ustaša, and the Četniks in Eastern Bosnia.

Steve Serdar, their leader, had already reported direct to Cairo in early May that the local Četniks were working with the Germans in Sarajevo and guarding the roads round Zvornik for them, and were collaborating with the Italian garrison at Više-grad.

In discussions with Serdar, we put together further evidence of the use by the German commands in East Bosnia of Četnik bands as auxiliaries.

On 29 July our mission signalled: 'Ozren and Trebava * Četniks 1,300 strong attacked Partisans west of Tuzla, helped by one battalion of 369 Division. Guarding the Doboj-Tuzla railway, and Tuzla town, for the Germans to whom they surrendered without fighting in May.'

On 15 August we reported again that these Četnik groups were armed with German rifles and supplied with food and pay. The evidence came from Serdar's mission in Bosnia, who collected it from prisoners taken by the Second Proletarian Division.

We were soon to see for ourselves.

At the end of July units of the First Division received orders from Tito to move to Bosanska Krajina, with two brigades originally formed in that area, to clear the area of Četnik and Ustaša units and to destroy the Sarajevo-Brod railway: the first sabotage operation with British explosives.

I have described how, together with the divisional commander and his staff, I watched the reconnoitring of the railway at dusk on 31 July.

During the action that night, Partisan troops captured the commander of the Četnik Zenica *odred*, Golub Mitrović, and two of his staff.

I was faced with this group of prisoners in a woodland clearing. It was proposed that I should interrogate them personally. This was the first, and only, occasion that such a situation arose. I refused. The British could not be a party to civil war. The evidence was clear. It was beyond my responsibility to be implicated in questioning Četnik prisoners about to be executed.

I turned away, and walked through the trees. A short burst of rifle fire closed the incident. We advanced past the three bodies a few minutes later.

* Two mountain bases to the east of the Bosna river.

This episode was ill-received by the Partisan command. I had long anticipated such a confrontation, and knew that I should have to assume such an attitude, from which I never deviated—at the price of lack of comprehension and a certain ill-will on the part of our Partisan allies.

They felt that we were fighting another war, that the British themselves bore a definite responsibility for the continuing civil strife by their support of Mihailović – and the Četnik movement – even when faced with its collaboration with the enemy.

Such a debate might well be conducted in Cairo. It was there, it seemed to me, that a decision should be taken and not by an officer alone in the field in the climate of a civil war, which as yet was not admitted by the British 'officially' to exist.

On returning to Tito's headquarters from this expedition, I signalled to Cairo on 12 August: 'The First Division has captured the staff of the Zenica Četniks, who were guarding for the Germans the approaches to Sarajevo. Documents taken are at my disposal. Textual translations follow showing collaboration with Germans and Ustaša. Staff offered that I should interrogate Četnik leaders. Categorically refused to have contact with them.'

The papers of the Četnik Zenica detachment were captured in this action, and were examined. They presented in miniature the tragedy of local conditions in Bosnia since the rising in 1941.

This small unit took its name from the town of Zenica, the centre of a complex of steel mills working for the Germans and whose production was a significant economic target. The Commander, Golub Mitrović, had originally led a company of one of the first Partisan units in the area. In the spring of 1942 he had broken away, and formed his own Četnik band. Shortly afterwards he captured and killed a group of Croat Partisans – miners from the coalfield of Husinja, a strong Communist district – and recently had ambushed a patrol of the Seventh Division, killing the commissar and the whole group.

This Četnik detachment was now one of a group operating in East Bosnia under the orders of Major Baćović, Mihailović's commander for East Bosnia and Hercegovina.

Most of these Četnik groups had already, as was clear from these captured documents, come to terms of mutual non-aggression with the Pavelić authorities, receiving, reluctantly on both sides, arms and supplies for anti-Partisan operations. But the shadow of the Ustaša massacres, which had provoked the original rising, Četnik and Partisan, in Bosnia in the summer of 1941, bore heavily on these compromises, and led to friction and resentment among the rank and file of these Bosnian Serb Četnik bands.

In a letter written by the commander of the Zenica *odred* on 18 October 1942, he refers to

misunderstandings between the staff and the Croat authorities. I have done my best to settle this difference and to improve relations between this detachment and the Croats. This staff has sought the mediation of the Germans at Zenica. The German command there has requested in writing that the Zenica Četnik commander should go under their protection to the German Divisional Headquarters in Sarajevo. This staff asked that they first obtained permission from their commanding officer Major Baćović, but the Germans answered that they have no time. This staff, therefore, decided to send Golub Mitrović to Sarajevo without awaiting permission.

On 4 May an agreement was drawn up between representatives of the Zenica Četnik staff and a Major Poche, acting for the German military authorities. Its main purpose was to make the necessary detailed arrangements for the Četniks to take over from the Germans the guarding of the railway line and bridges in this area. It was here that the Partisan forces found them.

During the late summer of 1943 another Četnik leader, Djuro Plečaš, was captured by Partisans near Knin in Northern Dalmatia. He was on his way to the headquarters of Pop Djuić, the main collaborator with the Italians, and Mihailović's commander for the area of the Dinaric Alps. Plečaš had first worked in Serbia for Kosta Pećanac, the official head of the Četnik organization on the outbreak of war, who had gone over to the Germans within a few weeks of the armistice.

In February 1942 he commanded a 'legal' Četnik detachment at Užice in Western Serbia and was under instructions from Pecanač to maintain correct relations with Nedić and the Germans. In the following August Plečaš was appointed by Mihailović as Inspector of his forces in Eastern Bosnia, and in February 1943 as his commander for Western Bosnia with orders to establish a Četnik 'Gavrilo Princip' Corps.

Plečaš had called a conference of local Četnik leaders to set up this command, to meet at the headquarters of Djuić, and conduct truce negotiations with the Ustaša. At this point, Plečaš, or at least his archives, fell into Partisan hands.

A series of messages had been sent by us to Cairo on the Četnik question in the light of captured documents, and frequent talks with the Yugoslav liaison officers attached to the British mission and Partisan commanders visiting General Headquarters.

These telegrams started on 3 August, following on the incident at Bijela Voda. Detailed material evidence was now available to us of the active collaboration of Četnik groups in Bosnia, Herce-govina, and Dalmatia, and of the direct and formal control of these bands by Mihailović.

Any illusion which might remain in Cairo and London as to a renewal of the negotiations with Tito and Mihailović in the winter of 1941 had been dissipated within the country during the previous two years.

In snatches of private discussion during these months, Tito described to me his personal encounter with Mihailović in the room of a peasant house in Western Serbia in October 1941. The manner of description was simple and human, quietly vivid in style, and not discoloured by strident or ideological rancour.

During the meeting of the two men, the Četnik leader perched on a box – his 'war chest' – seizing at intervals his field telephone and seeking to contact his local unit commanders, calling for reports on the number of men at their disposal. Tito listened to the brief phrases: ten, twenty, fifty troops appeared to be dotted in surrounding villages. The effect was not impressive. The strength of this embryo nationalist force was symbolic, but, to Mihailović, it represented the continuity and nucleus of resistance of the Serbian elements of the Royal Yugoslav army rooted firmly in a proud military tradition. To Tito, the officer facing him embodied the defeated forces of an alien and reactionary system with whom some improvised and even temporary accommodation might just be conceivable in the immediate moment in face of the punitive expedition of the German occupation divisions.

Proposals made by Tito for a joint operational staff included the nomination of commissars to joint Četnik–Partisan units. These were countered by the insistence by Mihailović that Partisan officers should hold whatever rank they had reached in the Royal Yugoslav army. Neither side could accept loss of control of the direction of combined operations. Nor would Tito yield on his demand for immediate and total commitment of all units to armed

resistance. Mihailović pressed for cautious and passive mobilization of the Serb peasantry for future action.

The deadlock was unresolved, and brief collaboration was
disrupted irreparably and tragically by Četnik treachery, and
ensuing civil strife.

Subsequent evidence, however, confirms that the initiative for
a common action in Western Serbia in these early days came
from Tito, and his impressions, as conveyed in our brief dialogues
nearly two years later, were conveyed to me in simple and un-
emotional terms.

In a signal of 28 August I referred indirectly to these talks.
There was no hope of any understanding between Četniks and
Partisans now, as Tito had stated in several talks with me in the
strongest terms. The Četniks were regarded by the Partisans as
open Axis allies since their conduct at Užice, and in the last
Axis offensive. Of the discussions between Tito and Mihailović in
October 1941, I signalled 'I have learnt several details, and will
report separately.'

The Bosnian Četniks, according to captured documents, had
contracted agreements with the Pavelić authorities. It was not
Mihailović's practice to maintain a personal link with his local
commanders. Contact was usually established by touring staff
officers.

At the end of August, in the light of these messages, I received
for comment a proposal from Cairo that those Četnik commanders
against whom there was such evidence that they were working
with Pavelić and the Germans should be denounced by name
over the B.B.C.

I replied: 'I feel that to attack the collaborationist Četniks on
the B.B.C. would be a definite step forward, but to do so without
implicating Mihailović would be a subtlety which would neither
be appreciated nor understood here. Captured documents refer
openly to legal Četniks, i.e. those allowed to work with Axis – as
distinct from illegal Četniks. But both are under the supreme
command of Mihailović.'

At the end of August, I signalled a summary of the Četnik
question as it appeared to us during the previous weeks of consecutive study and discussion.

The Četnik participation in military support of the Axis during
the recent enemy offensive on the Partisans cost the latter, since
January 1943, during the cycle of the 'Weiss' operations, heavy

The wooded slopes of Ozren and the Sutjeska river

The escape route to the north

Across the Sutjeska valley

Dragoš Sedlo

losses, about half of which were due to the Četniks' slaughtering stragglers and wounded.

Recently, the Četniks had taken the initiative in attacking the Partisans in the Lika. The headquarters of Djuić at Knin was situated within the Italian garrison. Documents showed that this attack 'coincides with a planned Axis offensive'.

There was no distinction between the Četnik position in Serbia and elsewhere. Those outside Serbia were under orders of Mihailović and proved to be close Axis collaborators. The Četniks of Bosnia and Hercegovina were operating under German orders with German pay and badges of rank. Mihailović and his commanders had often and conclusively stated that their main enemy was the Partisan army.

It was also a mistake to assume that the main strength of Mihailović had been always based on Serbia. Until the Četnik débâcle in Montenegro in the previous summer, the majority of their recruits were from Serb villages outside Serbia. The Mihailović organization as revealed in these documents consisted of small groups of such peasants.

'Such a policy logically had led to active Četnik collaboration with the Axis and this, coupled with repeated warnings from us not repeat not to attack the Axis until word was given, had destroyed any will to resist among Četnik ranks if it ever existed.'

On 31 August a final signal from us on this theme reached Cairo: 'Have no evidence of any resistance by Mihailović. It would help me in argument with the Staff here if you would keep me informed of any guaranteed instances of resistance by Mihailović commanders in Serbia as I am continually confronted by cases of false claims of action by Mihailović in this and other areas.'

The irony of this message masked our frustration. Perhaps, on the spot, the issue seemed miserably simple, and our constant awareness that any hope of a settlement between Četniks and Partisans had evaporated, if it had ever existed, two years before, was tinged with impotent bitterness.

We were still in theory cast in the role of national arbitrators as one Cairo message showed, which called on me to seek the intervention of Tito to halt clashes between Partisans and Četniks to the far south in the region of Priština, in the Kosovo region along the Albanian border.

The issue of Četnik collaboration with the enemy was closely

G

linked with that of our recent recognition, in B.B.C. broadcasts, of the military activities of the Partisans against the Axis.

I was continually being presented by the Supreme Staff with reports of laudatory references on the B.B.C. to the heroic deeds of those very Četnik commanders whose records were in my hands, and at a time precisely when I was making every effort to persuade Tito and his staff, in the light of my original instructions, to produce detailed intelligence regarding the strength of his own forces and their location.

Matters came sharply to a head when on 5 and 6 August the B.B.C. repeated two news items, which announced that two 'Mihailović brigades' had crossed from Slovenia into Istria. I signalled on the following day:

This is a deliberate and subtle lie. Two Partisan brigades did in fact cross the frontier some days ago and I was so informed. This transmission has got the whole staff on the raw and caused some unpleasant interviews, particularly as I persist in maintaining a correct attitude towards the Četnik question, in defiance of mounting documentary evidence here of their active collaboration with the Axis.

All are aware of the increasing military and political importance of this region (Slovenia) and distrust a deliberate attempt to undermine their position in a vital area. I have tried to minimize the importance of the affair by pleading lack of detailed information in London of the Partisan order of battle* but it is clear that weeks of work have been undone.

I proposed that the B.B.C. should be requested to correct this report, and asked for a date and time to be transmitted to the mission.

Such action was taken, but the 'battle of the air' was a continuing affray, and the B.B.C. struggled with contradictory directives, based alternately on reports from Mihailović and those from our mission and others in Partisan territory.

On 1 June 1943, nearly a week after our departure from Cairo, an urgent signal had been received there from the British Foreign Office requesting information as to the identity of the leader of the 'Partisans' and the location of their headquarters.

On that particular day, Tito and his Staff, together with the members of 'Typical' mission, were halted in a peasant farm among scattered hamlets on the wooded slopes to the north of Mount Durmitor.

* See p. 95.

Cairo had answered these queries to the limit of their knowledge. Tito was the name of the commander-in-chief 'at present in Montenegro'. This signal from London was not repeated to us, and even if this had been done, Stuart and I could but have confirmed the accuracy of this single statement.

To us, the man who had received us six days earlier was Tito, and very definitely the commander with a General Headquarters, directing in person and with absolute authority a major operation of war.

He was clearly not the mysterious Soviet functionary Lebedev, whose existence was hinted at in messages from Mihailović sources, nor an impersonal pseudonym for a secret revolutionary organization; but details of his identity were as yet not apparent to us.*

The portrait of the man to whom we were attached took slow shape in the early moments of personal contact. At our first encounter by the Black Lake on the evening of 28 May I had the impression of a deceptively quiet personality, used to imposing his authority with few words or gestures, commanding an instinctive and total respect from those around him, sure in judgement and deeply self-controlled. We had no time for discourse during the ensuing days and only physical images formed.

Tito's features were firm but not sharp; the eyes were light grey and fixing, his movements deliberate and restrained. His voice was calm and even in tone on all occasions. He seemed unruffled by the scramble of our constant movements, and took a deliberate and characteristic care of his personal appearance, impeccable and elegant in his neatness, with delicate nervous hands.

Although we moved and halted in small untidy groups, as we crossed the mountains and valleys of the battlefield, we shared together irregular meals, and at night sheltered within calling distance on the bare hillsides or in the patches of forest. From the first moment I decided that our daily intercourse should be marked by a simple formality. Although I could often see him a few yards away, shaving, or sitting on the ground surrounded by his immediate followers, I would never saunter over, but would send one of our escort to fix an appointment. It was a tidy arrangement; essential in the primitive ways of our daily life.

As our column moved northwards into Bosnia, pausing for days at a time in the local villages, we had more time to talk, apart

* See p. 203.

from immediate exchanges of information on the military situation or the arrangements for the first air sorties from Africa. In patient fragments, I began to form a personal impression of the man. We knew before our arrival that numerous Partisan bands were operating in Yugoslavia under the direct command of the General Secretary of the illegal Yugoslav Communist Party, although it was not clear that this figure was also Tito himself. But, in any event, one would expect to be dealing with a rigid doctrinaire, fanatic, harshly moulded by underground life, narrow in outlook, and impervious to open debate. Instead, the personality of Tito emerged as that of a man broadened by the experience of exile and prison, flexible in discussion, with a sharp and humorous wit, and a wide curiosity.

After the death of Stuart, who was a fluent Serbo-Croat linguist, I was obliged to conduct all business and conversation with Tito in German, which he spoke with ease with a slight Viennese accent. It became clear that he enjoyed argument and spontaneous discussion. I never asked him any direct personal questions, but at times he would talk about his own past and our conversation often ranged beyond the current technicalities of business, especially at mealtimes in peasant houses or under the trees. He liked particularly to speak of his days in Vienna and in Paris where he had organized, on Comintern instructions, the dispatch of volunteers to Spain. He himself was never sent there, as certain rumours have suggested. He could read English with some difficulty, and once mentioned that his favourite paper in that language was *The Economist*. He was keenly inquisitive about men and events but inevitably his vision and knowledge had narrowed since the rising in Serbia two years before. He had discovered that I had worked before the war with Mr. Winston Churchill as his literary assistant, and often questioned me about his personality and views.

Tito's only source of information on the general progress of the war came from Russian and occasional B.B.C. broadcasts picked up by his radio staff. Our arrival bringing our own wireless communications meant that we were able to pick up our own news whenever local conditions permitted the operation of our sets. There was thus constant exchange of news between us from a now wider range of broadcast sources, at times provoking sharp and spirited controversies.

Our talks were in general disjointed and fragmentary until, in mid-August, we settled for most of the month in relative peace on the plateau of Petrovo Polje. It was here that our first consecutive political discussions began, in an atmosphere of genuine confidence and personal terms which had been built up imperceptibly in the closeness of our daily company during the previous weeks of fighting. Tito seemed to expect little of us as an Allied mission as a source of material aid, but he was quick to realize the importance of our presence as witnesses of the conflict, and of the fighting qualities of his troops. At such a critical time a British mission was accompanying his headquarters as he travelled into new regions where the population could see that the British were physically represented as Allies and formally accredited to him as a national leader.

The first parachuting of supplies by British planes, although not, as it was hoped and planned, sufficient in quantity for the immediate needs of the Operational Group moving into Bosnia, had a very marked propaganda effect. Even when such sorties, for technical reasons, failed to arrive, or contained unsolicited and inappropriate material, Tito never commented on what were sometimes bizarre episodes. On one occasion we received a plane-load of atrobin, a drug for curing malaria, a disease unknown to us in the regions where we were operating. This operation had been conceived presumably by someone familiar with the Macedonian campaign of the First World War when the Allied armies on the Salonika front had suffered from this malady.

On another day we received a supply of boots which were badly needed as many of the Partisan troops were reduced to peasant slippers or were barefoot after the long marches over rough country. But this load consisted entirely of boots for the left feet. Included in the containers were also copies of the British Army newspaper published in Cairo, which featured a regular series of caricatures of dandified British officers known as 'the Two Types' with their sloppy trousers and battered caps. Mournfully I handed these papers to Tito who immediately began identifying, among the members of his staff, the Yugoslav equivalents, to their sharp annoyance as they could not follow our joking in German.

Our impressions of the composition of the Partisan leadership steadied as the pace of our movements slowed. In the long night marches, and during the daylight halts, chance encounters revealed haphazardly the identity of certain personalities in snatches of talk. These were simple accidents of human proximity, but, during the weeks following the mountain battle, the figures of

Tito's constant companions assumed a more rounded content, even though their individual functions could at first be but dimly perceived. We were dependent on the limitations of our powers of observation, and the need to exchange personal fragments of experience in moments of fear and stress.

The only names, some garbled and inaccurate, of Partisan leaders which had reached the British were, apart from Tito as a pseudonym, those of Arso Jovanović and a 'Professor' Djilas, whom Hudson had reported as his companions on his journey from Montenegro to Western Serbia in October 1941, and that of a 'Jewish photographer from Belgrade', Moša Pijade, mentioned by the Royal Yugoslav officer Rapotec on his arrival in Istanbul in July 1942.* Pijade, according to Mihailović sources, was the grey eminence of inconspicuous Communist bands which had made their disturbing appearance in Serbia during the autumn rising of 1941.

Such was the sum of British 'intelligence' on the Partisan leadership prior to our arrival.

I was to meet Pijade in the very first days when the British mission was crowded into the cave together with Tito and his Staff just below the village of Mratinje before the crossing of the Piva.

We sat among the scrub outside the shelter, and our first talk ranged over the nature of the rising in Montenegro in July 1941. This dialogue was a curtain-raiser to our ignorance, and one of many such conversations.

With a disconcerting honesty and realism, Pijade pictured the mistakes of the Montenegrin Communist Party leadership in imposing on the simple clan structure of the country ill-digested formulas of class struggle, alienating a majority of a proud and united population, and playing into the hands of local nationalist leaders, some of whom had co-operated in the spontaneous rebellion against the Italian occupation.

Pijade spoke in brief sentences in fluent French. He seemed to measure each phrase with quiet authority, and as I met him often in the ensuing months, he appeared as a rare combination of an intellectual and man of decision.

He was clearly very close to Tito, and almost of the same generation, though not an early associate in the small and illegal Yugoslav Communist Party between the wars, nor similar in

* See p. 206.

temperament. The relationship between the two men was created under special conditions. They had shared the constrained intimacy of prison life as Communist agitators, and these years were a critical phase in the formation of both personalities.

Pijade, who came from a middle-class Jewish merchant family in Belgrade, had been an art student and studied in Munich and Paris before the First World War. He was a painter of marked talent.

In 1919 he turned to journalism, and joined the Communist Party formed in the following year. He was the editor of the first Party news-sheets and numerous pamphlets, and during the 'illegal' period when the Party was banned by law after 1921, Pijade ran its underground press. He was arrested in 1925, and sentenced to twelve years' gaol. In the prison of Lepoglava he met Tito for the first time in 1930.

Pijade became the teacher of the 'prison school', which formed and held classes at Lepoglava. He had already translated Marx's *Capital* into Serbo-Croat at his previous place of detention – at Sremska Mitrovica – and, as the leading journalist of the early Party, was familiar with Communist literature.

This prison group formed a particular inner circle within the leadership of the later Partisan movement, not a neat clan but rather a secret human cell.

Later I was to meet others.

Pijade also shared with Tito experience of life outside Yugoslavia, though significantly in his case in the years preceding the outbreak of the First World War. But through study and reflection in long periods of prison (Pijade was released from Lepoglava in April 1939 and re-interned for several months early in 1940) his Marxist views were more flexible and more tempered by a sense of political realism than those of some of his present companions.

Pijade was essentially the original thinker of the Partisan movement, and the creator of its political structure. This general frame emerged to us in outline through observation of its grass roots in the regions through which we passed.

Throughout the months of our presence, Pijade became an increasingly familiar personage: unperturbed in crisis, quick in gesture and movement, quiet in speech, inquisitive in conversation, and sharp in dialectic; in physical aspect a schoolmaster of authority, with sharp grey eyes framed with spectacles perched on a beaked nose, his body thin and slightly hunched, dressed in baggy faded clothes and a forage cap.

'Professor' Djilas, whose name had emerged once in an early signal from Hudson,*also appeared in the early days after our landing. My first clear impression of him was in the last hours of the battle in one of the Bosnian villages north of the encircling ring, which had been just breached by Tito's forces.

Milovan Djilas was endowed with the outstanding physical courage of the Montenegrin clans, bred in generations of Komitadji bands raiding Turkish garrisons and repelling the Austro-Hungarian penetration of the barren fortresss of that region.

In the immediate moment of our tired escape from destruction, Djilas departed with a handful of companions southwards to the desolation of the battlefield. It was an unwritten law of Partisan war that in a lost free territory – in this case the stronghold of Montenegro – the bare elements of Party work must continue, and cells be re-formed in anticipation of a future return.

Djilas slipped from our company one evening on such a task. There were other Montenegrins engaged on similar missions but it was his departure which we witnessed. Saturnine and darkly handsome, he seemed to embody the legends of his divided land. This was the single impression first borne upon us.

Shortly afterwards Djilas reappeared at Tito's headquarters deeper in Bosnia. He was holding a bayonet, wrenched from a member of a German patrol which had been liquidated by his band on their return journey.

Djilas was a member of a group within the Partisan leadership which played a significant and decisive rôle in the whole movement, the Youth organization of the Party† and its guiding cells of university students in particular from Belgrade.

Djilas himself came from a family clan on the borders of Montenegro and Albania, and had been sent to Belgrade University where he studied law and philosophy. As one of the clandestine group of student leaders of the reconstructed SKOJ after 1937, he had come into personal contact with Tito, and by 1940 he was a member of the inner circle of the reconstructed and clandestine Party leadership.

* See p. 132.
† Known under the initials SKOJ (Savez Komunistiške Omladine Jugoslavije). See p. 92.

He had been sent as one of the organizers of the rising in Montenegro, where Hudson had encountered him.

By character intransigent, arrogant in the superficial certainties of Marxism as simplified in a student world, Milovan Djilas had been uncompromising and extreme, in Montenegrin fashion, in his participation in the July 1941 rising in this region. His nature was both complex and simple: rigid political beliefs of urban intellectuals had been imposed by a deliberate effort of will on the realism and honesty of a clansman. His countrymen were natural inheritors of an epic world of clean and simple loyalties and codes of honour, lit by a poetic insight into the nature of man.

The tragedy of Djilas was to emerge long after the events at hand: the irreconcilable conflict between a rigid and pitiless doctrinaire and the reflective imaginative artist of a mountain community of epic traditions.

It would be an impudence to imply that any trace or hint of such turbulent contradictions in the personality of Djilas could be perceived by his companions and least of all by alien and puzzled strangers during these days of struggle.

He was seldom in our company and engaged, with rare pauses, on restless missions as a leading delegate of Tito and the Supreme Staff.

The only remaining name merely known to us was also mentioned without comment by Hudson: that of Arso Jovanović as present at the headquarters of the 'Montenegrin Freedom Force' at Radovče in September 1941 * and one of the members of the party which had escorted the Englishman to Tito's headquarters at Užice the following month.

It had also been noted in Cairo that Jovanović had been denounced, at the request of Mihailović, on the B.B.C., together with certain other officers of the former Royal Yugoslav army, as a 'traitor'.

The existence of regular officers with undefined 'patriot' forces, revealed in this manner, also added a further note of confusion to the thin analysis of the Yugoslav scene available to the British authorities, and gave a certain plausibility to the vague theory that joint national-communist bands were in existence, and that some prospect might emerge of a united resistance throughout Yugoslav territory.

* See p. 127.

Arso Jovanović was present at the first encounter of the British mission with Tito and his Staff among the trees bordering the Black Lake within hours of our landing. The identity of other members of the group surrounding the Partisan commander impinged on us in gradual and fortuitous stages, but Jovanović was inescapable.

He appeared to be Tito's chief technical military adviser with the general functions of a chief of staff. In the scramble of the following weeks, Stuart (until his death) and then myself spoke almost entirely with Tito in short interchanges. But Jovanović was in daily and somewhat sullen evidence. He was clearly not accustomed to strangers, and his range of human experience was limited.

In the course of time, fragments of his past emerged. He had held the rank of captain in the Royal Yugoslav army, but had been one of a small group of officers and soldiers who had secretly joined the Communist Party before the Axis assault on Yugoslavia.

The Party leadership had formed a military committee in 1940 with the task of creating subversive cells within the Royal Yugoslav armed forces. This effort had been very moderately successful, but had provided a small cadre of trained military leaders at the time of the rising. Jovanović appears to have been one of this group.

He was a Montenegrin, and first appeared openly as the commander of a mixed local rebel detachment in Montenegro in the explosion of popular resistance to the Italians in July 1941. An improvised Partisan staff was composed of regular officers like himself, and including leaders of exclusively nationalist bands such as Djurišić and Stanišić who were later to form in the bitter blood feuds of civil war the Četnik organization in these areas. This original directing staff was also composed of members of the Montenegrin Communist Party and of Djilas as the delegate of the Central Committee.

Jovanović joined Tito after the escape of the surviving Serbian Partisan units into Montenegro in December 1941 and became, in effect, the Chief of Staff of the central group of the Partisan forces.

Our contacts with him were frequent but without significance. I never got to know him on relaxed personal terms nor conducted any business of import with him.

He appeared an obstinate and impulsive man, conscious of his military training, but, as far as we could perceive, a frustrated adviser on tactical matters, transmitting Tito's orders to visiting commanders, but not entrusted with decisions.

It was one of the prime tasks of the British mission to report on the structure of the Partisan leadership to whom we had been sent, and on its military formation and strength.

The conditions of our experience in the Sutjeska battle, and of our erratic moves through the forests and empty villages of Bosnia, did not permit any tidy and detailed transmission of such fragments of our observations. These were formed essentially during the weeks of enforced idleness on the plateau of Petrovo Polje, and in the relative calm of our existence at Jajce.

The patent inadequacy of W/T communications in such, or indeed any, circumstances prompted me to signal British Headquarters in the Middle East during August with the proposal that I should come out to Cairo and report on the work of the mission to date, and brief in such detail as was at my disposal the senior officer whom I had also proposed should now be sent to establish more formal liaison with a significant and predominant resistance force.*

In the event, the first proposal was not taken up by my superiors, and the second was implemented in mid-September without any prior contact between myself and Brigadier Fitzroy Maclean, my successor.

The information pieced together by the first mission on the basis of our directives of May 1943 was thus conveyed in hasty verbal summary to Maclean after his arrival, and, in immediate retrospect, in more detailed reports on my return to Cairo.

It is perhaps of some historical value, however, to record in narrative form, in distant reflection, and as perceived at the time without the benefit of hindsight or subsequent evidence, the lineaments of the military and political leadership of the Yugoslav Partisan movement to which the 'Typical' party had been sent.

The first query, so long unanswered and unrevealed, was simple to clarify. The 'guerrilla' forces were commanded by Tito with personal and absolute authority. He was surrounded by a group of advisers, not constant in its composition but altering frequently by the coming and going of commanders and delegates on special missions.

This body was novel and flexible in its structure, secret in its actions, and defied any precise analysis by inexpert strangers inevitably viewed with correct caution and guarded suspicion,

* See p. 107.

softened to some degree by the accident of shared peril and human comradeship in the bitter episode of a fight for survival.

The immediate companions of the commander were designated as the Supreme Staff, but such a term was misleading and it was clear to us from the beginning that it bore no relation to the structure of an army in the sense that an Allied mission could grasp with automatic understanding. Nor indeed was this 'Supreme Staff' of Tito conceived in any conventional terms.

The political and military aspects of the direction of the Yugoslav National Liberation Movement were deliberately and inextricably intertwined.

The military organization of the Partisan rising in July 1941 was the work of an inner group drawn from the Politburo and the Central Committee of the Yugoslav Communist Party, at that time hidden in Belgrade.

After the transfer of the central leadership to Western Serbia in September 1941, and the creation of the 'free territory' at Užice, the structure was revised at the village of Stolice at a military 'consultation' of the Central Committee with local Partisan commanders of the early detachments formed at the outbreak of the rising in various regions of the country. At this meeting was set up 'the Supreme Command of the National Liberation Partisan Detachments of Yugoslavia'.

It was then decided to set up headquarters in Bosnia and Hercegovina, Croatia, Slovenia, and Montenegro for the purpose of directing operations in those areas, whereas in Serbia, where the Supreme Staff was in direct charge, the headquarters was formed only after the retreat of the main Partisan forces from Serbia. The setting up of headquarters in the various provinces was rendered necessary by the lack of communications and by the need to promote a more rapid spreading of the uprising and a better conduct of military operations. Tactics were to be brought in harmony with the peculiarities of each respective area. The Supreme Staff continued to operate as the highest military organ making strategical and tactical suggestions to the various headquarters and co-ordinating large-scale military operations.

However, the Supreme Staff exercised also a political function, namely, as a State administration, and that of organizer of the people's authorities, because the majority of the members of the Politburo composed the Supreme Staff.*

---

* The historical origins of the Supreme Staff are best described in Tito's own subsequent account quoted above from a speech 'On the Tenth Anniversary of the Yugoslav People's Army' (*Speeches and Articles*, vol. V., pp. 290 ff.).

The structure of this Supreme Staff was never strictly defined as distinct from that of the Politburo and the Central Committee itself. Its members served on one, each, or all of these bodies, and in the turbulent mobility and sporadic hazards of Partisan war it was inevitable that individual functions and tasks were improvised and changing. A formal list of the membership of the Supreme Staff at any one time as a distinct body would therefore be misleading and unreal. In addition to exercising overall control of the military operations and organization of the Partisan forces, senior party leaders appointed to the Supreme Staff were frequently absent from headquarters on special missions.

The Supreme Staff was, at the same time, the military embodiment of the political leadership of the Party and the real strategic decisions at each successive phase of the rising were taken by an inner group formed by Tito, and drawn either from the Politburo, elected at the underground Party Congress in Zagreb in October 1940, or picked according to special duties from the Central Committee re-formed at the same meeting.

In practice these nominations related either to establishing the central authority of Tito and the Supreme Staff over the regional organizations, or to developing a 'technical' body such as the Medical section created by Gojko Nikoliš.* With certain members of the original inner group formed by Tito, the British mission was to come into varying degrees of contact between May and September 1943, as also with military and political delegates, who were appointed progressively to the Supreme Staff as an act of status rather than precise function.

We soon became accustomed to the sudden arrivals and departures of figures with whom we had brief personal interchanges, often stimulated and enlivened by mutual curiosity.

In the immediate entourage of Tito, one figure was constantly present and usually silent. He was first known to us as 'Marko'. His apparent functions were of a security nature, assisted by an élite Escort battalion drawn from the original Serb *odreds* of the rising. Alexander Ranković – his real name – was taciturn and unruffled, of great physical courage proved constantly in the early weeks in enemy ambushes and air attacks, aloof from contact with us, partly out of linguistic difficulties but also from a natural reticence and lack of fluency of speech.

Ranković gave the impression of an experienced Party worker,

* See p. 38 ff.

hardened to the subtle dangers of an underground world: the Communist secret agent of conventional legend of the kind our superiors would expect us to meet.

In a sense, this superficial image fitted. He came of poor peasant stock from Serbia and started his adult life in the 1920s as a tailor's apprentice in Belgrade. He became active in the craft unions in the Yugoslav capital, and joined the Communist Youth and the regional Party committee. He had a natural genius for political organization in 'illegal' urban conditions, and his activities were halted by a prison sentence of six years in early 1929. It was under these conditions that he met Tito and Pijade, and his real political education began at the 'prison school' of Lepoglava.

In terms of Marxist classification Ranković, although of peasant stock, was the only worker apart from Tito himself as distinct from the intellectuals in the Partisan leadership.

On the release of the prison group of the Yugoslav Communist Party, he became the specialist in the organization of the cadres and of work in the trades unions, and the boss of the small Serb regional leadership.

Although we did not know it at the time, merely sensing the seniority of his political function, Ranković was, when the British mission met him, the secretary of the Central Committee with the special task of organizing political work within the military units of the Partisan forces.

The extent to which the army of Tito was under firm Communist Party control was one of our tasks as a mission to elucidate. Our impressions were formed in fragments of experience in chance moments of accompanying Partisan brigades and smaller units, but a firm and general picture was to emerge during these months. The subject was never formally discussed, and we could but observe within personal limits.

Ranković could have supplied the answer, but the degree of Party control over the army throughout the regions of Yugoslavia was an intricate and delicate affair, and although the determination to exert the absolute authority of the Communist leadership over the National Liberation Movement as a whole was patent and clear, the extent was a constant and fluid concern which not even the Supreme Staff could have defined with precision during the period of our presence.

He remained a secret figure in our midst, with rare glimpses of a person. It was recounted to us that in April 1941 he had been arrested in Belgrade by the Gestapo and released by a dramatic raid on the main prison hospital by a Party action squad. We knew also that his wife, who had emigrated as a young Serb peasant girl to Belgrade and become a textile worker, had shared in his conspiratorial work and taken part in the rising in Serbia. She was killed a year before our arrival in a local clash with Četniks.

Ranković was aware of and not displeased by our presence in the circle of the Staff, and we were often in his company. It was he who took charge of our party within minutes when Tito was wounded and Stuart killed, and during the following days he was in effective and unobtrusive authority.

Our immediate survival was probably mainly owing to his nerve and promptitude. I remember him moving tirelessly, during the next hours, maintaining order among the scattered pockets of the Escort, dispersing without savagery the tragic menace of civilian refugees betraying our presence at night to the enemy by lighting fires for warmth, and ever at Tito's side.

In after years Ranković reminded me of the extent of our hunger in the form of an anecdote. He had for a brief while moved ahead of our party alone into a deserted village where the domestic pigs had gone wild. He shot one, and carried it back to our improvised encampment where the animal on a spit became the centre of our restrained but impatient attention. Apparently he watched me as my turn came to partake of this transient luxury, and my greedy haste was betrayed by the grease streaming down my uniform. Such are the small mental pictures which are preserved in the mind, obliterating episodes of more savage import and deeper significance.

Apart from Tito himself, Ranković, Pijade, and Djilas whom we had encountered in the first days, the inner political group of the leadership included two other personalities, one of whom came to be associated closely with the British, and the other in a lesser degree. They were Ivo Lola Ribar, and Edvard Kardelj.

Ivo Lola Ribar was twenty-seven years old at the time of the Fifth Offensive. He was the leading representative of the new generation of Communist youth, and secretary of the Central Committee of its organization in 1939. In the following year he was elected to the Politburo of the Party.

The members of SKOJ were to form the political cadres of the Partisan detachments, and in many instances rose to military commands; a particular group of future leaders formed by historical accident in Belgrade University.

Numerically this was a stronger formation than the Communist party itself, which had about 8,000 members in 1941. By the same year 30,000 young people, most of them university and high school students from the towns, had joined this organization. They were the essential core of propagandists and Party 'agitators'. About 15,000 were ordered to join Partisan detachments at the time of the rising, and it was their special role to proselytize the fighters. The girls served as nurses and ran unit newspapers, but many fought in the ranks.*

Lola Ribar was the symbol and idol of this youth, and, in a sense, the 'dauphin' of Tito, who had brought him into the reconstructed Central Committee of the Party as the leader of SKOJ.

Lola was a Croat and the elder son of Ivan Ribar, a Zagreb lawyer and politician, who had been President of the Yugoslav Parliament after 1919. By an historic irony the father was responsible for the passing of the legislation outlawing the young Communist Party, and, later, under the influence of Lola, he rallied to Tito and became President of the first provisional 'assembly' of the National Liberation Movement set up at Bihać in Western Bosnia in November 1942.

I was to meet and converse with both father and son on many occasions.

Lola was a dark restless young man, with a square strong countenance and unruly thick hair. He was of lucid intelligence and wide experience for his years. He had represented the Belgrade students at the Comintern-organized World Youth Congress in Paris in 1937 and had made international contacts at that time. He spoke accurate French, and was a lively debater, quick to take points but unshakeable in his set views. Tolerance of others was not his main characteristic, but his self-assured rigidity of outlook was softened by natural charm. Lola had iron nerves and will and survived cheerfully perilous missions, in particular to the underground Croat Party Committee and cells in occupied Zagreb.

I acquired respect and affection for him. In the event of a Partisan victory he would have been one of the leaders of the New

* 12,000 members of SKOJ were killed in the first nine months of the rising.

Yugoslavia. Fate was, however, to strike him down, a few paces from my side, in November 1943.*

Edvard Kardelj, in contrast to Lola Ribar, was one of very few survivors, politically and physically, of the older generation of the Yugoslav Communist Party. He was younger than Tito. A Slovene, from a working-class family in Ljubljana, Kardelj was born in 1910 and trained as a teacher. He was a militant in Party organizations from the age of 17 and served two prison sentences. He first met Tito in 1934 at a secret regional Party congress, and at the end of that year was sent to the Soviet Union where he attended the Lenin School in Moscow and lectured in the Communist University for Western Minorities.

He returned to Yugoslavia in 1937, in the same year as Tito. The two men were the only survivors of the Stalin purges which embraced the decimation of the Yugoslav Central Committee then based in Moscow.

Tito and Kardelj were linked by their Russian experience, an ambivalent education shared by hardly any other members of the reconstructed Yugoslav Party organization at that time.

Kardelj was not present during the early months of our mission in the country. I did not meet him until his appearance in Jajce in the autumn of 1943. His function was of vital import to the leadership as the head of the Slovene Liberation Movement, and responsible for an important strategic area of Partisan operations.

He seemed to be second only to Tito, and was in fact chairman of the Central Committee.

Presumably because of his previous Russian connections, Kardelj, for some months in 1942, was hidden in Zagreb in charge of the secret W/T transmitter working to Moscow. He once told me that this was a particularly interesting moment. We never found the time to enlarge on this tantalizing hint.

Kardelj was a short neat man, bespectacled with a trim moustache. He was not talkative, but when he spoke it was with quiet assurance and authority. He appeared deceptively to be a typical bookish Marxist intellectual, but his moral status as leader of Slovene resistance and his skill in creating the only genuine regional all-party United Front belied such a simple impression and revealed marked political skills and powers of leadership.

These men, Pijade, Djilas, Ranković, Lola Ribar, and Kardelj,

* See p. 252.

H

appeared to form the inner cabinet of Tito. There were others, both Party functionaries and military commanders, who were co-opted at times, and present on certain occasions. All major decisions of strategy, military and political, were taken by this circle within the Supreme Staff.

The Operational section headed by Arso Jovanović as Chief of Staff was responsible for planning and was essentially advisory.

Apart from Jovanović, there were two Vice-Chiefs of Staff, 'Veljko', Colonel Pavle Ilić, who had met us as Tito's personal representative at the landing ground where we had been dropped; and Colonel Velimir Terzić.

'Veljko', who acted for a time as liaison officer to the British mission, had been a captain in the Royal Yugoslav army. He was a Serb from the Roumanian border and had joined the Partisans in Serbia in July 1941, when he commanded one of the outstanding early detachments drawn from Kosmaj, a mountain area south of Belgrade. He was accepted into the Party the following year, and shortly afterwards was appointed to the Staff.

He was a friendly and open companion, tall and elegant in his uniform, a modest and efficient regular officer; one of those who had joined the Partisans in a mood of humiliation at the deficiencies of the Royal Yugoslav army command in the campaign of April 1941, and in the quiet conviction of the duty to continue the fight.

Terzić was, like Ilić, also a former Royal Yugoslav officer. A Montenegrin by birth, he had joined the 'military committee' which had organized the rising against the Italians in Montenegro in July 1941. As also in the case of Ilić, his first experience with the Partisans was as commander of a local Partisan detachment.

He appeared to act as Jovanović's second-in-command, and was personally closer to him than Ilić – in all probability because of their previous work together in Montenegro.

To the members of the British mission, Terzić was a familiar figure, and we were in frequent contact with him in the days of the Sutjeska battle, as he bore to Stuart or myself hasty reports of intended moves.

He was a bustling grave man, direct and simple in his dealings. We lost sight of him later when he was sent as Chief of Staff to the Partisan headquarters in Croatia.

Such were our impressions and the limits of our knowledge of

the Partisan leadership and the structure of the Supreme Staff
during the months of our mission.

What of the army itself and its military value? The British
government and Chiefs of Staff had authorized Cairo to send missions to territories which appeared to be outside the direct control
of Mihailović and where 'Croat and Slovene guerrillas' were dimly
reported to be operating. It was the task of such parties to report
on the nature and organization of such bands and, in the case of
'Typical', to investigate the position as seen from the central command of the 'Partisans', a loose term which was reluctantly employed in London.

The existence and location of a central command had been
discovered by the first exploratory mission of Canadian Croats less
than a month before we were dropped. 'Typical' mission had parachuted in May 1943, almost with innocence, into a battle for survival. It could at least be said that we came without prejudice, our
minds vacant and fresh, untrammelled by intelligence summaries.
Our observations would be from scratch.

In physical appearance it was a motley army, the troops
dressed in captured Italian or German uniforms, disconcerting
at times in abrupt encounters at close quarters in the woods, in
the grey service dress of the former Royal Yugoslav army, or in
peasant clothes. They were lightly armed with rifles or light sub-
machine guns with bandoliers of ammunition and some of them
with Italian hand grenades attached to their belts. The generations blended, ranging from veterans of earlier campaigns, of the
Balkan Wars and Salonika, to boys – and girls – in their teens.
Some units grouped the young in special battalions or companies.

The officers at this time bore no badges of rank; like their men
they wore a five-pointed red star on their forage caps, on varied
peasant headgear, or the leather peaked hats of workers.

Pictures formed, and impressions made patterns in the night
columns and the frozen still halts in daylight.

More ordered images shaped in immediate retrospect.

A considerable force of lightly armed and hardened fighters of
some twenty thousand men was engaged in a fanatic search to
outmanoeuvre a highly professional military operation of encirclement, conceived by the German command and conducted in the
main by élite S.S. and Alpine troops as part of a force more than
five times the number of their opponents, equipped with heavy

weapons and mountain artillery, supported by fighter and light bomber aircraft.

The strategic initiative lay with the Germans, and their lumbering precision might prove annihilating.

Partisan tactics were conceived in the counter image of the enemy, and the special style of their actions engendered the miracle of their survival.

Faced with the overwhelming numerical and logistic superiority of the Axis forces, Tito's troops exploited certain advantages, born of the sum of experience of previous actions, and the evolution of special technical skills.

The Partisans were moving on inner lines within a tightening ring. Lightly armed and familiar with the terrain, trained to operate instinctively in small and isolated parties, their units could evade encircling thrusts of the enemy. Skilled in ambush and experts in night fighting at close quarters – for which the Germans showed peculiar reluctance – the Yugoslav troops could often gain brief but vital local superiority. The protection of the general movements of their columns was decisive to the outcome of the battle. This narrowed to a race for the mountain crests, which dominated in scattered dots the river crossings and the upland tracks. Each height was the scene of hand-to-hand clashes without quarter, to be held at all costs in unison with the moving columns of the main group of Tito's forces with their sick and wounded.

The probing of the enemy circle was the supreme test of Partisan tactics. The decisions facing Tito and his Staff were brutal in their simplicity: to mislead the enemy as to the main direction of his forces seeking to break out of the ring, to preserve a striking force with the purpose of completing such an action, and at the same time to protect the columns of the hospitals.

The Germans were at certain disadvantages, and, in particular, in their profound underestimation as professional soldiers of the tactical skill of their enemy, and their contemptuous neglect of study of the special nature of partisan warfare. The Germans were also moving concentrically long distances, slow to block a thrusting assault at gaps in ragged terrain. Their columns moved encumbered with the impedimenta of a regular army.

Tito once described to me watching units of the S.S. division lumbering snail-like with their field kitchens bringing slow reinforcements to a critical sector. He recounted to me that the German planning was more sophisticated and effective than in the previous Fourth Offensive, but that they had missed the lesson of creating mobile units with special anti-Partisan training. German forward units were always pressing behind the Yugoslavs, and could never move with speed in self-contained columns to attack the Partisan forces from the rear. By not winning every grim race for each mountain crest, the German operation failed in its central purpose of annihilating the Yugoslav main operational group.*

The main operational group in the Sutjeska battle formed the central military force of the Partisan movement and, together with further divisions and brigades brought into the action, the Supreme Staff had at its disposal about twenty thousand fighting troops.

The first and essential characteristic of these military formations was their mobility and capacity to fight in independent units without awaiting superior orders.

Some understanding of the history of their formation, the peculiar structure of the Yugoslav National Liberation Army, and the characteristics of its commanders and officer cadres, was essential to the functioning of our mission.

During the three months between the epic of the Sutjeska and our sojourn at Jajce, I attempted to piece together from observation, and many chance conversations and personal encounters, an estimate of the numerical strength of the Partisan military formations, and their organization.

The designation of units – corps, divisions, brigades, and battalions – was deceptive and gave a first and transitory misleading impression of a regular army in the conventional sense. The National Liberation People's Army as it was now christened combined in a unique form 'regular' and 'guerrilla' components.

From the outset it was the intention of the Communist leadership to provoke a general military rising throughout Yugoslavia against the occupier, embracing all national and regional elements of whatever racial origin or creed. This required the creation of a military organization, which must be rigidly controlled by the Party at all levels, and be tightly woven into the several territories of the country in close association with the population. There would be a struggle of a strictly military nature against the occupiers and their satellites, and a simultaneous battle for the minds

* Interview of the author with Tito, 27 August 1967.

of the masses – and given the social structure and economy of Yugoslavia, this meant the peasantry.

In the late summer of 1941, at specific times varying according to regional conditions through enemy-occupied and partitioned Yugoslavia, 'rebel' and 'patriot' bands appeared in a variety of traditional forms and bearing names evoking historic memories: *Čete* (companies); *Komitadji* (irregular bands especially in Montenegro and Macedonia with long traditions of Turkish wars); *Komite* (a similar designation); and more novel *Odredi* (detachments).

The conditions of revolt varied by regions, and in the late summer of 1941 risings against the Axis occupation forces and their newly established satellites – Anton Pavelić in the 'Independent State of Croatia', and later General Milan Nedić in a rump Serb state – were in the main confined to Serbia, Montenegro, Bosnia, and Hercegovina.

In some areas bands formed spontaneously; in others mixed units under nationalist or Communist influence and many in uneasy collaboration coalesced, while in Serbia a calculated rising was organized by the Yugoslav Communist Party, who had set up a secret military committee in the autumn of 1940 to plan for the event of rebellion.

In Tito's words: 'After the capitulation of April the military committee was enlarged and named the General Headquarters of the Partisan Detachments of Yugoslavia . . . [following] the mass slaughter by the Ustaša of the Serb population in Croatia and Bosnia the Communist Party began to send its members to organize into guerrilla detachments the population which had fled to the woods.' [7]

These developments during the two years preceding the appearance of the British mission at Tito's headquarters were intricate, confused, and still defy precise analysis.

In essence, the evolution of the military structure was dominated by the need to maintain a simple territorial organization of local detachments, which would maintain a presence in times of enemy punitive expeditions, and act as a source of recruits when larger formations liberated and held, for a space, 'free territories' – essential bases for the regional extension of a centralized liberating movement.

The military shape of rebellion assumed varied forms and Tito was faced, after the collapse of the rising in Serbia, with the formidable task of welding together scattered elements of resistance and imposing upon them a rudimentary military organization, while at the same time hastening the process of establishing the control of the Communist Party throughout the areas of rebellion.

The rising in Serbia had been directed by the Central Committee of the Party, and to a less effective extent also in Montenegro. In Croatia the main Party Committee had been arrested by the local Royal Yugoslav authorities before 1941 and handed over to Pavelić in April. There was therefore no central impulse leading to an organized rising throughout Croatia. Early resistance in the regions of the Lika, Kordun, and Banija took the form of spontaneous reactions of defence by the local Serb population against the massacres perpetrated by the Ustaša of Pavelić in the Orthodox villages in the summer of 1941. Similar events took place in Bosnia and Hercegovina where again local Serb villagers took up arms against the new collaborationist regime.

The Supreme Staff which Tito had formed in Serbia in November 1941 had not the technical means of communication nor trained military personalities in sufficient numbers to impose a direct control over these local centres of resistance. The conditions for any national front under disguised Communist leadership, which the Russians persisted in urging, simply did not exist. The breakdown of the brief moment of co-operation between the Communists and Četniks in Serbia was repeated throughout the other Yugoslav provinces where there was a Serb minority. In most of these areas the Communist Party had little or no contact or organization, and the local Serb leaders were usually either former Royal Yugoslav officers or from the police force.

The task of setting up elementary military formations of the Party on a regional basis was primarily the work of roving delegates from the Supreme Staff whose direct control could only be extended painfully and gradually.

It was from the local village roots based on territorial companies, the *odreds*, that the whole Partisan organization was to rest, and to create, with the mobile Proletarian Brigades, the two most original forms of military organization.

The units formed spontaneously, sometimes joining a local Communist nucleus, and others created from the beginning by Party members. They were a vital and indeed the main source of recruits, and their structure was kept flexible. From these *odreds* also were drawn candidates for training as officers. They remained throughout the war the real focus of local military talent.

In the building up of the armed forces of the National Liberation Movement the shortage of trained military leaders was acute.
All Yugoslavs of whatever background had received a basic military training at some stage. But this related only to certain age
groups, and it was to a considerable and marked degree that the
youth rallied to the Partisan movement. The Party itself had an
effective but numerically small cadre of members who had served
in the Spanish Civil War in the Republican armed forces and they
provided an invaluable nucleus of commanders. The Party had
also some secret members within the former Royal Yugoslav
forces and they formed yet another group. In many cases, however, the local Partisan staffs were obliged to draw on the military
experience of former regular officers and non-commissioned
officers. Their presence within the Partisan movement provided an
essential military leadership in certain moments and also represented a lurking political danger. In many cases these men were
prepared to fight the occupier but not to accept the leadership of
the Communist Party. Some stayed in the Partisan ranks and
joined the Party as the leading resistance element in the country,
others went over to the Četniks or never left them, and their very
existence symbolized the deep cleavages in Yugoslav life in each
region.

Tito and his Staff had now formed a conception of Partisan war
which deviated both from past Soviet practice and present diplomatic tactics. The basic military difference of interpretation was
simple. To the Russians, the creation of Partisan units was as an
auxiliary weapon of a regular army to carry out certain tasks behind the enemy lines; to the Yugoslavs the Partisan units *were*
the army, organized in mobile formations and in territorial defence units, which together represented the morale and ideology
of revolutionary war. Tito believed from the beginning that he
was creating an experience in revolution which had no precedent.

The Supreme Staff, together with the group of Serb detachments from the 'Užice Republic' under its direct command,
crossed the river Uvac into the Sandžak on 12 December 1941.

The fighting in Serbia was the first experience of Partisan war,
and the measure of the natural tactical skill, and the example of
certain weaknesses, of military organization. Tito concluded, in a
later analysis:

It became crystal clear that we could not carry out large-scale operations with combined Partisan detachments and battalions, and that we had to undertake the gradual creation of larger, purely military, formations. This was necessary for the following reasons: it was very difficult to conduct a frontal warfare with scattered Partisan detachments; these were semi-military formations ill-adapted for fighting outside their areas, because many Partisan fighters still felt that they were fighting only to defend their own villages; the Partisan fighters were in constant contact with the members of their families, often slept at home and so on, which sometimes had very adverse effects, especially when they were killed fighting in front of their families. All this compelled us to begin the organization of purely military formations.[8]

On 22 December 1941 the first Proletarian Brigade was formed at Rudo in the Sandžak, 'a regular military unit which could be used in any theatre of war in Yugoslavia', and a Second Brigade was constituted from other Serb detachments on 1 March 1942. In the late spring of 1942, the Third Sandžak Brigade and the Fourth and Fifth Montenegrin Brigades were set up. Thus Tito now had under his direct command five such formations (about 800 to 1,000 fighters each). They were composed of the core of the West Serbian *odreds*, and those detachments which followed Tito into Bosnia out of the Sandžak, Montenegro, and Hercegovina. Henceforth they were to operate as grand companies, uprooted from their home territories, and as the military arm of a political revolution.

The myth of an élite proletarian guard had been created and the language is significant: 'The proletarian people's liberation shock brigades are the military shock formations of the peoples of Yugoslavia under the leadership of the Communist Party . . .'*

Simultaneously with their rôle as a military striking force, the proletarian brigades thus formed the political arm of the National Liberation Movement.

The immediate task, at its formation, of the First Proletarian Brigade was to ensure the hold of the Partisans over the key strategic area of East Bosnia, where the first local detachments were disintegrating.

By November 1942, when the Anti-Fascist Council met at Bihać, the Proletarian Brigades had increased to twenty-eight such formations. Grouped together they were now capable of undertaking more sophisticated military operations against the enemy, as in Bosnia in the middle of that year.

* Article One of the Statutes setting up the First Proletarian Brigade.

At the same time, the Yugoslav leadership decided to set up divisions and corps. The first two divisions, the First and Second Proletarian, were formed on 1 November 1942 and six more by the end of the year.

These units were mobile, small in numbers, and light in equipment. They were created, apart from the first two, on a territorial–national basis, and all local formations were subordinate to them.

In December 1942 a party section was attached to each division in charge of the whole structure of political work within the unit, and responsible direct to the regional Party committee or to the Central Committee.

Each division was a self-contained world with its own hospital, finance and supply organization, military court and police, its postal service in certain areas, and sometimes its band and choir.

Military expansion was closely co-ordinated with the major political rôle. It was in the ranks of these units that the ideal of a united Yugoslav movement was inculcated, 'expanding the liberation struggle and particularly in spreading and consolidating brotherhood and unity among the nationalities'.

These brigades were also the conquerors and guardians of 'free territories' from Užice to Foča and in the great march of the summer of 1942 to Western Bosnia, the Lika, and the Kordun, where, under their shield, the 'Bihać Republic', stretching over 45,000 square kilometres, was set up, and the political structure of the movement evolved in a firm pattern.

Such were the military formations, with which the British mission at times briefly found themselves moving in clashes with the enemy or visiting their staffs.

It was in particular with the First and Second Proletarian Divisions that our main experience was acquired.

The companies, battalions, and brigades were mainly composed of the survivors of the Serbian detachments and those from Montenegro and the Sandžak, and recruits drawn from territorial *odreds* during the long march of these formations from Bosnia to the 'free territory' of Bihać: Serb peasants from the Lika and Bosanska Krajina and Banija, the historic Croat military frontier, Dalmatians from their precarious footholds in the white limestone mountains behind the Adriatic coast.

The two divisional commanders were often in our company, and symbolized one special element in the Partisan military leadership.

At the head of the First Proletarian Division was General Koča Popović. He had been present at our first encounter with Tito and his Staff on the morning of our arrival, but his identity was not disclosed.

Taut, and deliberately controlled by a sensitive and disciplined mind and power of will, Popović was an intellectual soldier of outstanding talents, which were perhaps alien to his inner nature. He came from a prosperous Belgrade family and had broken away early from his domestic roots after his philosophical studies in the university. He moved to Paris where he frequented the circles of Surrealists, the Left Bank world of poets, writers, and artists. He was bilingual in caustic polished French, and his mental defences were impenetrable. His sarcasm was rapier-like, respectful of counter-thrusts, but he was never off his guard.

He graduated from youthful rootlessness into the discipline of the clandestine activities of the illegal Yugoslav Communist machine. Popović was drafted with a group of selected Party members to Spain, through the 'centre', under the charge of Tito, for Balkan volunteers established in Paris under the auspices of the Comintern.

Popović fought with the Spanish Republican forces, not in the International Brigades, and became an artillery captain. This experience was his military school, and he missed no aspect of the Spanish prelude.

He escaped through France at the close of the Spanish Civil War, and through illegal Party channels found his way back to Yugoslavia.

He once told me that he was mobilized as a reserve officer in the Royal Yugoslav army in 1940, and ordered by his colonel to watch out for subversive activities in the regiment.

After the surrender of April 1941, Koča Popović organized, and commanded, the Kosmaj *odred* during the rising in Serbia, the training cadre of many future Partisan commanders (including Pavle Ilić). On the formation of the First Proletarian Brigade, Popović became its commander, and, by logical progression, commander of the First Proletarian Division.

Popović was a lone wolf and a solitary man, with rare unguarded moments. He had a touch of military genius and a hatred of war. He was wary of friendship, and defended with devilish skill a total integrity of mind and heart.

As a divisional commander, with his sure instinct and lightning comprehension of immediate situations, Koča Popović, on his sudden initiative, sensed the weak point in the German encircling ring north of the Sutjeska, and was the immediate architect of our salvation.

I was frequently in his company, and grew to accept his contrived and polished sallies. Daring with cold deliberation, and secret by nature, he was the idol of his troops, but few men knew him.

His lack of fairness in private debate concealed, usually with success, a profound understanding of the reactionary capitalist British whom he was amused to assume that we represented.

The commander of the Second Proletarian Division, Peko Dapčević, had one special bond with Popović. They had both fought in Spain. It would be difficult to find any other personal characteristic which linked them, except a total indifference to physical danger.

Peko was the son of a merchant, and was born near Cetinje, the old capital of Montenegro. It was the ambition of every Montenegrin family clan to send its sons either to study law in Belgrade, or to enter the Serb military academy.

Indeed, the accident of fortune in this competition of careers, in the Montenegrin clans, marked the grouping and bitter divisions of the future local Partisan and Četnik leaders in those regions. The students became the former, and the regular officers the latter.

He studied law in Belgrade and was drawn into the group of progressive student clubs. He graduated in 1937, and, together with the selected band which included Koča, was passed through Party channels to Spain where he fought in the Republican forces. In 1939–40 he was interned in France, and returned through the same conspiratorial channels to Yugoslavia.

During the July rising in Montenegro Peko Dapčević commanded the Partisan Lovćen *odred* and acted as Chief of Staff to the early 'military committee' in Montenegro.

Peko was brought on to the Supreme Staff created at the Stolice 'military consultation' in November 1941 in Serbia, and after commanding the Fourth Proletarian Brigade on its formation out of the original Partisan detachments in Montenegro and the Sandžak, he took charge of the Second Proletarian Division on its creation in Western Bosnia in November 1942, absorbing his

brigade and adding to the Montenegrins troops from the Bosanska Krajina and Dalmatia.

Peko was a natural and communicative leader, a *Komitadji* from
the Montenegrin highlands formed in the progressive schooling of
Belgrade student associations.

Both open in character and shrewd in the judgement of men,
Peko was the Communist *condottiere*, deep in the primitive traditions of guerrilla war tempered by the more sophisticated experiences of Spain.

If he gave his trust and friendship, it was a timeless act. He had
an air of naughtiness, which thinly masked a sharp and cool brain,
and darting mind.

I enjoyed his company and even in moments of tension we
would quarrel very occasionally over his excessive Montenegrin
idolatry of Mother Russia.

The 'Spaniards', of whom Koča Popović and Peko Dapčević
were outstanding examples, formed a select but small cadre of the
Partisan military leaders. About 1,200 Yugoslavs fought in the
Spanish Civil War, and during the years after 1941 four of the
Army (Corps) Commanders were Spanish veterans and twenty-
nine became generals.

But this group was only one element in the military leadership
of the National Liberation Army. Especially in the early days of
the rising, the Partisan detachments and larger formations were
dependent to a marked degree on officers and non-commissioned
officers of the former Royal Yugoslav army. They were regarded
with political caution, but many worked their passage.

Each unit from the local territorial *odred* to the divisional and
later corps commands was flanked by political commissars and
Party sections, and by 1943 this process was in practice complete.

Military qualities determined the selection both of commissars
and a new generation of commanders. Training courses were held
in each territorial region and the building of cadres, military and
political, was a constant and preoccupying task.

Our own impressions were very general, and bore no relation
to the mythical formula of 'Croat and Slovene guerrillas', whose
existence our mission and others were originally instructed to confirm and define.

As the British mission attached to the Supreme Staff of Tito, our observations were circumscribed by the areas in which we moved. At no time were we in a position to acquire professional and detailed information as to a conventional order of battle of the Partisan forces. Our knowledge of events in Slovenia and Croatia, for example, was limited to chance encounters with visiting delegates of the Staff or commanders of units reporting to Tito.

The calculations which we attempted to summarize were, therefore, very approximate, but certain elementary manifestations were clear. Other guesses would need the investigation of hindsight.

At the end of August 1943, in the relative calm of Jajce, we concluded that about 75,000 men were organized in regular military units, in addition to a swarm of local detachments. Of this central military organization we reckoned that about three-quarters of the rank and file were not members of the Communist Party, but that they were firmly integrated under Party leadership.

Of the military units with whom the British mission to Tito had direct knowledge, the overwhelming majority were Serbs, either from Serbia itself or from the Serb villages in Bosnia, Hercegovina, and Croatia, or – in racial identity – Montenegrins from certain clans, and Serb peasants from the Sandžak.

This assessment included Moslem units from Bosnia and Hercegovina, historically of Serbian race, and Croats from other regions.

The composition and strength of the Partisan army formations in Croatia, Dalmatia, and Slovenia was beyond the range of our experience.

The central conclusion of our observations was that the National Liberation Army, in marked and forceful contrast to the pan-Serb, anti-Croat, and anti-Moslem obsessions of the Mihailović Četniks, was a *Yugoslav* military organization embodying a revolutionary political movement, which, in its turn, was conceived as a counter society to that represented by the Royal Yugoslav government in London, formally recognized by the British.

The inherent contradictions, which the British mission to Tito, and similar missions in Partisan territory, had brought to light would have to be considered and confronted on a summit level.

The deepest impression of Partisan military formations, which summed up our experience, was that each unit was a closed society, and a human refuge from the destruction of their villages and the slaughter of their kin. This climate was conveyed in their haunting songs. They were fighting to return to their homes, which would be reconstructed in a new and better world than they had known. In the mass, they represented the underprivileged and the neglected of a former society, the age groups and social categories untouched by the local organizations of the traditional political parties of the past. This was the basic strength of the movement: the mobilization of the youth, the women, and the aged, and the creation of a new kinship and a special indefinable morale.

An exploratory stage was over, and the National Liberation Movement was entering on a new phase of development. On 23rd August therefore I sent out the following signal:

As the result of several talks with Tito in the past week and a general study of the situation, I consider that the preliminary stage of satisfactory contact with Partisan headquarters has been completed and that work should now develop on an organized plan. I feel therefore that two steps should urgently be taken: a Brigadier should now be sent to establish high level mission; and that I come out early next month to report in detail on the Partisan army, its potential military value, and the question of supplies this winter. Also on the centralization of British missions to the Partisans.* There is now the possibility of supplies by sea.

After discussion I could return with the Brigadier or jump back. As to exit from the country, landing grounds accessible to us here are practicable. There would be no need to send anyone to take charge. I need not be away more than ten days. Consider it necessary that above points be fully discussed in Cairo.

Our collaboration with the Partisans should be carried out latest by the end of September, in view of the fact that they must make important decisions before the winter. This has not yet been discussed with the Partisan Staff here. Please comment and report.

By a coincidence unknown to me, a senior officer had been selected to head a new mission to Tito's headquarters, and his directive, drafted personally by the Prime Minister on 23 July, had

---

* During July and August, six British-led missions were sent to Partisan commands in Bosnia and Slovenia. Their radio links were direct with Cairo, and we had no contact with them, and but scant knowledge of their tasks.

reached Cairo. The text was agreed, and amended in final form, on 11 August, in consultation with General Maitland Wilson, the British Commander-in-Chief in the Mediterranean theatre.

Wroughton recorded on 22 August: 'Very exciting news to-night. A Brigadier is coming September, and the Major is going back for discussions.' This reference must have been to a Cairo signal which either crossed with mine of the same day or was a reply to it.

The appointment of this senior mission was the culmination of high level discussions on British support to resistance movements in Yugoslavia of which I was unaware, except from rumours re-counted to me by Major Basil Davidson, whose mission had para-chuted to us on 16 August. He had been in charge of the Yugoslav section of S.O.E. in Cairo, and we had worked together in the planning of the first missions to the Partisans.

Basil Davidson stayed with us for a few days before leaving on his appointed task of moving to the Vojvodina, the flat fertile land between the Danube and the Hungarian border, where, with the prior agreement of Tito, it was intended that this British mission would be infiltrated into Hungary through Yugoslav channels.

It was with excited pleasure that I awaited the landing of Basil and his party, and we profited by our brief encounter to discuss the latest news from Cairo, and the general impressions formed by our mission.*

Two other British officers parachuted to us at Petrovo Polje on the night before the arrival of the Davidson mission. Flight-Lieutenant Kenneth Syers, in Royal Air Force uniform, arrived as the military intelligence officer to replace Bill Stuart. He appeared at alarming speed out of the darkness, a frail figure with his legs spreadeagled, but with good fortune only sprained his ankle.

He was followed by Ian Mackenzie, a Major in the Royal Army Medical Corps, and an experienced and gifted surgeon. His orderly was dropped on the following night, incongruously ac-companied by anti-tank rifles and explosives.

The arrival of Ian Mackenzie was more than a symbolic appear-

---

* Basil Davidson has described the experiences of his mission in his book *Partisan Picture* (Bedford Books, 1946), which is the first published account of a British mission with the Yugoslav National Liberation Army, and an inspired historical record of the climate of the grass roots of Partisan war as seen by a British officer in the autumn and winter of 1943.

Tito and the author at Jajce

Tito and Koča Popović: Jajce 1943

ance of a British military doctor. His natural modesty and special skills endeared him to the Yugoslav medical staff, and in particular to Gojko Nikoliš, with whom he established a warm and close understanding. The work of Ian Mackenzie, operating on the wounded alongside his Yugoslav colleagues, in continuous enemy actions pressing against the edges of our central headquarters, reflected a moral credit on the British mission beyond the bounds of conventional tribute.

In conversations with Tito and his Staff on Petrovo Polje, the question was raised of American representation, and there were hints of British obstruction to such a proposal. There was every reason for representation, both to emphasize Anglo-American solidarity in our policy towards Yugoslav resistance, and to mark our co-operation by the presence of an American officer together with our own mission. I had signalled Cairo in this sense in early July, strongly urging that such a move should be made. On 7 July Wroughton noted that we were to receive 'American officers', and according to Vlada Dedijer, 'a member of the British mission' told him on 17 July that an American mission was now expected and would be 'under British command'.[7]

In the early hours of 21 August* the reception party stood by near the village of Oklinak on Petrovo Polje to receive Captain Melvin O. Benson of the American Office of Strategic Services.

His previous experience of 'Special operations' created an immediate bond between us. 'Benny' Benson had volunteered for this work, before the United States entered the war, and had been trained by the British in the delicate months before the Japanese attack on Pearl Harbour.

His superiors then drafted him to join an Anglo-American party to be sent to the Burma Road from a base in Java. He escaped from the Japanese invading forces of the island to Australia, and had arrived by slow boat – an additional shared experience – to Egypt in December 1942.

Benson was sent on a British parachute training course and to another specialist establishment dealing with explosives. At the beginning of July, possibly in relation with my signal, he was informed that he would be parachuted into Yugoslavia to join Tito.

---

* In Captain Benson's citation for the Legion of Merit the date is given as 21 August; in his report on his mission (22 June 1944), as 22 August. The date of 21 August is confirmed in Wroughton's diary.

I

To our mutual good fortune, the arrival of Benson strengthened
our joint task of reporting on the Partisan situation. We worked
as one mission, and shared without reserve our impressions and
information. It was agreed between us that he should use our
radio link rather than set up separate W/T communications.
There were practical advantages. We were operating in mobile
and uncertain conditions. The natural hesitation at O.S.S. Headquarters that the lack of an American set, operating independently,
would lead to an undue absorption of their representative by the
existing British mission and a mere repetition of identical reporting,
was quickly dispelled by Benson himself. His independence in
regard to the British mission never became an issue.

As he wrote in his subsequent report:

Being dependent on the British radio and operator was not entirely
satisfactory. Difficulties of keeping batteries charged, and the need for
minimum time on the air, coupled with the fact that quite often we
were moving from place to place, made a duplication of messages most
impractical. The British officer and I together obtained all the information which he transmitted, and although I called this to the
attention of my Commanding Officer at Cairo, I feel that my work was
judged by the few signals I sent rather than by the work done by the
Anglo-American mission.

On the evening of his arrival, Benson dined with Tito and his
Staff and was received with marked cordiality. The Yugoslavs
were in urgent need of publicity in the United States on the details
of their struggle, and in particular among the American groups of
Croat and Slovene origin, whose influence on official policy towards Yugoslav affairs was of special import and had hitherto
been orchestrated in an anti-Partisan direction.

Tito's first request to Benson was for the transmission of propaganda aimed at these groups in the United States, to counter the
powerful pan-Serb elements which were effectively dominating
the American press, both in the national and local language
newspapers.

Closely connected with this campaign, of vital concern to Partisan headquarters, was the evaluation of Četnik collaboration with
the Axis, and the transmission of the evidence now being assembled by the British mission – which was passed in its entirety
to Benson. This 'battle of the air' was parallel to that conducted
within the B.B.C., but of incomparably wider import in the United
States where counter-propaganda was skilfully organised among

PART I   III

the groups of Yugoslav origin backed by powerful political support in Congress and the Senate.

As Benson wrote in his final report on his mission:

> During my entire four months' stay with the Partisans, one thing that was always a source of embarrassment and annoyance was the misrepresentation of Yugoslav news over the New York and London radios. The giving of credit to the Četniks for Partisan victories and otherwise referring to them as Patriots, in an attempt to include the Četniks with the Partisans, was impossible to explain.

On 24 August the British mission was warned of an imminent and anticipated move from Petrovo Polje to Jajce, the medieval capital of Bosnia.

We walked into the town on the following morning. Life there seemed on the surface almost normal. There were fruit and vegetables in the market. Electricity functioned; the telephone lines were undamaged. The population were going about their daily business. It seemed, for a brief moment, as if we had walked out of the war: out of the armed clashes without quarter in the wilderness of the mountains, at times hand to hand in the forest glades and on paths in the hills, and into a tranquil provincial capital. It was a transient hallucination, but we were already used to living in the moment, and to busying ourselves with the simple facts of existence.

By the same evening Jajce began to assume the character of a military headquarters. Tito and the Supreme Staff took up their abode in the buildings clustered round the old Turkish fortress dominating the town, and units of the army camped on the outskirts, thrusting out patrols along the river Vrbas, protecting the whole of the valley.

The British mission, together with Ian Mackenzie, our surgeon, and Benny Benson, moved into a wooden cottage by the side of the river.

We had not lived in a house since leaving Africa. As Wroughton scribbled in his notebook: 'What a change. See no reason why we should ever go back to the old way of living . . . We are getting bacon and eggs for breakfast . . . These are all the things that we only dreamt and talked about two months ago.' And then he added: 'Of course, we may have to get out of here at any time.'

Two days later, I set out in a captured German staff car to

search for a landing ground and to organize the reception of the new mission. Instructions from our main headquarters, now in Italy, gave us as yet no details of the composition of this party, but indicated that they would attempt to land by plane if a suitable field could be located.

Daily bombing of Jajce by enemy planes, and air reconnaissance over the surrounding country, made it essential to fix a pinpoint at a safe distance away from our 'capital'.

There was a short break in the exchange of our messages. On 31 August we were instructed to be ready to receive the Brigadier's mission on 5 September, and, on 1 September, were asked for the co-ordinates of the field which I had just inspected, about fifty kilometres to the west of the area firmly held by the First Proletarian Division based on the town of Bugojno.

On the following day, I set out on the pillion of a motor cycle, to reconnoitre another landing ground nearer Jajce. The field was 1,000 yards long and 600 wide, but closely fringed by a steep range of mountains. This excursion proved fruitless.

The arrival of the mission would be preceded by supply sorties. At least some lesson may have been registered from the manner of our landing the previous May. These supplies were to be dropped at the field which I had reconnoitred at Bugojno, starting on 4 September, the night preceding the appointed arrival of the party itself, and I sent Thompson to the field to receive the stores.

Each schedule of our radio watch was being kept with tense anticipation, awaiting final instructions for the reception of the mission on 5 September, and details of its composition.*

That evening, 2 September, I returned from my trip on the motor cycle to our present house on the bank of the river across from Tito's headquarters.

We lived in one room. A single iron bed with a worn mattress, and one table and chair, represented our radio station. We played cards to win our turn to sleep on the bed, and tonight it was mine.

The others – Captain Benson and Sergeant Crozier, the W/T operator who had joined us in Eastern Bosnia† – were sleeping on the floor, folded in their kit and bed-rolls.

Just before midnight, there was the sound of steps on the

---

* A laconic signal had merely informed us that the name of the Brigadier was 'Lamhurst'.
† Near the village of Dragnić, on 19 July.

stairs. Ian Mackenzie, the surgeon of our mission, came into the room. He had been to operate on casualties in fighting on the previous day on the hills to the west of 'the Jajce Republic'. A tall girl in British battle dress was with him as an interpreter. Ian mumbled an inaudible introduction. She spoke in quiet and perfect English, with no trace of accent.

I motioned gallantly to the iron contraption in the corner, and our visitor, the first female presence in our company, stretched out on the mattress, overcome by instant and exhausted sleep.

Walter Wroughton was seated by the W/T set, tapping the call signs for a scheduled contact due at midnight. We were expecting the final instructions and technical details for the reception of the new mission. He had been on duty for long stretches, relieved at regular intervals by Crozier. He signed to me that a message was coming through, and I told him to hand it to me as he took down the first enciphered cable. I took over the decoding to share the work, and to lose no time at this moment of urgency.

The signal contained instructions to report any information that I could glean as to the whereabouts of the daughter of Nomčilo Ninčić, the Foreign Minister of the Royal Yugoslav government in London. Her existence was unknown to me, but a sudden intuition prompted me. I wrote down a simple coded sentence, and handed it to Walter to tap out on his set. It reads: 'Reference your signal. Stop. She is in my bed.'

No further messages came through, and the contact was closed down for the night.*

* My assumption proved correct. Olga Ninčić had been educated in London. Her command of English was so marked and unique, in the world in which we moved, that this clue had provoked my impudent identification. In the morning Olga, after a startled but gracious rebuke in Partisan style at my reactionary sense of humour, took the news in good spirit.

At Belgrade University before the war, she had enlisted in the Communist Youth organization and married a fellow student, a young Moslem named Avdo Humo, who was to become one of the leaders of the Party committee for Bosnia and Hercegovina to plan the rising in the summer of 1941.

Olga was arrested by the Pavelić police but, as she was pregnant, was taken under guard to hospital in Sarajevo.

She escaped, and after the birth of her child, leaving the infant with her husband's parents, took to the woods.

Later she was attached to Tito's staff and in June 1944 acted as his interpreter at the first meeting at Caserta between Tito and the British Prime Minister.

No further signals were transmitted to us on the next or the following five days.

On the morning of 8 September a message came in naming the Brigadier as Maclean and mentioning that he was a member of the Foreign Office and not a regular soldier. There were no details of his arrival.

That evening, 8 September 1943, the radio operators at Tito's headquarters in the fortress, and our own in the British mission house beside the river, picked up the broadcast news of the Italian surrender to the Anglo-American forces in Italy.

The future balance of the war in the Mediterranean and the Balkans was revolutionized. The first reaction in Jajce was of elation at a decisive victory which would have immediate and far-reaching effects on the whole theatre of war in Yugoslavia.

A signal from British General Headquarters in the Mediterranean did reach us in Jajce during the following hours, with a request to inform Tito that the commander of the British mission was instructed to negotiate an armistice with the nearest Italian commanders, carry out the disarming of the nearest Italian divisions and take charge of this enterprise.

This remarkable message seems to have been dispatched on the assumption that the British mission attached to Tito's headquarters was in some queer fashion in operational command of operational 'guerrilla' units.*

I sought an interview with Tito at his headquarters in the Turkish fortress across the river, bearing these instructions.

Tito has recorded his account of this meeting.†

The extent of ignorance in the West of our National Liberation struggle is shown in the following episode. An Allied military mission had arrived at the Supreme Staff at the time of the Fifth Offensive. One day, in the town of Jajce, at the moment of the Italian surrender, the head of this mission came to me and showed me a dispatch from his High Command in which he was to seek to disarm and take over the equipment of all Italian units. When he saw that I regarded ironically this request that all the war material should be handed over to the Allies, he raised his voice and said in formal tones that this was meant seriously. I asked him how he thought he was going to disarm the Italian divisions and go to Dalmatia from Jajce across a broad tract of

* Similar orders were sent to Colonel Bailey at the headquarters of Mihailović, and to the commanders of British missions in Greece and Albania.
† Tito, *Govori i Clanoi*, VI, p. 327.

difficult country to traverse, pointing out that the Germans would get
there before him. He did not know what to answer, but asked if he
could go at once to Dalmatia, against which, understandably, we had
no objection. He did not know that our units had already been dispatched there, and that they had already disarmed the Italians. He was
told: firstly, that we would disarm all Italian units; secondly, any
military equipment and stores from disarmed Italian divisions and
units belonged to us, as it had been used in our country, and against
our forces. We had no right to hand these stores over to anybody. . . .
It should be understood that new doubts had arisen as to the intentions
of certain Allied circles towards our country. We had enough grounds
for such suspicions. . . .

Tito mentioned this interview with me in an account written in
December 1951. I have no recollection of the precise text of the
signal I was instructed to deliver, but Wroughton, in his diary,
recorded on 9 September: 'Last night Italy surrendered, the
best news for a long time. We have been told to arrange the
armistice locally.'

I have reason to remember this interview. The episode seemed,
at the time, to reveal the extent to which our mission had not
succeeded in conveying to our superiors the reality of the situation
in Partisan-held territory since our arrival in May 1943. There
had never been any question of British officers taking command of
'guerrilla bands' in these regions. From the moment of our landing
during the Sutjeska battle, we had, on our own initiative, taken
the view that we were a liaison mission attached to a highly
organized and effective army. This should have been apparent
from our signals,* and Tito's outburst, on the late evening of 8
September, gave me the feeling that our mission had been in vain.

The history of this episode is of some importance as revealing the
extent of the lack of comprehension at British General Headquarters of the military strength and capacities of the Yugoslav
National Liberation Army, and the rooted suspicions of Tito as
to Anglo-American political intentions in regard to the Partisan
movement as a whole.

This meeting was the only occasion since our arrival when
Tito displayed, in my presence, an explosion of temper.

Faced with the lightning counter-measures of the German
divisions southwards along the coast to disarm their Italian

---

* It does not appear, from Fitzroy Maclean's account in his book *Eastern
Approaches*, that he was ever shown these messages.

allies of the day before, and with the scramble of Četnik units in Montenegro to achieve the same object, Tito was placed at a sudden and critical disadvantage. Possession of the equipment of the Italian divisions in Yugoslavia would alter the whole balance of military and political power throughout the country. The British had seemingly so little confidence in Tito as an ally, in spite of the presence since May of a British mission at his headquarters, that they withheld vital information at such a moment.

The request, as conveyed in the signal of which I had informed Tito, seemed to confirm that, as in 1941 and 1942, and throughout our mission, the British had continued to play a double game. The conspiracy to promote Mihailović as the military and political leader of Yugoslav resistance had now been brought into the open, and the opportunity had been created by the Italian surrender.

Tito seems also to have suspected that the British had deliberately leaked this news to Colonel Bailey at Mihailović's headquarters in advance of the radio broadcast at 5 p.m. on 8 September. This question was put to the latter at his trial in Belgrade in 1946.*

There is no evidence that any such move was made. Bailey merely received simultaneously a copy of the same signal that had been dispatched to us at Jajce.

At the time, I had no hint from Tito of such a precise accusation; from the outset, our mission had never been in any contact whatsoever with Bailey.

My memories of this talk with Tito coincide, in the main, with his account. I stressed that it was inconceivable that, if I had received any prior warning, I should not have communicated it to him at once. The true explanation that this silence could only be for technical reasons of W/T security, to avoid any risk of interception by the Germans, seemed to carry little conviction. But this did not explain the instruction to our mission to sign an armistice and take over the Italian equipment.

* Trial of Dragolub-Draža Mihailović (Stenographic Record in English) op. cit., p. 211. Mihailović could not answer the question. He merely stated that Bailey left with the Četnik commander for the Sandžak, Colonel Lukačević, to negotiate the surrender of the Italian 'Venezia' division.
See also Phyllis Auty, Tito (Longman, 1970), p. 218 and note 16.

I could only suggest that there was little point in bitter re-
crimination. I knew no more than I had already said. Could we
review the immediate situation? I was aware of the critical
implications involved. Some repair to this damage, caused by the
unfortunate signal, might be carried out if I could witness and
report on the next moves on which Tito must make an immediate decision.

He seemed to relax, and his stiff and cold manner began to
soften.

Together we studied the map.

By paper calculations the Germans would be in Split, the headquarters of the nearest Italian division and Corps Command, in
two days, and the main Yugoslav striking force, the First Proletarian Division, stationed round Bugojno, was three or even four
days away.

Tito intended to order its commander, Koča Popović, to beat
the Germans in this grim race by forced marches.

I was anxious to dissipate and refute, by some quick counter-
move, at least some of the weight of the suspicions and accusations which Tito had just flung at me as the British representative
at his headquarters, and in particular on the eve of the arrival of
the Maclean mission. My only asset was personal: an element of
confidence which Tito had, without exception, previously shown
in my integrity.

I proposed on the spur of the moment that I should leave at
once with the First Division to witness events on the coast and
the surrender of the Italian forces in Split to Tito's troops. I
would take with me Captain Benson as the American representative attached to the British mission, a W/T set and operator, and
report direct to British headquarters on this enterprise. Tito was,
as always, sharp to take the point. He had not – as he wrote in his
subsequent account – already made his tactical dispositions.
Popović was still at Bugojno. An objective report, on the spot, of
the race for the coast might undo part of the present damage in
his relations with the British. As proved to be the case, the negotiating of an armistice with the local Italian command, in due
form and in the presence of Allied witnesses, could only be to his
advantage, as commander of the National Liberation Army,
whose status, in the appreciation of the Anglo-American headquarters in the Mediterranean, appeared to have been insultingly
and deliberately disregarded.

Tito agreed that I should join the Staff of the First Division, and leave at once for Bugojno.

I returned to our headquarters across the river, and signalled, in the inadequate space of a radio signal, that I intended to leave at once, subject to confirmation from headquarters. I had not yet been informed of the precise date for the arrival of Brigadier Maclean, nor received a reply to my proposal, in my previous message of 23 August, that I should come out to Cairo and make a full report to my successor to put him in the picture before his departure.

Early on the following morning, 9 September, a series of signals were passed to our headquarters. One was signed by General Maitland Wilson. It was drafted in Serbo-Croat, and instructed me to inform Tito officially of the imminent arrival of the mission of Brigadier Maclean. Another stated that the party would consist of eight members, and that the plan, considered at the end of August, that I should come out to Cairo prior to the dispatch of the new party was 'cancelled'.* No date for the reception of the mission was communicated.

I took these messages to Tito at his headquarters, but have no record or memory of our conversation.

I signalled to Cairo that all preparations were ready at the appointed airfield for receiving the Maclean mission. Lieutenant Thompson, who had parachuted to join us at Petrovo Polje as my assistant, was moving together with Colonel Velebit, as Tito's representative, to supervise the final arrangements at the airfield near Bugojno, and to receive the time and signals for the reception party. I would continue with the proposed expedition to Split.

After careful thought I had decided to risk my plan, and gamble on being able to return in time to receive the Brigadier. If I succeeded, by continuing to Split, in my purpose to restore an element of confidence in the relations between Tito and the British, the task of my successor could only, to that extent, be facilitated.

Without waiting for a reply from Cairo, I left with Captain Benson on the following evening, 11 September, for the headquarters of the First Division at Bugojno.

---

* Wroughton's diary, under an entry dated 10 September. It appears from this record that our headquarters had not considered for a moment that I should come out as I had suggested.

This expedition upon which we now embarked was to be the last act of our original enterprise, and closed the first stage of exploratory contacts by the British with the leadership of the Yugoslav National Liberation Movement, in preparation for the arrival of the Maclean mission, with firm directives from the government in London, at the headquarters of Tito.

PART TWO

Behind the decision in May 1943 to send a military mission to Tito lay an intricate series of historical events relating to British policy towards Yugoslavia since the outbreak of war in September 1939.

The British Chiefs of Staff had outlined a general policy of support to resistance groups in Axis-occupied Europe as early as June 1940. British strategic planning, in the early stages of hostilities, did not conceive that there would be an early and massive invasion of the European Continent. The rôle of subversion in British military thinking was defined in Mr. Churchill's own words as 'the corpus of a liberating offensive' which, it was hoped, would come as the culmination of the war against the Axis.

After the fall of France, a special 'Fourth Arm' for the promotion of clandestine warfare was set up by the Prime Minister, known as the 'Special Operations Executive' and placed under the direction of Mr. Hugh Dalton, the Minister of Economic Warfare.

This organization was to conduct sabotage against the Germans in occupied Europe, to support and aid resistance groups should they form, and to collect intelligence regarding the enemy. It had its origins in 1939 as the D section of the War Office. There was no precedent for such a specialist section, nor was irregular warfare a subject which had attracted in the past the attention of the British Chiefs of Staff. A small group of officers was responsible for the first efforts in this field.

But lack of experience was made up by enthusiastic improvisation and optimistic unawareness of the difficulties, both technical and human, which were involved. There was no general overall plan for Europe, and such action as was taken in the field of clandestine warfare was the work of dedicated amateurs.

The task of D Section in the Balkans during the period of the 'phoney war' from September 1939 to June 1940 was directed to propaganda and sabotage. The main effort was concentrated on attempting, in the case of Yugoslavia, to prevent the alignment of the Royal Yugoslav government with the Axis, and, if possible, to bring the country actively on to the Franco-British side. At the same time, possibilities of sabotage were explored, and many lessons – even if negative and unrewarding at the time – were learnt. Yugoslavia, in event of the war spreading to the Balkans, would be of considerable significance to both belligerent parties. The main rail communications from Central Europe to Greece and the Eastern Mediterranean lay along the river valleys of Yugoslavia. The Bor copper mines in Serbia were the largest in Europe. Bauxite and chrome mines were of almost equal value. The Danube waterway was the route bearing Roumanian oil and wheat to Germany and Central Europe. The first sabotage plans were concentrated here on the tugs and barges of the Danube shipping companies. This was considered as a long-term operation, and in practice not put into effect. Any action would require the consent of the Yugoslav government, and by the time of the fall of France in June 1940 any co-operation, which had tacitly existed in certain government quarters with British officials on the spot, ceased. The first stages of the propaganda battle were over – and lost by the British.

After June 1940 the Special Operations Executive, operating under the control of the Ministry of Economic Warfare, absorbed the original D Section. Action was now concentrated on preparing acts of sabotage in the event of Yugoslavia joining the Axis, and exerting pressure in certain political circles to restrain the government from taking such action and, in the worst event, assisting its overthrow. Having failed to secure collaboration, the emphasis now lay on resistance. From what elements in Yugoslavia would, in the opinion of the British representatives on the spot, such active resistance come?

The early British contacts were chiefly with the leaders of the Serb Peasant Party, who were opposed to the policy of good relations with the Axis; and with the so-called 'nationalist associations' which grouped together the patriotic and ex-servicemen's institutions, whose national president was perhaps the closest associate with the British.

These British links with Yugoslav personalities and associations were exclusively Serb, nationalist, and conservative in politics. There were few similar contacts in other parts of Yugoslavia, particularly in Croatia, though certain relations had been established with patriotic organizations in Slovenia.

Such was the extent of British activities in Yugoslavia at the time of the German assault and occupation of the country, together with the Italians, in April 1941. Official representation was withdrawn from Belgrade and a dark curtain of enemy occupa-

Tito : Foča, 1942

Tito speaking during the AVNOJ celebrations, Jajce, November 1943

Moša Pijade

tion came down over the country. Nothing had been achieved in the way of a stay-behind organization, and no clandestine wireless communications had been set up in advance.

King Peter of Yugoslavia and his ministers, headed by General Simović who had played a leading part in the *coup d'état* of March 1941, were established in London as the Royal Yugoslav government in exile. It remained to await news of any guerrilla or underground action against the Italians and Germans from inside the country.

The headquarters of Special Operations for the Balkans had been established since April 1940 in Cairo.

The first scraps of information about the situation within Yugoslavia after Axis occupation began to trickle through via Istanbul when occasional couriers arrived during August 1941.

The first reports reached Turkey early that month. Guerrilla bands were reported near Suvobor in Western Serbia. The name of a certain Colonel Mihailović as their leader appeared for the first time in a report dated 15 August.

But the picture presented was too fragmentary; the first essential step must be to renew the broken contact. Since 22 June 1941 the British had been allied with the Soviet Union. It might well be that our new ally would also have views about the general position in the Axis-occupied Balkans.

The Russian government had recognized the Royal Yugoslav government in London, and their Embassy in Moscow, which had been closed after the March *coup*, was re-opened on 19 July. Diplomatic relations were formalized at the end of August; Dr. Milan Gavrilović returning to Moscow as Yugoslav minister, and Mr Bogomolov being appointed on 3 September as Soviet minister to the Simović government in London.

During October several meetings took place between Eden and Maisky on Yugoslav affairs. Mihailović had been in radio contact with the British since September, and, as both the Russian and British governments formally recognized the Simović administration, it seemed logical that Moscow and London should work out a joint policy aiming at the creation of a united resistance movement in Yugoslavia under the leadership of Mihailović as the acknowledged representative on the spot.

A series of early approaches were made by the Foreign Office to the Soviet Government, urging the Russians to bring pressure

K

to bear on the Yugoslav communists to put themselves at the disposal of Mihailović as a national leader.

But chances of any effective joint action were far ahead.

The autumn and winter of 1941 reflected a dire defensive scene. The continent of Europe, with the exception of Sweden, Switzerland, Spain, Portugal, and European Turkey, was under Axis control.

Only vague rumours reaching Cairo and London hinted at the early organization of guerrilla bands of opposed and clashing political views, which had emerged on a regional basis in the chaos of the early stages of enemy occupation of a country ill-equipped with any network of up-to-date road and rail communications. It was known that there had been a spontaneous rising in Serbia, and any differences between the resistance elements were cloaked under the vague appellation of 'patriot' forces. Similar events appeared to have taken place in Montenegro, following the Italian occupation, but no clear picture had emerged either there, or in Serbia, or anywhere else in the country.

General Simović appealed to the Prime Minister to send urgent aid to these scattered groups.

On 28 August 1941 Mr. Churchill sent a minute to Mr. Dalton: 'I understand from General Simović that there is widespread guerrilla activity in Yugoslavia. It needs cohesion, support, and direction from outside. Please report briefly what contacts you have with these bands and what you can do to help them.'

Two days later Mr. Dalton reported to the Prime Minister that such plans were in hand. The sum of £20,000 was being sent to Mihailović by courier from Istanbul, and a mission was to be dispatched to study the situation inside the country.

On the evening of 20 September 1941 the British submarine *Triumph* landed a party on the Montenegrin coast near Petrovac.*

---

* H.M.S. *Triumph* left Malta on 16 September. The submarine log contains the following statement. 'Captain Hudson and his three Serbs set off . . . in great heart. . . . They had been sent on the expedition at short notice, and their equipment had to be substantially supplemented from ship's resources.' I am much indebted for this information to Miss L. Farrow of the Naval Historical Branch of the Ministry of Defence, and also for her patient researches into the details of the landing of the Atherton party at the same point on the coast of Montenegro on 4 February 1942. (See p. 155.) A British officer accompanied the Hudson mission to the coast. He is not named in the report of the Commander of H.M.S. *Triumph*. He was Captain Julian Amery.

The mission was a mixed one. It consisted of Captain D. T. Hudson, and two Royal Yugoslav officers: Majors Zaharije Ostojić and Mirko Lalatović. They were also accompanied by a Royal Yugoslav non-commissioned officer, Veljko Dragičević, as W/T operator, with two radio sets.

The party were picked up by local guerrilla units who were posted in the hills overlooking the coast, and taken to the village of Radovče near Nikšić, some sixty miles inland.

The first radio message was received on 26 September from the party by a Special Operations W/T station in Malta. It was reported that they were with a local band of about a hundred men, and that the leaders were named as Arso Jovanović and a certain 'professor'. A further message revealed the name of the latter as Djilas.

Rumours of rebellion against the Italian occupation troops who had moved into Montenegro after the capitulation of the Yugoslav forces in April 1941 had reached Cairo and London before this Anglo-Yugoslav mission had been dispatched by air from Alexandria on 13 September and onwards from Malta by submarine. But nothing was known of the political complexion or the military organization of these groups. The King and members of the government of General Simović, who had taken over power after the *coup d'état* of the previous March, had been escorted by the British from Greece to the Middle East and on to London. Their representatives had already, in the early summer, been placed in Istanbul and Cairo, as the two watching and listening posts for the scanty intelligence which filtered out of occupied Yugoslavia after April. The task of maintaining links with the country was the joint function of these Royal Yugoslav officials, who were mainly regular army officers under the control of Jovan Djonović, who had been appointed the official representative of the Royal Yugoslav government in Cairo. On the British side, this task was the immediate responsibility of the Balkan Section of S.O.E., most of whose members had already experience of Yugoslav affairs inside the country before the Axis invasion of the previous April.

The first reports upon conditions within occupied Yugoslavia came by courier links to Istanbul, where they were intermittently intercepted by the British but in general passed to Djonović in Cairo, whose close relations with Tom Masterson, the head of the S.O.E. office there, made it just possible for the British authorities to assemble fragmentary evidence. Both Djonović and his agents in Istanbul were naturally anxious to keep the organization of links with possible developing resistance groups in different regions of his country as far as possible in Yugoslav hands. But his dependence on British material support for organizing any operations obliged Djonović to filter such information as he saw fit to the British authorities.

In early September, therefore, it was decided to send in the first experimental mission. It was intended, at first, that this should be a purely Yugoslav affair. Majors Ostojić and Lalatović were chosen for this adventure, and they received their instructions via Djonović from General Bogoljub Ilić, the Minister of War in the Yugoslav government in London, and the man who hoped to keep a tight control over any future such operations back into Yugoslavia, with the intention of rallying whatever scattered resistance groups might have formed after the dissolution of the Royal Yugoslav Army during the Axis invasion. Such operations were thus planned as an exclusively Royal Yugoslav military mission.

In April 1941 Ostojić was a Major on the General Staff of the Royal Yugoslav Army, and one of the group of officers involved in the March *coup d'état*. At the end of hostilities, he was given the mission of 'directing' Prince Paul to Greece, where the latter and his family were placed under the responsibility of the British authorities. Ostojić travelled to Cairo, with the members of the Simović government, and stayed there with the newly-formed mission headed by Jovan Djonović.

Major Lalatović was a Royal Yugoslav Air Force officer, who had flown with a squadron of planes from the air base at Nikšić in Montenegro to Greece. He joined up with a group of brother officers who had escaped from the country in April and reached Cairo.

The intricate events of the March *coup d'état*, the personalities of the officers involved, and their mutual relations, strongly influenced the attitude and mentality of the military clique now forming in Cairo, and the evolution of the policy of the Royal Yugoslav government which moved to London. Conflicts and intrigues, which created rival factions in Cairo and London, were in a sense a reflection and prolongation of the circumstances surrounding the events of 27 March in Belgrade.

Although the personal sympathies of the British officials from S.O.E. responsible for carrying out the directives of their own authorities to report on, and ultimately to bring aid to, resistance within Yugoslavia were closely bound up with their Yugoslav opposite numbers based on shared experiences during the *coup d'état*, it was clear from the start that the British must insist on sending in their own observers.

Twelve hours only before the dispatch of the Yugoslav military group, the S.O.E. section in Cairo instructed Captain Hudson to accompany the party, thus transforming the first mission into a joint one. He received only a very general briefing on what to expect on landing at the point chosen in Montenegro. His directive was in the vaguest terms: to contact, investigate, and report on all groups offering resistance to the enemy, regardless of race, creed, or political persuasion.

Bill Hudson was of a roving disposition and inured to hardship. He had formerly been a mining engineer in South Africa. From his school days in England he had developed into a fine athlete, and was a boxing champion – skills which he could and did apply with effect on occasions. He was a young man of outstanding physical courage and a rough independence of spirit. Bill Hudson had been a consultant mining engineer in Belgrade and elsewhere in Serbia for several years before the outbreak of war, at which moment he was working at the antimony mines in Western Serbia. He joined the Yugoslav D section (the original War Office nucleus which formed the basis of the future S.O.E. organization) shortly thereafter. He was fluent in the language and had valuable experience of conditions in Serbia.

Hudson was not aware of the secret instructions of his two Yugoslav colleagues, who appeared to have received certain directives from General Ilić, the Minister of War in London.

General Simović claimed, in a post-war statement, that

the mission was sent without my knowledge but on the basis of my preliminary talks with General Ilić. Before I went to London the Yugoslav command in Cairo, in agreement with the British Intelligence Service, sent Ostojić and Lalatović into the country . . . with the task of making contact with the forces of resistance in the country and to send reports on the situation there. I heard later that they had received certain instructions but what and from whom is unknown to me. . . .

Representatives of the (British) Intelligence Service let it be known that secure communications with Yugoslavia could only be set up if they sent in their people with a W/T set and the necessary ciphers and did not ask for my agreement.[1]

The mission was a joint British–Royal Yugoslav operation and there was no question of command.

The safe arrival of the party at the Montenegrin village of Radovče was immediately reported to London. Brief messages followed from Hudson, saying that small bands of *Komitjadi* existed everywhere in the neighbourhood and that their total strength seemed to be about five thousand men. The village of Radovče lay in the mountain region of Piperi some ten miles north of the Italian military headquarters at Podgorica.

The history of the early days of this mission, and the fragmentary nature of the surviving radio signals received from the group, remain unclarified. The 'Montenegrin Freedom Force', to which Hudson referred in one of his first messages, and its leaders, represented the remnants of communist-led Partisan bands who had withdrawn to the hills and areas isolated from the towns of Montenegro after the suppression of the general popular rising against the Italians in the previous July. These bands had been fighting against the Italians in loosely-knit co-operation with the similar nationalist groups led by former Yugoslav officers and N.C.O.s, with no central direction or formal agreements. The explosion had been spontaneous, but with the re-assertion of Italian control, especially in the towns, rifts were widening and clashes developing between the small communist and nationalist groups. Hudson's first impressions were that the communist units were the stronger and the more aggressive, and he reported to Malta in these terms, suggesting that aid should be sent to them.

Ostojić and Lalatović, however, had secret instructions from their superiors, which were unknown to Hudson, and which ordered them to contact and reveal the exclusive existence of national bands loyal to the King and led by their fellow-officers from the dissolved Royal Yugoslav army. They had been informed in Cairo that a certain Colonel Mihailović was at the centre of a skeleton nationalist resistance movement based on the heights of Suvobor in Western Serbia, and their orders were clearly to proceed, through nationalist channels in Montenegro, to Mihailović's headquarters. The very existence of the latter was unknown to Hudson before his departure, but on 10 September a chance radio message picked up in Malta revealed to the British the presence of a Colonel Mihailović in Western Serbia. On 9 October Hudson received a signal from Cairo via Malta, ordering him to move as fast as possible to Serbia, as Mihailović was signalling messages *en clair* and urgently needed safe ciphers.

In the meantime, his two Yugoslav colleagues had not been inactive and had contacted, with the knowledge and consent of the small Partisan command at Radovče, a recently formed committee of former Yugoslav officers 'who were aware of the outlook of the Royal Yugoslav government'. The Partisan guerrilla staff raised no objection to this move, as they seemed to be aware of contacts in Serbia between Mihailović and their own central leadership. But this climate of co-operation soon proved to be fragile and fast dissolving.

On 16 October Hudson reported on his set: 'The communists who are well organized are now leading an action in Montenegro. They want everybody to unite in the fight against the occupying authorities. Numerous national elements are standing on one side and are waiting. Must urge on nationalists to organize for the struggle'. *

He had already received orders from Cairo to move to Serbia, and on 20 October the S.O.E. station in Malta received an urgent message from Cairo asking whether Hudson had taken with him ciphers which could be worked to London, and whether Malta had arranged 'inter-communication with Draža Mihailović'. Cairo also asked for a landing point for a possible further submarine operation, and expressed the hope that supplies would be sent in shortly.

Lalatović and Ostojić were pursuing a somewhat different course of action. On 13 October the following summary of messages was sent to Malta in French, and presumably over Hudson's set from Montenegro:

Instructions have been delivered to our group which is operating in Montenegro not to co-operate with those leaders of Četnik *odreds* who do not recognize the Yugoslav government. No other report which you have received and which states the contrary should be dealt with.

It has equally been so settled that Colonel Mihailović is receiving orders to refrain from sabotage except against railway tracks, locomotives, etc., where explosives are not needed, so that the population will not be too exposed to reprisals. The group has been ordered to confine itself for the time being to preparations and collecting material

---

* The mission and its W/T traffic had been given the code name 'Bullseye'. The above telegram was marked 'Bullseye' No. 25 and dated 16 October 1941.

with the aim of co-ordinated and well organized action at a moment which will be ordered later.

We have received a telegram which confirms that this message has been received by the group in Montenegro.*

On 19 October Hudson sent his last message from Montenegro before setting out on his journey, which referred to the existence of 'patriot forces' in the area of Danilovgrad, a town lying just to the south of the road from Podgorica to Nikšić. He must have informed the local Partisan command of the orders which he had received to move to Mihailović's headquarters, and he set out, together with Ostojić, under Partisan escort, on or about 13 October. The party travelled through an exclusively Communist Partisan-controlled liberated zone, which stretched from the areas which Hudson had visited in Montenegro, across the Sandzak to the valley of the Western Morava river. Three local senior Partisan representatives travelled with the party: Arso Jovanović, Milovan Djilas, and Mitar Bakić.

Although Hudson probably did not realize at the time the real function of these men, their presence on this occasion is significant, and the reasons for it clear. Jovanović, a former Royal Yugoslav officer who had gone over to the Communists, was one of the leaders of the July rising in Montenegro, and in fact military commander of what were still called their guerrilla units; Mitar Bakić had been Secretary of the secret military committee of the Yugoslav Communist Party, which had been set up in 1940, and he was a leading organizer, on the Party side, of the Montenegrin rising; Milovan Djilas was the delegate of the Central Committee of the Party for the whole region of Montenegro and the Sandžak, and therefore the link with the leadership of the movement now located in the town of Užice in Western Serbia, close to the headquarters of Mihailović in the nearby hills of Ravna Gora to the south of Valjevo. Reports reaching Montenegro from Serbia, from both sides, Partisan and nationalist, hinted at early negotiations for a common resistance front, and it was therefore natural, and indeed important, that the Communist leaders in Montenegro should accompany this Allied mission on

---

* This message (contained in the Mihailović files in Belgrade) raises unsolved problems relating to the W/T contacts of the Hudson mission. The few surviving telegrams seem to have been sent in accordance with the 'Bullseye' wavelength and code, at times by Hudson and at others by his Royal Yugoslav companions without his knowledge. The above signal is clearly an example of the latter case.

its journey, and bring them in the first instance to their own headquarters.

The story of the competition between Communist and nationalist groups within Yugoslavia for Allied aid and recognition begins with this journey of the first mission to the centre of events.

It is significant that Lalatović and the radio operator of the mission, Dragičević, did not travel with the main party but stayed behind in Montenegro and retained the two radio sets of the mission. One of these had already burnt out, and the other was an obsolete and heavy Mark III set. The party had also landed without a charging engine.

Lalatović was clearly bent on establishing channels of communication overland which would be exclusively nationalist in character, in anticipation of the landing of British supplies to Yugoslav resistance groups on the Montenegrin coast, and to ensure that no further contacts would be established by the British with local Communist Partisan units in that region, and that the lines of communication Cairo–Malta–Montenegro–Serbia would from the beginning be securely held by supporters of the Royal Yugoslav government.

On 24 October the following signal was received in Cairo, presumably from Lalatović: 'Everything is ready to receive material aid at Radovče according to the plan drawn up, which will be valid on 21–22–25–26–27 October.'

The message provokes speculation. Hudson had already left, with a Partisan escort, for Western Serbia. Does this signal refer to arrangements made by him before leaving to send supplies to the headquarters at Radovče? Was this village the base for a joint Partisan–Četnik command? Or did the message come from Lalatović on his own set and refer to separate and secret arrangements to send supplies to other nationalist bands in the area?

Hudson's first impressions of the superior strength of the Partisan organization in the areas through which he travelled were confirmed during the course of his journey. They were the sole force in evidence in the areas of Montenegro through which he passed.

They were the only people who seemed organized in that part of the world. I passed right through them, and I formed a high opinion of them. From point to point every night when we stopped there were the familiar nucleus of men with rifles, women with typewriters, organization, passing out propaganda, and raids. . . . I do not think that Mihailović had his links and organization running through that part of the world then.*

Hudson, Ostojić, and the group of Communist leaders from Montenegro reached the central headquarters of the leadership of the Partisan rising in Serbia at Užice on or about 25 October. The town itself, and the surrounding villages and countryside, formed a 'free territory' and base. It was already known by the Partisans as 'Užice Republic', with a skeleton political administration and military headquarters. The Germans had withdrawn from the town under rebel pressure, leaving intact the most important arms factory in Serbia – a vital asset in the hands of the Partisan command.

Hudson now met the leading personality of this movement, who was presented under the code name of Tito.

There are no documentary records of the first meeting of these two men, but it is possible to reconstruct in approximate terms from fragments of their later recollections. Hudson had arrived in Western Serbia on direct instructions from Cairo to contact Mihailović at his headquarters, which the former had been merely informed was somewhere near Suvobor, a mountain region in the Šumadija to the south-west of the town of Valjevo. The British in Cairo and London had, from the meagre information so far at their disposal, no intelligence in regard to the location or activities of the Partisans in Serbia, nor the identity of their leaders. Bill Hudson had been told, while in Montenegro, that a large-scale rising had taken place in Serbia, and his first impressions were to be formed in Užice.

He had already come to the conclusion, based on what he had seen in Montenegro and the Sandžak, that the Partisan bands, whose structure and organization he had not yet had the opportunity to study, nevertheless warranted British material aid, and the first step towards procuring any supplies, either by submarine to the Montenegrin coast or by air sorties inland, depended on the establishment of radio communications.

In his first talk with Tito at Užice, Hudson offered the necessary technical data (wavelength, times, and ciphers) to establish a W/T link with Cairo, if Tito could supply the necessary set, as some supplies had recently been captured from the Germans.

* Intervention by Colonel Hudson at a conference held at St. Antony's College, Oxford, on Britain and European resistance (1962).

Hudson also pointed out that Cairo would be interested in such a direct radio link with the Partisans, with a view to Tito expressing his side of the confused picture of the rebellion in Serbia, and making his own case for receiving Allied support, in the same way as Mihailović was now doing through his improvised radio messages in clear, about which Hudson had already been informed. Presumably also this was known to Tito. Hudson formed, however, the impression that Tito was hoping, and would prefer, that any Allied support to his movement would be coming from the Russians. From other sources it was clear that at that time the Partisan command in Serbia, encouraged by their early successes against the German occupation forces, and in the profound belief in an early Allied victory on the Russian front, did not display any immediate enthusiasm for establishing early links, in whatever form, with the British.

Hudson did not conceal from Tito that his orders were to proceed to the headquarters of Mihailović, and this news came at a moment when the relations between the two rival leaders were at their most delicate and menacing. The talk between the two men was cordial, if non-committal on the Partisan side. Tito understandably was reluctant, in view of the state of his relations with Mihailović, to disclose at this stage to Hudson any details of the strength of the Partisan groups operating in Serbia. Hudson on his side stressed that the British were interested only in the unification of all Yugoslav resistance, and were therefore equally concerned with the reasons for the dissension which was deepening between the various elements.

Tito seems to have talked directly and openly about his own reactions to Mihailović, and gave the definite impression that his main aim was to avoid trouble with the Četniks. As he put it to Hudson, he had 'nothing against the Old Man personally, but the Yugoslav Officer Corps as a whole was compromised'. The humiliating collapse of the leadership of the Royal Yugoslav Army at all levels during the April campaign was without doubt a real element in the situation. At this particular moment, Tito was perhaps considering that some compromise arrangement for a joint organization of resistance in Serbia could still be achieved, but told Hudson that if Mihailović would not co-operate, all that Tito asked was that the former would not interfere with continued Partisan operations against the Germans.

There is as yet no further evidence, apart from Hudson's

personal recollections. He had no W/T contact with the British while at Užice.

Tito himself refers to one talk with Hudson. 'In answer to my question how was it possible that in London Draža Mihailović has been proclaimed a national hero when he was in no sense fighting against the occupier, Hudson recounted this episode. "The British government has not the slightest idea about Mihailović. The affair started . . . from some American journalist* in Turkey who wrote a long article in which he wrote about the heroic resistance of Mihailović against the occupier." ' [2]

The prevailing climate was one of confusion and incipient crisis. Hudson saw some fighting from the Partisan side round the town of Krupanj, and on returning to Užice met Ostojić, who had already travelled to Mihailović's headquarters and came back with a message for Hudson asking him to go there urgently. Tito raised no objection to this proposal, and in fact supplied Hudson with Partisan travel documents. The latter left Užice on or about 25 October, presumably accompanied by Ostojić and some form of escort.

In the meantime, Lalatović had reached Užice from Montenegro, together with the radio operator Dragičević. The latter had already fallen out with both Yugoslav officers attached to the mission, and refused to follow Hudson to Ravna Gora. He was to remain with Partisan headquarters and to become their chief radio operator. Lalatović seems to have made his way to Mihailović on his own, and without hindrance.

Hudson arrived at the headquarters of Mihailović on 25 October at the village of Brajići on the foothills of Ravna Gora, and on the eve of the second personal meeting between Mihailović and Tito, which took place there two days later.†

At the first encounter of Hudson and the Četnik leader, whose very existence had been unknown to him before leaving Cairo, Hudson was immediately criticized for 'having been with the Communist rabble'. News of Hudson's favourable impression of the Partisan organization in Montenegro had of course already reached Mihailović through Ostojić, and it is possible that there was also some internal radio or courier communication between Ravna Gora and Montenegro. Hudson explained that his in-

* His name has not been identified.
† Precise details of dates are difficult to establish in light of fragmentary and conflicting evidence.

structions were to report on all resistance elements, and that he intended to visit Tito from time to time; to which Mihailović replied that he would break off relations in such a case. Hudson probably also knew that Tito and his close advisers were due at Brajići in a matter of hours. But he was told by Mihailović that the presence of the British officer was not necessary as the talks were an internal Yugoslav matter, and in fact the discussions took place in the schoolroom in the village, with Hudson sitting in isolation in the next room. After the meeting he saw Tito for a moment, and found him non-committal but good-humoured.

The Brajići talks proved to be the last attempt to organize a joint Partisan–Četnik command, and a provisional agreement was drawn up. The physical presence of a British officer in the region must have exerted a temporary restraint on Mihailović, who was encouraged by the reports of Ostojić and Lalatović that he had the official backing of the Royal Yugoslav government in London as the official leader of resistance within the country – a situation which was also confirmed by the exchange of radio messages via Malta since mid-September, in which General Simović had assured Mihailović that he would soon be receiving material aid from the British and recognition of his official status. But the position of his own forces in Serbia in relation to the Partisans, leaving out of account the German occupation units, was not such that he could undertake immediate and open hostilities against Tito. The latter was prepared to accept a joint operational staff, but had no intention whatsoever of placing himself under the command of Mihailović. Nor was he in any way ready to countenance the latter's determination to desist from immediate attacks upon the German occupation troops, an attitude in which Mihailović was encouraged by messages from London, and to an extent justified by the mounting reprisals against the Serb population, particularly in the lowland valleys.

The situation throughout the area was one of lurking civil war: the Partisan headquarters was firmly entrenched in Užice, and in certain others towns joint Četnik–Partisan units were in temporary control. In the countryside small units owing allegiance to one side or the other were scattered and engaged in sporadic activities against the Germans. Hudson was without any means of independent radio communications; the fate of his Mark III set, which had been brought up from Montenegro by Lalatović and Dragičević and left in Užice, has not been completely clarified.

It seems that Hudson fulfilled his instructions in handing over safe codes for Mihailović's own wireless traffic, which now opened up with Malta in cipher under the code name 'Villa Resta', and it is certain that Hudson retained in his own possession separate ciphers, which he used for the first messages which he was now to send out to Cairo during these critical days. He had of course not been able to communicate during his brief stay in Užice, for obvious technical reasons, and therefore the British had no reports either of the existence of Tito and his staff or of the strength of the Partisan movement in Western Serbia. Their only source of information between Hudson's last telegram from Montenegro dated 19 October, and the first messages from Ravna Gora, had been from Mihailović himself and from two written reports brought out by agents, one via Turkey and the other through Lisbon, to London between September and early November.* All hopes in London were directed towards an effective working agreement between Partisans and Četniks in Serbia.

On 29 October Mihailović sent a telegram in his own code, which had just been supplied to him by Hudson, which read: 'In the name of God send help while the weather is good. In a short time we could form an army corps. Ostojić and friends are here. Signed Colonel Mihailović.' This gave, as was intended, the deliberate impression that offensive action against the Germans was imminent, and also, incidentally, revealed the presence of Hudson at his headquarters. But in the days following the Brajići meeting with Tito, Mihailović, spurred by his advisers and in particular the two new arrivals, instigated the first open-armed clashes between his units and certain Partisan bands still associated informally with his own. These attacks took place on 2 November near the town of Ložnica, below one of the contested mountain bases of Cer, and on the edge of the Mačva lowlands to the north.

Precisely one week later, Mihailović, in the presence of Hudson, received the first British air sortie from Malta, bringing in one token supply of funds.

Of the messages which passed between Hudson and Cairo, in his ciphers but on Mihailović's set, few remain. Hudson was faced, alone and without instructions or official backing from his own superiors, with making a desperate and lone attempt to prevent the first isolated clashes between both parties ending in full-scale civil war. Mihailović, secure in his correct understanding

* See p. 203.

that he was already the legal representative on the spot of the Simović government, and convinced that the first sortie of British supplies by air meant that the British authorities had accepted the same position, felt free to ignore the existence of Captain Hudson at his headquarters as an official British representative. But he underestimated the man.

Hudson had already indicated that clashes had taken place between both sides, and some message seems to have been sent from Cairo proposing that Hudson should act as some sort of mediator. In an undated signal, he radioed that it was now 'impossible to establish communications with the Partisans. Mihailović insists that communicating your message will end relations between us. Fighting between Partisans and Četniks broke out yesterday . . .' *

On 13 November a message was sent by Hudson with the following warning:

I suggest that you tell Mihailović that full British help will not be forthcoming unless an attempt is made to incorporate all anti-fascist elements under his command. This attempt is to be made by me personally going to discuss terms of such incorporation with the Partisans at Užice, and reporting to you via our Mark III W/T set there, and his [Mihailović's] W/T set here. Such an attempt should be preceded by a strong appeal for unity by a Moscow broadcast to the Partisans.

Mihailović had already informed his government, in very different terms, of the rapid deterioration of the situation in Western Serbia, accusing Tito of initiating armed clashes with Četnik units. This accusation should have revealed, both to the Yugoslav and British authorities in London, that any supplies of arms, under such conditions, to Mihailović would be used in civil strife. There is no evidence that this point of critical importance for the future was immediately appreciated, at least by the British. But the decisive value of Russian mediation in the crisis was acknowledged as being urgent and evident.

On the same day that Hudson had dispatched his warning telegram, 13 November, Simović wrote to Eden:

I have received the following telegram from Colonel Mihailović. 'The Communists have attacked us and forced us at the same time to be obliged to fight against the Germans, Communists, Ustaša and other factions. In spite of this the whole people is with the King.

* Internal evidence would suggest that this signal may have been sent on 1 November.

Hundreds of thousands of our people are unarmed, and those who are have no ammunition. The Communists are concentrated in the valley west of the Morava with main centres of resistance at Čačak, Požega, and Užice.'

One British officer has the impression that it is the Communists who are leading the Partisans, also against the Axis forces, and that Montenegro is organized on the Partisan side. Četnik leaders are talking openly that they would rather come to terms with the Germans than the Communists. Colonel Mihailović and his officers are faithful to the King. Many fighters who are now with the Communists will come over to the Četniks as soon as the latter receive the promised aid from the British. Civil war would last long and in the meantime nothing would be undertaken against the Germans.

Diplomatic moves were made both to the Soviet Ambassador in London and to the government in Moscow on these lines, and on 16 November Hudson received a further message from London:

His Majesty's government now consider fight should be Yugoslavs for Yugoslavia, and not revolt led by Communists for Russia, if it is to prosper. H.M.G. therefore asking Soviet government to urge Communist elements to rally Mihailović, collaborating with him against Germans, putting themselves unreservedly at disposal of Mihailović as national leader. Simović will also instruct Mihailović to refrain from retaliatory action.

The presence of Hudson as a witness on the spot, the basic military weakness of the small Četnik bands, and the chance of Russian pressure on Tito, constrained Mihailović, against his instincts and the counsel of his advisers, to refrain from further attacks on Tito's forces. The following days passed in tense anticipation in both rival insurgent camps.

But in reality there was merely a thin prospect of a temporary truce between rival factions. The personal relations of Mihailović and Hudson were irretrievably damaged. The latter had revealed the existence of incipient civil strife, which the former had endeavoured to conceal from the outside world in a gamble to acquire British arms to liquidate his Communist rivals and on the false pretence that this aid was needed to organize resistance against the Germans. His game had been called. The acceptance by the British of Hudson's recommendation to withhold further air sorties pending the creation of a joint resistance command was regarded by Mihailović as sabotage.

On the Partisan side, Tito was aware that it was Mihailović who had deliberately excluded Hudson from the Brajići talks on 27 October. 'It is interesting to note that Draža Mihailović firmly rejected my proposal that the British Captain Hudson, who was sitting in another room, should be present at the discussions.'[3]

But Tito could not have been aware that the British air sortie on 9 November had been made against the latter's urgent appeal, nor that Hudson had proposed to come for mediatory talks to Užice, and had been prevented by Mihailović. Any fleeting relationship of cautious trust between Tito and Hudson had equally evaporated.

Nevertheless, on three occasions after Hudson had settled at Mihailović's headquarters, he did take part in joint conferences to seek a formula at least for a temporary truce in face of the increasing signs of German military punitive expeditions to clear the Morava valley and the areas of Western Serbia now out of their control.

The first of these meetings was held on 20 November at the town of Čačak, nominally in the hands of Četnik units. Hudson reported the next day to Cairo on this latest development, and within the frustrating limits of an enciphered message, attempted to convey the true positions of the two parties:

My attitude to Mihailović has been that he has all qualifications except strength. At present the Partisans are stronger and he must first liquidate them with British arms before turning seriously to the Germans. He told me today that lack of ammunition will force him to retire from Ravna Gora if Partisans continue to fight him. I attended a Četnik–Partisan conference, and conveyed your attitude. The Partisans insist they keep their identity under any joint arrangements with the Četniks. They consider Simović's lack of reference to the Partisans' leading part in the revolt shows Yugoslav government's ignorance of the situation.* The Partisans consider that the people have lost all confidence in the former Yugoslav officers who were responsible for collapse. They suspect Mihailović of helping Nedić and other pro-Axis elements in fighting the Communists. The Partisans will continue to fight Mihailović unless he combines on their terms.

After this conference Hudson remarked to one of the Partisan delegation: 'The British General Staff wants to know that there can be a lasting agreement between Četniks and Partisans.'

The latter were prepared for the creation of a joint operational staff, but at no moment were agreeable to accept the command of

* In a broadcast over the B.B.C. on 15 November 1941.

L

Mihailović, as he had implied in his telegrams to London, and the British in their diplomatic moves in Moscow.

The Russians seemed to have assumed that the British Foreign Office had been successful in imposing this solution in Serbia, which fitted with their own short-term conception of popular fronts in enemy-occupied territories. Radio Moscow announced the news with apparent satisfaction.

On the same day the agreement of 20 November was mentioned in the Partisan newspaper *Borba*, published in Užice. 'On the occasion of yet another agreement, the signing of this act is a reflection of the sincere readiness of the leadership of the military Četnik units to abandon fratricidal war.'

General Simović in London was making a determined effort to prevent a final rupture. On 21 November he cabled Mihailović, in Hudson's cipher: 'We have taken measures for the Partisans to cease unnecessary action and place themselves under your command in the sense of my speech of the 15th. You must endeavour to smooth over disagreements and avoid any kind of retaliation.'

Mihailović seems to have taken this marked hint that, unless he did reach some form of short-term agreement with the Partisans, he might not be able to count on the unqualified support of his own government together with the British.

On 22 November, therefore, he informed his government in London: 'I have done all in my power and have succeeded in ending the fratricidal strife provoked by the other side. In the fighting against the others [i.e. the Germans] I have almost exhausted my ammunition. I have made all efforts to unite all popular forces and to complete the organization of the decisive action against the Germans.'[4]

Hudson had a brief moment of qualified confidence. On 21 November he signalled: 'Mihailović has now agreed to recognize the Partisans; I told him that if both sides turned against the Germans I believed that immediate British aid would be at his disposal, and we could help to establish him as unconditional commander-in-chief.'

But during these days Mihailović had been engaged in taking certain precautionary measures of fatal and decisive import for the future, on the assumption that the German punitive expedition now penetrating the areas where Partisan and Četnik bands were still roving would achieve Mihailović's real purpose for him – the early disruption of Tito's organization – before the latter, in the event of an irrevocable breakdown of the fragile truce negotiations, liquidated his own movement.

Tito's troops had sallied out against Mihailović's headquarters in Ravna Gora in early November, and, in spite of help from the Serb gendarmerie, had nearly captured him and his staff.

Emissaries from Mihailović had been in touch since August with representatives in Belgrade of General Milan Nedić, the German-sponsored head of the administration of a truncated Serb state, and secret joint plans were now drawn up to 'legalize' the Četnik organization of Mihailović in event of the Germans overrunning the whole of Western Serbia. The majority of the officers who had rallied to Mihailović, and some other ranks, would thus disappear into the ranks of the Nedić gendarmerie and State Guard* and tacitly refrain from any further armed resistance against the Germans. They would build up a new underground organization to be mobilized on a more propitious occasion.

There were immediate signs that Tito was restive, and that his forces might take the initiative in breaking the existing stand-still agreements. He could not afford to lose such initiative as remained to him in face of imminent German attack, nor under any conditions subordinate his units to Mihailović's command.

On 25 November Tito radioed to the Comintern a message giving information on Mihailović and the Četniks 'because Moscow Radio is putting out terrible nonsense about D. Mihailović . . . worse than that put out by London.'[5] Hudson was aware of Mihailović's fears, and had wind of the latter's recent covering-up negotiations with Nedić. On the same day, he reported to Cairo that the majority of the Partisans were not Communist. The Communist Party organization had been the first to show fight – hence its popularity. Kosta Pećanac, the leader of the 'official' pre-war Četnik organization, compromised the 'true' Četniks who looked to London as their signal star. He had thousands of Četniks helping the Germans against the Partisans. A police officer, Dangić, was commanding Četnik groups in Bosnia under Mihailović. There were several pirate bands of Četniks of no import. Draža Mihailović said that he had planted many officers with Nedić, and four thousand Nedić gendarmes awaited his words. 'Mihailović says that he is not yet in a position to receive persons landing in Montenegro.'

---

* A Serbian defence force which the German authorities in Belgrade permitted Nedić to raise for 'security' actions.

On 11 November 1941 Mihailović and members of his staff, unknown to Hudson, had met representatives of the German Command at the village of Divci near Valjevo.* He hoped to procure from the Germans those weapons which the British were temporarily withholding, and to co-ordinate the actions of Četnik units with the Germans in combined operation to destroy the Partisan movement. Pressure from Berlin, where the Serb organization of Mihailović's Četniks was regarded as essentially pro-British and an ultimate threat to German control of Serbia, led to the breaking off of these secret talks.[6]

In the event the issue in Serbia was decided by the Germans, pursuing an indiscriminate military expedition to clear Western Serbia of all rebel bands, Partisan and Četnik.

Meanwhile, in London, on 28 November the Prime Minister, Mr. Winston Churchill, minuted: 'Everything in human power should be done to help the guerrilla fighters in Yugoslavia. Please report what is possible.'

On the same day Mr. Eden wrote to General Simović reiterating the importance of creating a 'united front of all patriots in Yugoslavia', and suggesting that a message of congratulation should be sent to Mihailović also informing him that material aid and funds would be sent to him, 'but that the furnishing of our aid will be directly related to the maintaining of a united front under his leadership. . . . We are asking the Soviet government to persuade the Partisans to maintain a united front under the leadership of Colonel Mihailović.'

The following message was then dispatched from London to Hudson, in his cipher, to be handed as a personal message from the British government to Mihailović.

H.M.G. send heartiest congratulations to Mihailović on understanding reached with Partisans. They will be grateful if Mihailović will convey congratulations to the Yugoslav leaders who have contributed towards understanding. Help in material and money will follow within one week, weather permitting. It is intention of H.M.G. continue send Mihailović all the help they can but he must clearly realize this will depend on maintenance of united front between all patriots in Yugoslavia under Mihailović's leadership.

* On 12 November the Foreign Office instructed the British Ambassador at Kuibychev, Sir Stafford Cripps, to urge the Russians to bring pressure on the Yugoslav communists to put themselves at the disposal of Mihailović as the national leader, the day after this Divci meeting.

This telegram was dated 29 November.

In spite of obstruction from Mihailović, it seems that Hudson maintained contact from time to time with Tito in Užice. It is probable that he was on such a trip, or on a local tour of inspection, when the laudatory telegram from London arrived at Ravna Gora, for on 1 December Mihailović cabled on his own set: 'The morale of my troops remains excellent. Captain Hudson has not returned. He is cut off from us. Telegraph us in Serb. Mihailović.'

On the morning of 29 November German troops had entered the Partisan 'Republic of Užice', and the main surviving body of Partisan units withdrew westwards into the Sandžak. In the confusion Hudson found himself caught up with Tito and his staff, and it is improbable that the London telegram was ever delivered as intended.

On the previous day, 28 November, Tito had telephoned to Mihailović asking him what he proposed to do, and received the reply that the Četnik *odreds* would 'return to their territories, and carry out suitable guerrilla action until conditions for a general rising existed'.[7] This brief interchange marked the end of any further contact between the two men.

On 30 November Mihailović held a meeting of his commanders on Ravna Gora and it was decided to 'legalize' the Četnik units in agreement with Nedić and in common action against the Partisans.

On the same day Mihailović signalled to General Simović that 'the Communists have evacuated Užice and their whole force is withdrawing to Zlatibor [a mountain range on the borders of Western Serbia on the route to the river Drina]. . . . They are few in numbers and badly led.' He, Mihailović, would continue 'Četnik warfare': the morale of his troops was excellent. He endeavoured to convince London that the Partisans, and in particular their leadership, no longer existed as an organized force in Serbia and that he was persistently working for 'the unification of popular forces and the creation of a Balkan front'.

On 2 December Mihailović signalled that he was 'at war with the Germans and had entered into complete guerrilla warfare'. On the following day he issued orders to attack the Partisans. The breach was complete and the assumption clear: by parallel action with the German operations the menace of Communism in Serbia, which had threatened since September to master control of the rising, was at an end.

On 5 December Mihailović radioed that he could not maintain radio communications. The last contact with Malta was a message received that evening. He was retreating, and was unable to receive any supplies until he could make fresh contact. 'I am continuing guerrilla warfare as it suits the reality of the situation.'

Hudson accompanied Tito and his remaining forces 'in a two-day rout' across Zlatibor mountain. After crossing the Uvac river on the borders of the Sandžak, Hudson decided to return on his own to Serbia. 'I got the impression everywhere that British help was best concentrated on Mihailović if he still exists independently of Nedić. I told Tito and Co. this and made my way back in a wave of Germans and Quislings.* Hudson was travelling unescorted and was captured three times on this fearful journey. He reached Ravna Gora on the night of 7/8 December 1941 during the German encircling assault on Mihailović's head-quarters. 'I found no remains of Mihailović's men except himself and a few officers. Everyone else having converted themselves into Nedić men and departed to the complete frustration of the Boche.'

According to the official account of this German operation, the Četniks had ten killed and 350 prisoners. Among the latter was Lieutenant Mišić, Mihailović's personal A.D.C., the son of the national hero, Vojvoda Živojin Mišić, of the First World War. Together with most of the officer prisoners, he was shot by the Germans. His brother was with the Partisans.

The Germans also captured 330 rifles, five machine guns, 11,000 field telephones, one W/T set, and a safe containing 203,000 dinars.

Mihailović refused to see Hudson after the German withdrawal, and denied him the use of radio communications. Hudson had somehow dragged his own set with him back from the Sandžak, but had not had time before leaving Cairo to learn to operate W/T transmissions; his operator Dragičević had stayed with the Partisans in Užice in the previous October.

Mihailović vanished with a small band into East Bosnia, leaving Hudson as a lone fugitive in peasant clothes to pursue a bare and hunted existence in the scattered settlements of Ravna Gora for the following months.

The message of 1 December from Mihailović announcing that Hudson was cut off and had not returned to Ravna Gora was the

* These signals form part of the series which Hudson was able to transmit in February 1943. See p. 195.

last news received in Cairo of the whereabouts of their representative. No reports of his fate reached the outside world until the following spring.

The only British witness of events on the fringes of Mihailović's headquarters during this time, but with no means of radio communications, was an officer who had been captured by the Germans on Crete and had escaped from a train in Serbia carrying prisoners of war to Germany. His name was Captain Christie Lawrence, and he later wrote a perceptive account of his stay with the Četniks.* It seems that Mihailović even wanted to replace Hudson by Lawrence, who was, however, shortly afterwards recaptured by the Germans. It appears that, through Polish sources, Mihailović even put out a rumour that it was Hudson who had been captured.† In fact, the two men never met.

Mihailović spent the early weeks of 1942 in Montenegro and the Sandžak, establishing his direct control over the local Četnik organization, and creating a mountain base from which the Partisans were driven to move their main forces north into Eastern Bosnia. The Mihailović organization in Serbia remained as a passive territorial structure, mainly on paper, and with the protective cover of Nedić's political and military structure. In Montenegro Mihailović hoped to build a more effective striking force based on the Četniks now in control of this territory and on their comrades in the Sandžak and Hercegovina. These areas, during the early months of 1942, had become a Četnik 'free territory' and in a series of 'parallel' expeditions, this time with the Italian occupation forces, the Partisans were either driven underground in small cells and roving bands, or left to concentrate in Bosnia.

In April 1942 Mihailović sent a message to Hudson, who was still alone, in banishment,‡ to join him at his headquarters, then

* Christie Lawrence, *Irregular Adventure* (Faber & Faber, 1947).

† A Polish group of escaped officers and men, with a W/T set, were present with the Četniks in Serbia.

‡ Hudson had slowly made his way south-east from Ravna Gora, presumably with the help of friendly Četniks or peasants, ending up in the remote township of Ivanjica, in the far south-eastern corner of the Sandžak where it meets Serbia proper and what was then known as South Serbia (i.e. Macedonia) a few miles south of Raška. Here, for nearly four months, he had dragged out an appalling existence, living mainly on potatoes, and, what must have been worst of all, entirely without news of the outside world. It is little wonder that he could never rid himself of the after-effects of this traumatic experience.

It was during Hudson's 'Siberia' that the Atherton mission was sent in to try to discover what had become of him.

in a village on Čemerno mountain, near the town of Gacko in Hercegovina.* Hudson was asked to travel in disguise, presumably because of the embarrassing consequences if an identified British officer fell into Italian hands. There was no sartorial difficulty, as Hudson's uniform had been captured in one of the incidents during his journey back to Serbia the previous December. Presumably with 'legal' Četnik escort, Hudson travelled in Italian lorries through the Sandžak to Mihailović's new headquarters.

At the end of the month, the two men reached a temporary brittle understanding, and Hudson was given limited use of Mihailović's radio communications. No messages, however, seem to have reached Cairo in the ensuing days. Indeed, Mihailović's own W/T contacts had ceased during early December after his expulsion by the Germans from Ravna Gora and flight westwards.

The maintenance of radio contact on the only link available to the British was a matter of special concern, and the only source of information at that time available to Cairo and London. The total breakdown at the end of the previous year was sinister, and led to several speculations by the British authorities, including the possibility that Hudson was no longer alive, and that Mihailović was being controlled either by the Italian or German intelligence.

The W/T set at Mihailović's headquarters had been working since October 1941 using British ciphers delivered by Hudson and therefore under British supervision. The code name 'Villa Resta' was allotted to this series. The first messages had been picked up in a commercial Marconi code with the call sign YTHS in September 1941 in Malta. In early November, the British listening station there picked up similar signals. On 6 December Malta signalled to London 'YTHS call sign heard. Different note from that associated with Mihailović. We are not satisfied as to the identity of sender. May be Hudson using Mark III set.' London instructed Malta to send out the following on the same wave length: 'Please give us something to establish your identity. Where are you now?'

These messages passed at the precise moment of the German assault on Mihailović's headquarters at Ravna Gora. Hudson arrived from the Sandžak during the action: the Germans did

---

* He was about to move to Golija mountain where Italian aid was being brought in for the so-called Third Offensive to clear Montenegro of all Partisan influence.

capture 'a W/T set'. Were they playing it back? The local developments were of course unknown to the British.

On 7 January 1942 (when Hudson was a fugitive in the hills of Ravna Gora), a message was picked up, ostensibly from him: 'At the moment there are no Communists on the ground. On account of their inexpert handling, they were dispersed by strong German forces. Their leaders have retreated to Montenegro.'

Hudson was alone and out of touch at this moment with Mihailović. He may have clung to his set, but had not the technical training to operate it.

The first purported message from Mihailović's 'Villa Resta' set since 2 December was picked up in Malta on 6 January 1942 and suspicions were aroused in British circles that he was in enemy hands.

A cryptic message was sent about a dog and some element of confidence was restored by the reply. But Mihailović was again off the air until 22 March.

On 29 March Mihailović signalled: 'Captain Hudson is with us, and hidden in a safe place. The Germans are organizing a special chase for the British . . .'

This message lacked accuracy, and was intended to mislead London. Hudson did not reach Mihailović until some time during the following month.

Hudson's first signals since November 1941, in his code (series 'Bullseye'), were not received until June.* He reported that he was again on terms with Mihailović.

Anxiety as to the real state of affairs at the latter's headquarters, and lack of reliable evidence as to the situation in Montenegro (which only Hudson could supply) lay behind the message from London, sent on 4 June, which announced that Hudson had been promoted to the rank of Major and awarded the D.S.O. It was also proposed to send to Mihailović a new W/T set 'for direct contact with Cairo'.

Hudson now set about studying on the ground the situation in Montenegro, and the extent of Četnik organization and control of the territory. He reported during June and July that he had proof of the collaboration of the local Četnik leaders with the Italians: in particular, Djurišić and Stanišić. They commanded only about 2,000 men but were in control of the areas visited by Hudson.

* It is possible that some were sent after his arrival in Montenegro in April, but they have not survived.

He also stressed that Mihailović himself attached 'the greatest importance to Italian equipment'.

In August S.O.E. Cairo decided that a special British signals mission must be sent in to establish W/T communications both with Hudson and Mihailović on a secure and regular basis.

Lieutenant Lofts, with two British radio operators and improved sets and equipment, was parachuted to Sinjajevina, a mountain plateau on the borders of Montenegro and the Sandžak, at the end of the month.

Mihailović, while welcoming the re-establishment of firm radio links with his government, was also aware that he could no longer conceal from the British the extent of Četnik collaboration with the Italians nor the awkward evidence about his main enemy – the Partisan forces of Tito.

In April 1942 he had received a message from London asking for details of the Partisan leadership and the strength and location of its units, but this inquiry was conveniently left unanswered. A British official in London reported to the Royal Yugoslav authorities that Mihailović was again out of radio contact since 12 April – the date of the message listing an elementary questionnaire about the Partisans.

The arrival of the new British signals mission meant that Hudson would transmit disturbing revelations. The state of Mihailović's anxiety is shown in a signal dated 24 August:

We have no difficulties whatsoever in co-operating with Major Hudson. He carries out his work and has his separate cipher, which is not known to me, nor have I sought to ask for it. But I do need my own cipher for direct communication with the (Royal Yugoslav) General Staff and head of the government.

With Major Hudson we are doing everything to facilitate his work as everything is a joint Allied affair.

Hudson had already reported in July that Mihailović was not undertaking any military activities and was increasingly concerned with gaining political control of Yugoslavia, based on exclusively pan-Serb elements, and that there were further indications of Četnik collaboration in the areas which Hudson had toured.

But the secure Četnik hold on the mountain strongholds oɩ Montenegro, with the centre at Žabljak and round Mount Durmitor, where Mihailović now had his headquarters, and the marked fighting qualities of the Montenegrin leaders, especially

Djurišić, might provide the conditions for a revival of a new resistance movement. By assembling the Četnik bands in Hercegovina to the east and from Eastern Bosnia in the north, and ignoring Partisan activities which had been moving away to new bases in Western Bosnia and Croatia, there seemed to Hudson just a chance to back a Četnik enterprise.

The Montenegrin Četniks were able to maintain their position and reinforce their strength by the very nature of the Italian occupation, which was confined to certain towns with their main headquarters in Podgorica, and a string of small garisons to keep open the few lines of communications across the region. In addition, as auxiliaries of the Italians to the extent of receiving food supplies, and cautious deliveries of arms and ammunition, the Montenegrin Četniks were thus to control, in their own and the Italian interest, a firmly held free zone.

It would be a delicate hint to the British that they should condone such collaboration with one of the Axis powers. But there might be, as it seemed to Mihailović, something in the argument that, as the British had sent no supplies to enable the Četnik organization to maintain any semblance of activity,* it was only realistic to collaborate on a limited basis with the Italians. The arms thus acquired could be used to send parties back into Serbia to undertake those sabotage tasks which were of increasing concern to the British.

Djurišić seems, although the evidence is thin, to have hinted at some such deal to Hudson during the summer of 1942. If the British would turn a blind eye to the existing links between his commanders and the Italians, and supply some arms and especially considerable funds, Djurišić would be willing, even in defiance of Mihailović, to experiment with such an action.

British money would be used to buy weapons, by double-crossing or bribery of the Italians, to be used for an expedition to Serbia.

On 17 July Hudson radioed that a large arms drop was needed, and that he could hold a landing ground near Žabljak and lead personally 'a thousand men' to protect the dropping zone.

In response to this appeal S.O.E. dispatched a mission consisting of two Royal Yugoslav officers carrying four million lire, to the area indicated. By October, a series of supply sorties had

* Between February 1942 and January 1943 there had, however, been 25 air sorties to Mihailović.

dropped some thirty million lire and a considerable sum of U.S. dollars in the same zone.

The Djurišić 'plan' proved to be a passing and dangerous illusion: and Hudson was not a party to it.

S.O.E. policy still concentrated on the preservation of Mihailović's movement as the ultimate resistance force, and these odd summer air sorties may have been simply designed to prop up the only temporary Četnik 'safe harbour' in existence within the country.

Mihailović continued to veto any sabotage actions on the main railway communications running south through Serbia. On 4 August he signalled to his government in London: 'As to the appeal in Hudson's message that I should prepare sabotage action on the line Belgrade–Niš, a sortie will be needed with explosives and inflammatory material. Until I confirm to you that everything is ready do not drop any supplies.'

On further study of the military capabilities of the local Četniks, Hudson cabled in early September: 'In general the Partisan organization is miles ahead of Mihailović's, and, after chasing each other round Yugoslavia, the final scene will probably take place in Belgrade. Mihailović intends to set up a military dictatorship after the war, and this had been accepted by the Montenegrin leaders since the Communist withdrawal from this region (in the spring of 1942).'

Djurišić seems to have persisted in his 'plan', for Hudson reported at this time that the former had asked for direct British support to him independently of Mihailović for 'only a limited thrust into Serbia'.

But on 15 November, Hudson sent a considered and perceptive summary by radio of the situation as a whole:

Mihailović is supported by Vojvoda Pavle Djurišić, who is the most important Četnik leader in Montenegro, controlling important areas of this district and commanding the allegiance of many of the peasants. In return for this support Mihailović has secretly promoted Djurišić and has given him the prestige of his name, as well as considerable financial assistance. Mihailović has also agreed to adopt the policy of collaboration with the Italians pursued by the Montenegrin Četniks . . .

Mihailović and the Montenegrin leaders are essentially opportunists and will not risk their at present comparatively secure positions for the sake of what they would call 'adventures'. Djurišić sometimes goes to (Italian-occupied) Cetinje but Mihailović says that he may come and spend the winter at his headquarters. His [Djurišić's] original plan had been to follow up the retreat of the Partisans through Hercegovina right up to the Lika, but he was prevented by the stubborn rearguard actions of the Partisan forces.

Mihailović remains opposed to undertaking sabotage against the Italians. He insists that they will collapse shortly, when he expects to secure their arms and equipment, with which he plans to defend Montenegro against the Germans. He argues that if he were to take action against the Italians now, the Germans would occupy Montenegro and he would thus lose the chance of securing Italian arms. He also fears that sabotage would lead to his losing the support of the people, who would blame him for Italian reprisals, as well as to the cessation of Italian food supplies for the Četniks.

. . . In Serbia, Mihailović's groups, although outlawed by the Germans, have considerable freedom of movement in large areas. They are, however, little more than symbols of resistance. The peasants are in general favourable to Mihailović, but they have been told that no action can or will be attempted before the Axis is on the point of collapse.

I am personally convinced that these Četnik groups in Serbia could organize derailments at points where the Germans would not be able to take reprisals on Serb villages. No serious attempts however have yet been made to investigate the possibilities of carrying out such operations. The poor sabotage results obtained hitherto are due to lack of willingness on Mihailović's part and to lack of energy. When I press for continuous large-scale sabotage, the General and his entourage reply that half a million Serbs have already been killed in the fight against the Axis and that they cannot risk reprisals; they emphasize they will not depart from this standpoint for the sake of any outside interest.

. . . We cannot expect much in the way of results from this half-hearted activity, but I believe that if it were made clear to Mihailović that continued support for him from the B.B.C. was dependent on his readiness to undertake sabotage, he would realize the importance of attempting such operations even at the expense of his main objective of securing the support of the masses.

. . . I am convinced that the mood of the people, as well as the nature of Mihailović's organization and personal ambition, will oblige him to undertake a 'grand finale' against the Axis. When the General is satisfied that victory is certain, blood will not be spared, but until then I consider him perfectly capable of coming to any secret understanding with either Italians or Germans, which he believes might serve his purposes without compromising him. Any such understanding would be based on his conviction of an Allied victory and would be directed to the purpose of smashing the hold of the Communists on the people. I do not know whether Mihailović has an agreement with the Axis involving his inactivity in Serbia and their anti-Communist drive in North West Bosnia.

On 22 November 1942 Hudson added that Mihailović did not advertise his presence in Montenegro, but preferred to work there, and in Dalmatia, through local Četnik commanders who were in touch with the Italians. He was merely awaiting the Italian collapse and their weapons. He had 'so far not thought out practical plans for defending anything bigger than a hill top'.

In September, General Alexander, supported by an exhortation from the Royal Yugoslav government in London, had sent a message to Mihailović, calling on him to sabotage Axis communications, and had met with the response that, without adequate British material aid, he was not able to act.

Relations with Mihailović had reached a point where, whatever formal obligations of the British government to the Yugoslav King and his advisers in London committed them to supporting the Royal Yugoslav Minister of War as the symbolic leader of resistance within the country, there was an element of tragic farce. Hudson had been placed in a position, for over a year, which had reached the limit of human endurance. The attempts to infiltrate other missions to contact him, and to report on conditions over a wider area of the country, had failed.

The direct information reaching the British authorities from Yugoslavia was confined to the hectoring outpourings of Mihailović, and an intermittent series of messages from Hudson over the latter's set since April, and through Lieutenant Lofts' station after August, limited by circumstances to the Četnik position in Montenegro.

The complete blackout which descended on the sole W/T links between Hudson and Mihailović with Cairo in early December 1941 had given rise to the disquieting and correct implication that the Germans had broken up and driven in scattered and unknown directions the forces of both Mihailović and Tito, and all contact was lost with events now taking place within the country. The whereabouts of both Mihailović and Hudson were unknown, and there were no reports to show what had happened to the Communist bands, of whose strength, location, and leadership only a shadowy picture had hitherto been pieced together in Cairo.

S.O.E. therefore decided to try to send in three parties, in an attempt to renew contact, to locate any surviving resistance groups inside the country, and in particular to trace the fate of Hudson and Mihailović.

On 17 January 1942, the submarine *Thorn* left on patrol from Alexandria carrying on board two of these missions. The first consisted of two Royal Yugoslavs: Lieutenant Rapotec and Sergeant Stevan Shinko, both Slovenes. It was intended that this party would be put ashore near Split, where it was supposed, from courier reports, that a group of Mihailović supporters existed, could establish W/T contact with this area, and collect information on the situation in Croatia and, if possible, in Slovenia. Rapotec had also a radio set and a sum of money in Italian lire.

The second party was commanded by a British officer, Major Terence Atherton,* together with a Royal Yugoslav Air Force Captain, Radoje Nedeljković, and an Irish radio operator, Sergeant Patrick O'Donovan. Their task was to land as near as possible to the same place where Hudson and his party had come ashore in mid-September 1941.

The first mission, which bore the code name 'Henna', was put ashore on the Adriatic island of Mjlet early on the morning of 27 January 1942, and was expected to find its way by ordinary ferry traffic to the mainland. No news was received of it for many months.

The second mission, code-named 'Hydra', landed by rubber boats shortly after 9 o'clock on the evening of 4 February, near Petrovac at almost exactly the point where Hudson had landed. This mission never established radio contact with Malta or Cairo.

A further group, consisting of a British officer, Major Cavan Elliot, two Royal Yugoslavs, Lieutenant Pavle Crnjanski and Sergeant Miljković, and a British radio operator, Sergeant Robert Chapman, was parachuted 'blind', on the night of 5 February, by a British plane based on Malta, to Romanija mountain near Sarajevo in Eastern Bosnia. The code name of this party was 'Disclaim'.

A fourth mission, as yet undesignated, was being planned by

* See p. 8.

S.O.E. Cairo to be parachuted into Montenegro if favourable reports were received from the 'Hydra' party.

The dispatch of the first three groups was part of a co-ordinated plan by the British in Cairo to obtain a broader and more accurate picture of resistance groups believed to be operating in several parts of the country, and about which only vague information had hitherto been received from Serbia, through Hudson and Mihailović, and brief hints from the former during his short stay in Montenegro.

The 'Hydra' party, like that of Hudson, was a joint British–Royal Yugoslav operation and the two officers, Atherton and Nedeljković, had been briefed separately and in different terms: the former by S.O.E. Cairo; the latter by the Minister of War in London, General Bogoljub Ilić, through the Royal Yugoslav military mission in Egypt.

Atherton had worked in Belgrade for ten years before the war as a free-lance journalist, and later as the managing editor of the *South Slav Herald*. He was married to a Moslem girl from Sarajevo.

In April 1941 he had escaped from Yugoslavia through Greece and by caique to Egypt. He succeeded in being accredited as an official war correspondent to our forces in the Middle East, representing the *Daily Mail*. While in Jerusalem, in December 1941, he found means of volunteering to return to Yugoslavia. To a journalist, such a mission had every chance of developing into a major 'scoop'.

An attempt during that month to land a Royal Yugoslav mission by submarine on the Montenegrin coast, to contact those 'patriot forces' located by Hudson in September, failed. The submarine was recalled urgently to Malta for convoy operations. Atherton was then given charge of this party, and briefed on his mission.

Hudson's last message from Montenegro had been received in Cairo on 19 October 1941. He had reported that 'patriot forces' were operating in the Danilovgrad–Podgorica area in Montenegro. The purpose of Atherton's mission was to contact this group and to establish a coastal supply base in the area to bring in arms and support. There were no specific instructions to reach Mihailović, and the party was to remain in Montenegro and await further orders. He was to trace the whereabouts of Hudson and Mihailović, to report on the latter's relations with the Partisans, and on the location of their headquarters and the identity of their leaders.

Sava Kovačević

Peko Dapčević

Ivo Lola Ribar

Alexander Ranković

Atherton and his companions were picked up in a few hours by a patrol from the Lovćen * Partisan *odred*, the same group which had found the Hudson party.

The local Montenegrin leaders were suspicious at first, and their attitude curt and correct. They were at once reminded of the intrigues of Major Lalatović with local Četnik officers in the previous September and suspected that the arrival of this second mission implied the renewal of an attempt to contact the Mihailović organization in Montenegro, with which the Partisan staff in the same territory was at that moment engaged in a ruthless struggle for mastery. News of the breach between Tito and Mihailović in Serbia had filtered into East Bosnia and Montenegro, where Mihailović's emissaries were now actively at work in building up the Četnik structure and dispersing the Partisan forces.

Against this background, Atherton and the other two members of his party were escorted to the headquarters of the Partisan Montenegrin staff based on the village of Gostilje, near Nikšić. The senior personality, Ivan Milutinović, was now the delegate of the Central Committee of the Yugoslav Communist Party for Montenegro in place of Milovan Djilas, whom Hudson had met in the previous year.†

On 13 February Milutinović sent by courier to Tito at the Supreme Staff headquarters, then at Foča in Eastern Bosnia, the following message:

During these last days a British mission has arrived here consisting of a British major, one Yugoslav captain, and an Irish W/T operator. We have detained them at the Staff and will keep them until we tell you what they are up to. They want to go to our Supreme Staff and to talk personally to Tito, according to what the major says. We have informed them in detail about the situation and Partisan strength and asked for their help in sending in war material. Today they have gone off to visit Radovče‡ to see how material could be dropped.

We have discussed this with them and they have agreed to give us arms, especially automatic weapons; some clothing and boots for the army, and later further aid. . . .[9]

* Named after the mountain shrine of Montenegro, on the summit of which stands the tomb of the Prince Bishop Njegoš.

† See p. 132.

‡ The village where the Serbian headquarters had been established in the autumn of 1941 to which Hudson had been escorted after his landing.

The news of the unheralded arrival of a mixed British–Royal Yugoslav party in Montenegro coincided with a plan to secure the dispatch of a Soviet mission to Partisan-held territory, and aroused in Tito at once perplexity and suspicion.

During these days he had received reports of overflying of un-identified planes in the region of East Bosnia and near Sarajevo. Were they carrying the long-awaited Soviet emissaries, or were they British aircraft seeking to drop parachutists and supplies to reinforce Mihailović and Hudson?

The delegate of the Partisan Supreme Command for Bosnia and Hercegovina, 'Tempo',* who was precariously hidden in enemy-occupied Sarajevo, reported on 12 February to Tito, almost simultaneously as the news of the appearance of the Atherton group in Montenegro reached Foča.

Yesterday all Sarajevo was buzzing with the news of a landing of parachutists on Romanija mountain. This colonel tells us that two British and two Yugoslav officers with a complete radio station, some machine guns and stores have been captured. It is thought that the plane came from the Morava valley near Čačak to Romanija. During their interrogation both Yugoslav officers state that they have come from Benghazi. The British officer states that he has nothing to say. The Germans think that they have arrived from some airfield in Turkey as they are all very fit and fresh and not tired after the flight. They have all been transported to Belgrade.

The source of 'Tempo's' information in Sarajevo was a Partisan agent working as a staff colonel at Ustaša headquarters, Suleiman Filipović. Later their informant was obliged to flee. I met him later in Bosnia as a Partisan officer.

This was the 'Disclaim' mission, which had been captured on 7 February, three days after landing, by Ustaša patrols, and handed over to the Germans.

On 16 February, Tito replied to 'Tempo':

As to the aircraft you write about, they were observed here and over Gorazde and we were convinced that these planes were our brothers or allies. I am sorry that this equipment has fallen into the hands of those Ustaša bandits, I was sure that these planes were coming in accordance with my request to 'Djeda' (the Comintern), but unfortunately this episode has happened during this offensive, and partly due to our feebleness for it should have been possible for our people to have given

---

* Svetozar Vukmanovic – Tempo, at this time delegate of the Supreme Staff in Bosnia and Hercegovina.

some sort of signal which we had agreed for the drop instead of lighting
fires. From now on we must take this business more seriously so that this
does not happen again.[10]

This letter from Tito reveals that the 'Disclaim' party landed at
a point in Eastern Bosnia near the village of Sokolac where there
was a landing ground * already fixed with Moscow for the reception of a Soviet mission, and possibly jointly with the British, since
in a letter of 23 February Tito commented on this affair:

The Yugoslav officers say that three British planes were involved. I
would be surprised if they have come precisely at my request to our side.
[Indeed, he had had no contact whatever with the British since Hudson
left him in the Sandžak in early December 1941.] I have reported to the
Comintern not to send such guests, since we had enough trouble with
them in Serbia [a reference to Hudson]. They have arrived at the most
unfavourable time when the enemy hold this territory in their hands.[11]

Tito was urgently concerned with reconstructing a new 'free
territory' in Montenegro in fear of stronger Četnik elements, and
had sent Moša Pijade as his personal delegate to carry out this
task, and also to prepare to receive near Žabljak the long-awaited
Soviet mission – an operation vital to the recognition of the
Partisan movement by the Allies, in particular since the confused
and inexplicable disappearance of Hudson to Mihailović's headquarters and the absence of any further sign of a British attempt
to renew contact with the Partisans.

On 25 February Tito sent a courier with a message to Pijade.

Our headquarters in Montenegro have written that again a British–
Yugoslav mission has arrived in the same way as the first one; only this
time there are two British and only one Yugoslav. They ask to come to
our Supreme Staff to talk to me, and at the same time to learn what has
happened to their predecessor, Hudson. They say that another similar
mission has landed in Dalmatia.†

At the same time they say that a plane of theirs will land shortly at
Žabljak. You should be warned that you do not fall on their necks
thinking that this [group] are those whom we are awaiting. If something
like this happens, hang on to the party and tell us. I am telling the
Comintern about the whole question and have asked them what to do.

* In a message from 'Tempo' to Tito dated 6 February 1942 the former wrote:
'Make every effort to ensure that we get the "post" [courier] from Zagreb.
They certainly have news there for "Djeda" [Moscow]. If Sokolac is to be
captured, this area must be cleaned up urgently on account of the business
which we know about.'
† This refers to the 'Henna' party (Rapotec).

This mission which is coming to us must be sent to me by safe channel and unhindered.[12]

The mystery of this fourth mission has never been clarified. Had the Russians and the British secretly mounted a joint operation?

In the meantime, Tito ordered Milutinović to send the Atherton party to Pijade in Žabljak en route to Foča.

The Montenegrin Partisan staff were reluctant to obey these orders, suspicious that the Atherton party were a provocation and that their real purpose was to locate channels of communications, as Lalatović had done the previous year, with local Četnik commanders.

On 7 March Milutinović sent this message to Tito:[13]

We are sending the British to you, but would like to stress to you that the whole time they have been with us they have not succeeded in making W/T contact. Although they have several times been given dispatched signals, they have never told us whether they have received any replies. This seems suspicious to us, and they have not been able to explain why they cannot make contact. We don't want to repeat the views which we have already expressed, but we do consider that one must be very cautious with them – the British major knows very well conditions in the provinces of Yugoslavia – and even people – he is a very sly character. The Serb (Nedeljković) seems very suspicious and scared. We have, in an earlier letter,* tried to give you a general directive as to further handling of these guests.

The Partisan Supreme Command was still awaiting with strained impatience the arrival of a Soviet plane. Such a mission, it was hoped, would clarify misunderstandings between Moscow and Tito which had not been resolved in radio messages between him and the Comintern.

Apart from the technical difficulties of parachuting a delegation or supplies at such a distance from the nearest Russian air bases, there was also the criticism directed by the Soviet authorities against Tito as to the manner and the nature of the Partisan rising, in particular the allegations by Moscow that Tito bore some responsibility for the breakdown of negotiations for common action with Mihailović at the end of 1941. The Russians were anxious that any rebellion on Yugoslav territory should appear to represent a national front, and seemed to reject Tito's thesis of Četnik collaboration with the Axis.

* Not traced.

On 11 March 1942 Tito wrote to Pijade at Žabljak:

Your comment on the common action of the Yugoslav government, Draža, Nedić, and the occupier is correct, but the Comintern is reluctant to believe this. Some days ago I received a letter, miles long, telling me that the material evidence which we are sending gives the impression that our Partisan movement is proceeding too much under Communist leadership, because otherwise how is it possible that the supporters of London are organizing the Četniks against us? They (the Comintern) further ask: why has it been necessary to create a special proletarian brigade? We ought to revise our policy and set up a broad national front . . .[14]

Pijade replied in a letter dated 15 March, saying that he was still awaiting in vain, after twelve nights, the arrival of a Soviet mission, and that he 'did not think that our political line was mistaken'. The tactics of the Mihailović organization were, through the local formation of joint 'volunteer units' in Bosnia and Montenegro, to break the structure of the Partisan movement.

On 20 February a Partisan unit near Nevesinje in Hercegovina had captured Mihailović's personal regional delegate, Major Boško Todorović. He was carrying papers which allegedly revealed the links between the Royal Yugoslav government in London and the Italian forces of occupation. Documents also showed the manner in which the B.B.C. news was exploited to support Mihailović, and convey code messages to him from the Royal Yugoslav government in London.

This evidence was sent by courier to Tito. As Pijade put it in a letter of 6 March, referring to these documents: 'It should be the moment for Radio Moscow to bring a campaign against Draža, or at least against the Četniks, and to give daily publicity to us, and stress that the Četniks are more than ever attacking us today led by officers under Draža's command, and in agreement with the occupier.'[15]

The arrival of a Soviet mission was essential to clear up the whole situation, and the Russians must be persuaded to press for at least the dismissal of Mihailović as Minister of War in the London government, thus removing the basis of his prestige within the country.

There remained the mysterious hint, reported by Atherton on his arrival at Partisan headquarters in Montenegro, that a British plane was due to parachute a party to Žabljak.

If separate Russian and British missions, or perhaps a joint one, should arrive at such a moment, this might mark a decisive and revolutionary turning point in the isolated position of the Partisan movement. Anticipation, suspicions, and puzzled excitement were intense among the Partisan leaders.

On 5 March Tito had sent a message to Pijade:

Last night at 1 a.m. a plane was heard again flying over Čajnice and Goradže (in the neighbourhood of Foča). Has anyone reached you?

The Comintern have now answered that the British mission should certainly come to see me, and that I should talk to them, but that I must be cautious and get out of them what they really want. They (the Comintern) ask further that I keep them continuously informed of the position, and add that nothing is known of the arrival of this mission in Yugoslavia. From this one sees, for example, the confidence expressed in this ally [the British].

As soon as they arrive, send them on.[16]

The delay in Atherton's departure from Milutinović's head-quarters caused Tito impatient anxiety, and probably a lurking fear that the Montenegrins might dispatch the party in another manner. As Tito wrote to Pijade: 'Take urgent action that the British mission once and for all comes on here. Inform the comrades that they will answer with their heads that this mission arrives here in one piece, as I want the whole matter finally cleared up, as does the Comintern.'[17]

These orders were more promptly noted by the parties con-cerned, and Atherton, Nedeljković, and the radio operator O'Donovan reached Žabljak with an escort, probably on the evening of 14 March.

Pijade sent a courier to Tito with a letter dated 15 March.

This morning I had a brief talk with Captain Nedeljković. He assures me that the whole mission has arrived from the British government and not the Yugoslav, except for himself. The British Captain speaks good Serb: he has lived in Belgrade and remembers having seen me at the Café Milanović, and mentioned certain Jewish journalists who were friends of his. I have the impression that he knows with whom he is dealing.

Pijade informed Atherton that he would be going on to Tito's headquarters at Foča.

It will be important to show him clear evidence regarding 'His Excellency the Minister of War'. This mission find themselves in an uneasy position if one asks them why are they so ill-informed in

London that they still accredit him (Atherton) to the Minister? Every opportunity must be taken to influence this mission to prove that our Partisan movement is the only patriotic army. I asked the Captain why up till now they have not helped us with arms and munitions. He says that it would be possible. You will be even better placed to extract from them clearly whether or not some of their colleagues have arrived at Žabljak.

Atherton had left his charging engines for his W/T set with Milutinović, who had promised to forward them to Žabljak 'within four days'.* The British officer also told Pijade that 'he did not much care for the fact that his party had already been in the country for the month and had still not been with you. I convinced him that they will leave tomorrow, the 16th. We have treated them correctly, and, on the advice of Milutinović, we have not been playing stupid tricks on them.'[18]

During his brief stay in Žabljak, Atherton learnt something of the strength of the local Partisan forces, and visited the political authorities and the military hospital in the Hotel Durmitor.

On 16 March Pijade wrote again to Tito.

The mission is leaving here on the 17th and should reach you on the afternoon of the 19th.

I think this: that they have come from the British government, that they should be asked clearly why they have been sent and to show their instructions. If they have come to co-operate and exercise some control, they must be told that we will gladly accept allied representatives, but not from one side, but from all the Allies; the British, the Americans, and the U.S.S.R. should send military and political representatives to us as a joint delegation. Second proposal: without regard as to whether or not they have come to co-operate or to convince us to work with Draža, we must make the request that Draža should be expelled from the Yugoslav government as a traitor and that our Partisan army and Supreme Staff should be recognized as the only patriotic army and leadership of the rising; that London radio should cease to give publicity to Draža.

The Captain (Nedeljković) tells me that the London government is poorly informed about the situation in Yugoslavia, and that by appointing Draža they hoped to show the British government that they were not simply an exiled government, but had one minister and some forces on the ground. I said that it could easily be proved that this minister is working with the occupier.[19]

On the evening of 20 March, Atherton and his party reached

* There is no evidence to show that this was done.

Foča with an escort of Partisan couriers from the Durmitor *odred*, and, after a talk with Tito, joined the Supreme Staff at supper.

Atherton had arrived by chance during a Četnik offensive against the Partisans in Montenegro; he was shown by Pijade the results of the recent Partisan efforts to restore the military and political situation in the Durmitor region, and learnt that the arrival of this British mission coincided with a determined attempt by Tito to clarify his position with Moscow.

Tito hoped to use the fortuitous arrival of Atherton to inform London of the strength of the Partisan movement, to send proof of Mihailović's collaboration with Nedić and the occupier, and to propose the recognition of the Partisans as the sole element of Yugoslav resistance. At the same time Tito, urged on by Pijade, pointed out to the Russians that the presence of a British mission made the dispatch of a Soviet delegation to Partisan headquarters even more pressing. As Pijade put it in his letter of 16 March: 'We must propose to them [the Russians] that they send their representatives to us and that we are not faced only with the British, that there should be a joint Allied mission with our Supreme Staff. We have sufficient free territory, and the means to hold it. Djeda could have had one man with us. Let him be dropped to us, and all will go smoothly.'

By the end of March, however, radio messages reaching Tito from Moscow made it clear that no parachute mission with supplies could 'for technical reasons' be sent in, and Pijade was instructed to disband his night watchers on the airfield near Žabljak. On the night of 27 March British planes flew over the zone, arousing hopes, but they were on a mission to scatter leaflets across the whole territory to commemorate the *coup d'état* of 27 March 1941.[20]

Unknown to the Partisan command, the Russians were considering the simultaneous dispatch of delegations, to study the position on the spot, both to Mihailović and to Tito. The refusal of the Royal Yugoslav government to accept the former proposal seems to have been the main cause of delay in sending a Soviet mission to the Partisans.[21]

Atherton's presence in Foča assumed an unforeseen significance as the only immediate, if faint, means of making contact with the British and pressing on their authorities evidence of Četnik collaboration with the Axis and the need for a new Yugoslav government, which would include some representatives of the Partisan movement on the spot.

There is no direct evidence of the discussions which took place between Tito and members of his staff with Atherton at Foča during the following days.

But a signal to Moscow over Tito's radio set, now functioning at Foča, stated: 'A British mission has arrived at the Supreme Staff. Wants to know facts about Yugoslavia. British have been shown evidence about Draža Mihailović. They state that this is not known in London, who are wrongly informed, and that the Partisans are guilty of not getting across their propaganda abroad.' [22]

Colonel Vladimir Velebit, who had just arrived at Foča from a perilous underground mission in Zagreb and was attached to the Supreme Staff, had been instructed to provide Atherton with all captured material relating to Mihailović, and to the collaboration of his commanders with the Axis.*

On 24 March, Tito again signalled to the Comintern:

The British mission agrees with the Central Committee of the Yugoslav Communist Party that a new Yugoslav government of democratic elements inside and outside the country should be formed.

After Atherton had studied material proof of Četnik treachery, he stated that the [Royal Yugoslav] London government were in error, and he could not understand their support of Draža Mihailović. [23]

But the behaviour of this British–Royal Yugoslav mission proved to be beyond rational analysis.

In early April Tito wrote in a letter to Pijade:

Something is not in order with the British. They squabble among themselves, but up till now we have not succeeded in unearthing what it is about. The squabbling has gone so far that our lieutenant [Nedeljković] comes alone to us to lunch, and they do not go about together. The Englishman tells me that they have no confidence at all in the London government, and I keep pressing that the government should be changed, as it is in the Allied interest in today's conflict. I have told the Comintern that I consider that a new popular government should be created, most of whose members should be in the country, and which should issue a proclamation calling on the people to conduct an

* See the letter by the Secretary of the Association of Yugoslav Journalists in London, S. Sudjić, in the *Daily Telegraph* of 16 February 1948. This included the documents recently captured from Major Boško Todorović, the personal representative of Mihailović for Bosnia and Hercegovina.

energetic armed struggle against the occupier. I have told this to the British. There has as yet been no answer from Moscow.

In another telegram to the Comintern I have reported that we shall be forced openly to attack the [Yugoslav] London government if they continue to retain Draža Mihailović and behave in a hostile manner towards us. I have also sought their advice and they have not yet replied.[24]

A dramatic episode now added to the complications of the scene. On the night of 15 April Atherton, his radio operator O'Donovan, and Nedeljković, together with a certain General Novaković and a small party, left their lodgings in the town telling the owner that they were going to the Supreme Staff headquarters. They disappeared into the woods surrounding the city 'in an unknown direction'. They left behind them their radio set, and a letter from Novaković to Tito.

The former was a local nationalist leader who had been captured recently by a Partisan unit and brought to Foča.

General Ljubo Novaković might have been an important figure in the history of Yugoslav resistance, and his adventures after April 1941 reveal little-known and vivid glimpses of the struggle for leadership amid the various nationalist bands sprouting in Serbia in the summer and autumn of 1941. He had a strong claim to assume a commanding position. He was the only Royal Yugoslav General on the active list to escape internment by the Germans, and to remain in the country.

He escaped from a military hospital at Valjevo in May 1941, and found his way to Ravna Gora, where he was coldly received by Colonel Mihailović as a potential rival. Novaković drafted a plan 'for Četnik action in Yugoslavia' which assumed the creation of a series of separate and independent territorial commands. This project was promptly rejected by Mihailović, and Novaković departed in mid-June from Ravna Gora in a huff to contact the official leader of the pre-war Četnik organization, Kosta Pećanac. The latter put him in charge of the 'Sumadija Staff of Četnik *odreds*' as a direct rival to Mihailović's skeleton organization. This was a brief and unfortunate episode. When Pećanac put his 'official' Četnik organization openly at the disposal of the Germans, Novaković broke off all relations with him.

Novaković seems to have been an ambitious, violent, incoherent and somewhat mentally confused character, obsessed with his military seniority and seeking restlessly for an independent and leading position in the creation of a resistance movement. Having been born in Montenegro, he moved back there with a small band of personal followers out of Serbia in the hope of setting up his own organization.

News of his existence reached London in September 1941, and he was reported to be leading 'an official Četnik group in Hercegovina'.

He was well known to those senior officers of the Royal Yugoslav army then in London, and his fellow general, Bogoljub Ilić, now Minister of War, sent a radio message to Mihailović at the end of October ordering the two men to work together.

Ilić correctly saw, in the dimly reported activities of Novaković, a disruptive threat to a central national command in Serbia under the direct control of the Royal Yugoslav authorities in London.

Tito thought likewise.

In early September 1941 Novaković had a secret meeting in Belgrade with representatives of the underground Communist Party Committee, and during the course of the next month was in imtermittent contact with local Partisan *odreds* in Šumadija, issuing joint proclamations calling for a general rising against the Germans.

But, after attempting and losing an over-subtle game of acting as an intermediary between Mihailović and Pećanac with a view to shelving both of them and emerging as the successor of the latter as head of a united 'official' Četnik organization, Novaković departed in the direction of Bosnia, and disappeared for a time from the scene.

He seems to have had schemes for rallying the Serb nationalist bands in East Bosnia, which were active on a small scale against the Ustaša and the occupier and for a time in uneasy association with the Partisans.

Combined Četnik–Partisan *odreds* were formed from Serb villages as 'volunteer units' under the nominal command of the Partisan headquarters, as an expedient and a remnant of their brief collaboration in Serbia, and held temporarily together by the penetration of Bosnia by the Ustaša and their massive slaughter of the Serb population.

During the crisis which divided the Partisan movement in East Bosnia under the pressure of Četnik penetration, Novaković appeared at the head of a small band of his own. At the beginning of January 1942, this group had been disarmed by partisan units and brought under escort to Foča.

Apparently under Tito's orders, he moved freely in the town, and seems to have frequented the Atherton mission without surveillance.

There is little evidence of events in Foča which followed the arrival there of the British mission. Atherton professed agreement with Tito's proposals, communicated by radio to Moscow, for reconstructing the Yugoslav government in London, denouncing the collaboration of Mihailović and his commanders with the Axis, and establishing some form of political representation of the Partisan leadership within the country as a section of a new administration in London and recognized by the British and the Russians.

Even if Atherton had sincerely accepted this solution of the crisis enveloping the Partisan movement, his W/T set could not be operated, and Cairo was unaware of his whereabouts and fate.

As to Novaković, Tito may have felt that, as in Serbia in the autumn of 1941, this 'general without an army' * might play at least a temporary rôle in rallying the Bosnian Četniks under Partisan command and disrupting the menacing extension of Mihailović's control in that region, and throughout Montenegro.

But any interpretation of what passed during these days in Foča can only be based on speculation. Atherton was in daily contact with members of the Partisan Supreme Staff, and in frequent private consultation with Novaković.

On the evening of his disappearance, Atherton had dined with Velebit, and given no hint of his intentions. At day-break bustling confusion was noted at Tito's headquarters. The head of the recently formed security section of the Staff, Pejo Penezić, was seen galloping out of the town in an easterly direction, with a patrol.

On the next day, 16 April, Tito sent a message to Djilas, the special envoy of the Supreme Staff to the Partisan command in Montenegro, giving general instructions for the reorganization and purging of the Party and of the military units in that territory, and for the preparation of military action against the occupying and Četnik forces. In this letter he wrote:

Our British guests have sprung a great surprise on us. Last night all

* A phrase of R. Colaković. Zapisi I, p. 457.

three of them vanished without trace together with that old fox General Novaković and a couple of civilians. I think that they are making for the Sandžak or Montenegro although that old skunk of a general left behind a letter in his room in which he threatens us with some 5,000 Bosnian Serbs. Do everything you can on your side to catch them if they appear on your territory.[25]

On 16 April the Partisan Supreme Staff sent a message to the neighbouring Jahorina *odred* giving details of the disappearance of the group from Foča. This unit had recently been the object of successful penetration by local Četniks, probably in contact with Novaković, and its commander was himself to desert at the beginning of May.

Atherton may have been impressed by Novaković's evidence on the pending collapse of the local Partisan military organization throughout Bosnia, and have wished to study the situation himself.

On 17 April Dedijer noted rather oddly in his diary: 'Atherton and Novaković are somewhere in the woods near Slatina (a hamlet about twelve kilometres east of Foča.) They have been observed by one of our patrols. It may happen that the bandit Novaković and Nedeljković will kill the British, and take their cash.'[26]

Partisan patrols along the river Drina failed to discover any trace of the party, and it could only be assumed by Tito and his staff that the whole group would reach Mihailović's headquarters. Suspicions already aroused that the British were engaged in a sinister and extensive game of building up decisive support for the Četnik organization seemed to be once and for all confirmed.

Atherton had boasted to the Partisan staff that he was in command of four missions. Tito already knew of the existence and fate of Major Elliot and his party, which was believed to have been parachuted with the intention of contacting Četnik bands in Central Bosnia. Reports had also reached Tito, at the end of March, that another British mission had landed in Dalmatia.*

On 8 April 1942 Tito had written a confidential letter to the Central Committee of the Communist Party in Croatia.

For your own information, but not for general publication, we have to acquaint you with some very interesting matters which we have

---

* This was the 'Henna' party of Rapotec. Tito seems to have thought that this group was the mysterious group which Atherton mentioned as being expected to arrive at Žabljak. In this letter he wrote: 'This is the mission which our guests have talked about.' (Tito to the delegate of the General Staff in Montenegro, 28 March 1942, Zbornik II, 30, p. 253.)

established beyond the possibility of doubt. We have now certain proof that the British, through their agents in Yugoslavia, are working not to remove, but rather to intensify, the differences between ourselves and other groups such as the Četniks. England is supporting different Četnik bands just as the Germans are doing and egging them on to attack us.

We have proof that British policy aims at sabotaging and compromising the struggle for national liberation so that when the situation is favourable and Italy leaves Hitler and comes within their grasp, the British will land troops in Dalmatia and elsewhere and appear as 'liberators' to save the country from chaos. To this end about ten so-called 'military missions' have already arrived and are doing their dirty work in different parts of Yugoslavia. One such mission has arrived at our headquarters, another has landed in Dalmatia and others are in different parts of the country, exactly where we do not know.

What they are aiming at can clearly be seen from what has been happening in Montenegro. Round Kolašin and elsewhere there suddenly appeared strong and well-armed Četnik bands, led in the main by pro-British leaders and assisted by the Italian occupation forces who are cunningly turning the situation to their advantage. These Četnik bands fell upon our Partisan troops at Kolašin, captured the town and shed the blood of many of our best fighters. As you know, the only fighting force up to now in Montenegro has been the Partisans. Yet here are Četnik bands suddenly springing up throughout Montenegro under the leadership of Fifth Columnists and pro-Britishers. This cannot be explained away simply by Italian guile. It is quite clear that the pro-British elements who have hitherto fought on our side have not suddenly turned against us overnight on orders given by the Italians. A hint must have been dropped in London.

You must be on your guard against this happening in Croatia. If any missions arrive, see that you are not taken in by them. Find a way of denying them direct access to the people and keep them well under your own control. Each mission has its own wireless transmitter. They keep in direct touch with their parent organization, the Intelligence Service. Any attempt at reviving the Četnik organization in your territory must be nipped in the bud. In Croatia, the military missions will probably try and make contact with members of the Croat Peasant Party, the Independent Democrats and the Yugoslav Nationalists, with whose help they will attempt to undermine your influence and the struggle for national liberation.

I must emphasize again that all this is not for general publication, but the confidential information of leading persons in the Army and Party.

In public, the alliance between the Soviet Union, Britain and the United States must continue to be stressed, and the latter two Powers are to be depicted as our allies. But their agents and pawns inside our country must be opposed, just as we oppose the henchmen of the invaders and the enemies of the people who are out to crush our struggle for national liberation.*

Two days later, on 10 April, Lola Ribar, a member of the Central Committee, who had just returned to Foča from a mission in occupied Zagreb, outlined the same suspicions.

'For your personal information, and not to be announced . . . various British missions are not only with us but in various parts of the country. From what we now know, it emerges clearly that the flaring up of civil war, in regard to the attempt to liquidate the Partisan movement in Yugoslavia, is to a large degree the intention of their superiors and equally of the Yugoslav government in London.'[27]

This interpretation of British plans was in great part due to the crisis in East Bosnia, Hercegovina, and Montenegro and marked signs of a rapid extension of Mihailović's activities in these regions, which threatened by his present numerical and military superiority to break up the very existence of the Partisan movement.

It could be logical to assume that this situation had arisen not only because of the marked success of Četnik propaganda and the corresponding failure of the Partisans in this bitter and competitive struggle for the support of the population, but also because a sudden increase in British material and psychological aid to Mihailović added to his prestige as Minister of War in the Royal Yugoslav government.

These letters of Tito and Lola Ribar were written during the presence of Atherton in Foča. It seems therefore at least likely that some of the suspicions harboured by Tito and his Staff sprang from the ambivalent behaviour and remarks of Atherton, and even more so of Nedeljković. Tito had reasons and evidence to fear that some plot was being hatched between Atherton and Novaković, which included the intention to contact Mihailović. The abrupt flight of the party may have been due to their realization that the Partisan staff were aware of some such scheme and intended to arrest them.

The effect of the episode is beyond doubt, and its impact on Tito

* Quoted in Stephen Clissold, *Whirlwind*, pp. 86–7, without indication of source. This letter is of historical importance as a summary of Tito's reactions to the abrupt appearance of British missions, and his analysis of the political intentions behind these operations.

and his Staff was to persist until the arrival of our mission in the following year.

The fate of Atherton himself and his radio operator O'Donovan was pieced together later from Mihailović sources.

News reached the latter's headquarters in an unusual fashion. Major Ostojić, who had joined Mihailović together with Hudson in October of the previous year, and was now the commander of the main Četnik forces operating on the borders of Sandžak and Montenegro, picked up a wandering Yugoslav officer, who turned out to be Captain Nedeljković.

On 15 May Ostojić sent the following radio message to Mihailović:

'Yesterday, on 10 May, Captain Nedeljković came. He is a member of the mission which landed on 4 February 1942, and was in the hands of the Partisans until 15 April. The mission included a British major named Atherton 'who is even worse than 'Marko',* and is asking for help for the Communists but has no contact with Malta. He wants to see you. At the moment Atherton is somewhere in Bosnia, and he has instructions to do all in his power to support the struggle against the invader.

Atherton was set free by Ljubo Novaković, who has sent to you an apologetic letter.†

Mihailović immediately signalled to his government in London: 'It has come to my knowledge that yet another British mission is in the country, but I do not know where they are nor have I been informed about them either by you or on the British side. Please act as soon as possible on this message.' ‡

Shortly after Mihailović received a letter from Atherton 'somewhere in Bosnia', saying that he was trying to reach Mihailović's headquarters, and on 24 May the latter again signalled to London: 'I have received during these days a letter from the British Major Atherton after his escape from Communist detention. I am taking all necessary measures to locate him.'§

* The name used for Hudson.
† Ostojić to Mihailović 15 May 1942. ('Mihailovic Telegrams'. Files in the Institute of War History, Belgrade. Part of the text of this message is quoted in Mihailović's post-war trial. See also the stenographic record in English (Belgrade, 1946), p. 386.) Novaković was married to Ostojić's sister.
‡ Mihailović to Jovanović, 15 May 1942 (Mihailović Dispatches, ibid.).
§ In Atherton's letter to Mihailović (preserved in the Belgrade Archives), he asked the latter to send a radio message to Cairo to drop a new W/T set for him to Mihailović's headquarters.

Bill Stuart and Vlada Dedijer

Tito's radio station, June 1943

Walter Wroughton, Glamoč, October 1943

Hudson, who was with Mihailović and learned of these developments, set out for Ostojić's headquarters to question Nedeljković.
The latter reported, in a letter of 26 May to Mihailović, his
conversation with Hudson and an other British officer who called
himself 'Radovan'.*

According to Nedeljković, Hudson asked why he had not come
with Atherton and O'Donovan, and received the reply that they
had separated from him and 'left in the direction of Serbia'.
Atherton had told Nedeljković that his mission covered Bosnia,
Hercegovina, and Montenegro, and that he had orders also to
collaborate with the Partisans.

Hudson was said to have retorted to Nedeljković that only the
Partisans were fighting against the Germans and Italians. The
British were not prepared to help those helping them, and Hudson
himself was treated by Mihailović as a prisoner.

On 27 May Hudson reported over Mihailović's set, but in his
own cipher, the first results of his inquiry. Three days later,
Mihailović received a signal from London: 'Atherton is our man.
He was sent in January. Help him and take his advice.'†

On 12 June Mihailović signalled to London that he was
pursuing inquiries but that a mystery surrounded General
Novaković 'who was last seen in the district of Foča'. The latter,
however, had sent a letter, abject in its terms and pledging co-
operation in the future. ‡

Prompted by Hudson, and pressed by London, Mihailović
ordered a formal inquiry into the fate of the Atherton mission on
20 June, to be carried out by a gendarmerie officer at his headquarters, Captain Uzelac.§

A summary of the results of this investigation was sent by
Hudson to Cairo. According to this message, Atherton and his
party had escaped from Foča on the night of 15 April, 'escorted
by the Četnik leader Spasoje Dakić', and the enterprise had been
engineered by Novaković who was planning to set up a Četnik
group in Bosnia independent of Mihailović's authority, and

* Nedeljković letter (Archives of the Institute of War History, Belgrade).
  'Radovan' has not been identified. There were two British officers who had
  escaped in Serbia after being captured by the Germans on Crete.
† Mihailović Trial Records, p. 386.
‡ The original is in the Belgrade Archives.
§ Copies of the original documents relating to this inquiry are in the possession
  of the author by courtesy of the Institute of War History, Belgrade.

presumably in association with Dakić who headed a small Četnik band in East Bosnia.

For seven days the party hid in a cave near the village of Čelebić on the river Drina. On 22 April, according to Hudson's telegrams, Atherton, 'whose attitude to the escape was not known', decided to move on into Serbia after quarrelling with Nedeljković and Novaković. The latter was 'now a prisoner of Mihailović in Hercegovina'. Nedeljković ultimately reached Mihailović's headquarters, but was subsequently encouraged to desert to Serbia – presumably to Nedić 'on account of his unreliability'.

Atherton and O'Donovan, his radio operator, left Čelebić on 22 April for the village of Tatarevina, and were escorted part of the way by Dakić. They were never seen again. Dakić, who later appeared at Mihailović's headquarters in possession of Atherton's binoculars, and wearing his boots, had probably murdered both men and stolen the large quantity of gold sovereigns which Atherton was carrying.* He was only 'nominally a Mihailović Četnik', but Hudson had the impression that Mihailović 'knew something about the matter'. This summary completed such evidence as Hudson was able to assemble up to July 1942.†

Mihailović's first reaction to all these happenings was to insinuate to London, as an astute propaganda move, that the British members of the party had been killed by Partisans. He stated this in a message, dated 27 May, at a moment when in reality he and the British military authorities in Cairo had every reason to believe that Atherton was alive. At the end of the signal Mihailović announced that, because of these murders, 'he had declared open warfare on all Partisans'.

Strangely, a similar report came from the leader of the 'Henna' party, which had been landed from the same submarine that carried Atherton and his mission, on the island of Mljet.‡ This officer, a Royal Yugoslav naval lieutenant and a Slovene, Lieu-

---

* Atherton was carrying one million lire and nearly 2,000 gold sovereigns. His fate was a direct lesson to future missions, who were never endowed with such funds.

† After Colonel Bailey arrived at Mihailović's headquarters in December 1942 the case of Atherton was re-opened. There was no trace of the bodies and no clues. It was, however, proved that they were alive on 23 April 1942, when Nedeljković and Novaković left them.

‡ See p. 155.

tenant Rapotec, reached Istanbul in early July 1942 on a faked
Italian passport, and was interrogated there by British officials.

The statement of Rapotec was the first of several, from Četnik
sources, which accused the Partisans of responsibility for
Atherton's disappearance. This campaign culminated in a letter
from the Yugoslav Prime Minister in London, Professor Jovanović, to the Foreign Office, dated 31 July 1942, stating that,
according to a report from Madrid, ' "Aterton", the brother of a
Labour peer, had been killed by Partisans, who had seized his
funds which were destined for Mihailović.'

An earlier Četnik version was more circumstantial. Atherton
had been arrested by a Partisan *odred* commander and he and his
party executed and their bodies thrown into caves between
Žabljak and Šavnik.

These Četnik propaganda stories came to the notice of Tito and
his staff in an odd manner.

An article in the *New York Times* in February 1943, which is
quoted in Dedijer's diary, from their London correspondent, C. L.
Sulzberger, stated that 'last year Partisans had killed some
British officers, among them the former correspondent in Belgrade,
Atherton'.[28] Tito was obligingly informed of this article by
Moscow. The story had been spread by Royal Yugoslav circles in
London, but seemed to have escaped the notice of British head-
quarters in Cairo.

On 8 February 1943 'Free Yugoslavia' broadcast from the
Soviet Union the following statement: 'It is true that Atherton
came with Nedeljković and 'Patrick' (Sergeant O'Donovan) to
our headquarters, but they left as freely as they came, although
playing an obscure rôle. Only our obligations towards our Allies
induce us to keep silence about Atherton's role. The aim of his and
two other visits * is completely revealed, and we may have the
opportunity of explaining it after the war.'

An element of mystery still surrounds the details of the disappearance of Atherton and O'Donovan. Circumstantial evidence
is, however, strong that they were murdered by Dakić. The latter
was killed in 1946 in 'special operations' conducted by the
security forces of Tito against the remnants of the Mihailović units.

The fate of Novaković is known. After leaving Atherton, and
presumably not daring to face Mihailović in view of their personal

---

* Only Captain Hudson had visited Tito's headquarters in October 1941.
The reference to two visits has not been elucidated.

relations and rivalry in the events of the autumn of 1941 in Serbia, Novaković went into hiding in his native village in Montenegro after this episode, and was later active in collaboration with Četnik and separatist groups, attempting to take over the leadership of the latter. At the end of 1943 he was captured and shot by units of the Fifth Montenegrin Brigade.

Nedeljković, who was described by Mihailović at his trial as a 'peculiar person . . . who suffered from persecution mania',[29] disappeared shortly after his arrival at Mihailović's headquarters. There is some evidence that he was caught, possibly by anonymous denunciation, by the Germans and imprisoned in Belgrade. He has never been traced.

Before the 'Typical' mission left Cairo in May 1943, we were aware of Hudson's investigation of the Atherton affair, and of later efforts by Colonel Bailey. It had been accepted that Atherton and his radio operator had been murdered by a Četnik leader named Dakić, who might have been operating in some loose association with the movement of Mihailović.

But Stuart and I did not know that the disappearance of Atherton and his party from Foča in April 1942, and the absence of any British attempt to contact Tito again until precisely one year later when another mission parachuted 'blind' into Croatia, had been interpreted by Tito to mean that the British held the Partisans responsible for the killing of Atherton.

At our first meeting with Tito, Stuart and I were confronted with this version, which we felt able firmly to deny. We were not aware, however, at the time that, on the arrival of the first Canadian–Croat mission at Partisan headquarters in Croatia near the village of Brinje in the Lika a few days previously, Tito had sent to his headquarters for Croatia the following signal:

23 April 1943 – Tito to G.H.Q. Croatia: Hold the so called delegates with you until we discover what it is about. Don't let them in any way again commit some provocation such as last year Atherton did – which compromised us with world opinion. They are our guests, look after them well, and see that they do not travel on further from us. Send us regularly their comments and eventual intentions.[30]

It was thus in the light of such an interpretation of the fate of a previous British group to have reached by chance Tito's headquarters that our own mission began.

Shortly afterwards I had an opportunity to question on the fate

of Atherton the former Četnik commander of Žabljak, a Royal
Yugoslav Air Force officer, Captain Franc Berginec, who had
come over to the Partisans in March 1943.

Berginec confirmed, from his previous knowledge of Četnik
sources, the version already known to us. During the following
days he was critically wounded, and committed suicide to avoid
capture by the enemy.

The attempts made by S.O.E. Cairo during the course of 1942
to re-establish contact with Bill Hudson by sending in further
parties, and to obtain a wider picture of resistance elements in
other regions of the country outside the immediate areas of
Western Serbia where Mihailović was assumed to be operating, had
been without success. The curtain was impenetrable, the picture
dark.

It was therefore decided to parachute a senior mission to
Mihailović's headquarters, to establish the true state of affairs
and to report, after careful analysis, on the chequered experiences
of the only British witness – Bill Hudson – of the events of the
critical year of 1942. This task was assigned to Colonel S. W.
Bailey, a former member of the staff of the British-owned Trepča
mines in Serbia, with a fluency in the language which enabled
him to pass as a Yugoslav, and a specialist in the affairs of the
country. He had headed the S.O.E. staff in Belgrade in the summer of 1940, and was an expert on the politics and personalities
involved in the *coup d'état* of March 1941 in Belgrade. In the
autumn of 1942 he was attached to the S.O.E. headquarters in
Cairo for briefing and parachute training, in preparation for his
present undertaking.

His mission was devised at an unrewarding moment, in the face
of complete lack of response from Mihailović to British requests
for active collaboration; in the knowledge that the Partisans were
increasingly clashing with the Axis; and when the realities of civil
war throughout Yugoslavia imperilled the unity of the country.

Bailey's directive was a mixed one. He was to report on the
military value of the Četnik movement as a whole and to persuade
Mihailović to undertake active sabotage. He was also to study its
political intentions and propose how British policy, still constructed in its original form of creating a united resistance front,
could be implemented.

On Christmas Day 1942 Bailey and his W/T operator were

parachuted to Mihailović's headquarters at Gornje Lipovo, ten kilometres north of Kolašin on the borders of Eastern Montenegro and the Sandžak.

Bailey was an ambassador with a platitudinous political brief sent on a military mission without the means of calling on significant aid to support his task. He was to inform Mihailović of 'the world strategical and political developments, and to discuss maximum Yugoslav assistance to the Allied war effort'.

He was also, somewhat cryptically, to consider the possibility of turning Mihailović's organization into a general Balkan movement. The precise meaning of this latter objective was difficult to comprehend. It might simply imply that an agreement with Tito should be still considered as a possibility, and that, in spite of all evidence to the contrary, Mihailović would emerge as the acknowledged leader of Yugoslav resistance, or it could be interpreted as an instruction to Bailey to study the possibilities of developing the tenuous links which it was known that Mihailović had formed with individual personalities in Bulgaria, Greece, and Albania, so that some truncated Southern Balkan Federation might emerge, abandoning Croatia and Slovenia to an undefined political future.

On 26 December Bailey presented his credentials to Mihailović at his headquarters and early the following month, on 10 January, the British mission established its own separate headquarters at a suitable distance near by. During the ensuing days, Bailey conducted a series of talks with Mihailović, and intensive private discussions with Hudson, whom it was intended to evacuate in due course, for rest and leave.

Bailey toured the immediate areas under Mihailović's control, and with thoroughness and objectivity prepared a detailed and provisional summary of his impressions, embodying also the unique experience of Hudson's mission.

At the end of January, Bailey began to transmit by radio to Cairo a series of considered reports. His early impressions of the Četnik organization were generally favourable, though Mihailović's staff officers seemed 'lazy and inept'. Mihailović claimed to command 120,000 front line Četniks, and was exploiting B.B.C. broadcasts and meagre British supplies to win over Partisan supporters from their hard rôle of maintaining resistance against the Axis.

On 22 January 1943, Bailey summarized the essence of his first impressions in the form of a proposal which he considered might resolve the deadlock of British policy in regard to Yugoslav affairs, which was still based on the creation of a united resistance front within the country.

Bailey faced this central problem from the start. Mihailović was 'determined to eliminate all rivals before attacking the armies of occupation, and was convinced that all Croatian guerrillas not under his direct command were a hundred per cent Communist and must be destroyed'. Bailey and Hudson agreed that there could be no reconciliation at this stage between Mihailović and Tito, and that the only solution lay in arriving at some formula whereby the two forces could be physically divided from each other in territorial terms.

According to Bailey's calculations, based on fragments of evidence inevitably from Mihailović sources, Tito commanded about 4,000 Partisans in Western Bosnia, the remnants of his forces from 1942, together with a further nucleus of 10,000 troops who were interested in fighting the Germans but politically nationalists and could be won over to Mihailović.

The latter was convinced that all Croats were Communists, but Bailey hoped to receive evidence from Cairo that non-Communist guerrillas did exist in Croatia.

The area of Western Bosnia, admitted to be under Tito's control, was of direct concern to Mihailović, both on national grounds and because of its important strategic position along the foothills south of the Kupa and Sava rivers.

Bailey's plan, now put forward to his superiors, was to seek to encourage Tito to move his main forces west of Zagreb to the hill country between the Sava and Drava and to envisage the creation of two independent 'republics – Tito based on Western Croatia, and Mihailović on Serbia. The nationalist organization of the latter would include the Serb enclaves in Bosnia, and he should be allowed to move his bands into this region from Hercegovina and the Dinaric Alps.

It would be necessary only for the 4,000 professed Communists under Tito to evacuate those areas of the Pavelić State which he now held, as Mihailović claimed that he could probably rely on support there from the 10,000 other guerrillas.

Such a settlement would establish a united nationalist organization throughout Serbian territory, and at the same time the appearance of Partisans in Croatia would confront the Germans with fresh disturbances in that area.

The advantage of such a delimitation of spheres of influence would be to deprive Mihailović of his principal excuse for not fighting the Axis, and at the same time the recognized presence of Tito in Western Croatia would create a source of trouble for the Germans in these regions.

Bailey suggested that Hudson might act as emissary to Tito 'who both likes and respects him'. Mihailović himself would thus not be compromised by direct negotiations with the Communists, 'and we should retain direct control of subsequent developments in Croatia'.

Bailey also made the point that Anglo-Soviet planning was essential on an equal footing. There was a danger of Yugoslavia 'becoming a second Spain'.

He was aware, in general terms, that the Germans and Italians were engaged in a major offensive to annihilate the 'Tito State' based on Bihać in Croatia, and in the gloating atmosphere of Mihailović's headquarters he was understandably influenced by the optimistic reports reaching Lipovo of the menace facing Tito.

On 14 February Bailey had signalled that Mihailović claimed that the Partisans still existed only in East Bosnia. 'Recent arrangements made between the Četniks and Italians for transportation of Četniks both from Nikšić and Kolašin to Bosnia were cancelled at the last minute, probably at German insistence. The Germans may not desire to have concentrated Četnik forces in Bosnia in view of their apparent intention to clean up the whole area as far as Split.'

Following on these proposals, Bailey reported that he had succeeded in persuading Mihailović to accept sub-missions of British officers in Serbia to carry out independent sabotage against agreed targets.*

Sir George Rendel, the Ambassador to the Royal Yugoslav government in London, was, however, against the proposal to transfer Tito to Croatia. This would not only aggravate the national rivalries of the Serbs and Croats, but would go a long way towards setting up a Communist regime in Croatia, which by reason of its geographical proximity to Hungary and Austria might form the nucleus of a Communist central European bloc.

The Foreign Office, where a special meeting was held on 18 February 1943, feared that there might be a future embarrassment for the British in facing a hostile Partisan force should there

* The first British sub-missions arrived in Serbia in April 1943. See p. 183.

be landing operations on the Dalmatian or Croat coast, but also Bailey's scheme had overwhelming disadvantages on other grounds. Serb–Croat rivalry would be aggravated, and the spread of Communism facilitated, leading possibly to a clash between Tito and the Croat Peasant Party of Maček in place of that between Tito and Mihailović. Slovenia would be virtually sacrificed to Communism. A complete rupture with King Peter was implicit. The effect on Greece and our other Allies would be disturbing.

The Bailey scheme should therefore be dropped at once, but the British government was now obliged to face alternatives; Russian co-operation, which was now unlikely; all-out support for the Partisans – not desirable as Mihailović definitely controlled most of Serbia and it would involve a complete break with the King; total backing of Mihailović, which was also impossible as it would lead to a clash with Russia, and ultimately a pan-Serb Yugoslavia; or a policy of drift which would combine all the disadvantages inherent in the present situation.

The Foreign Office was thus faced with evolving a cautious policy of support for both sides. It was agreed that, if diplomatic approach to the Russians failed, negotiations with Tito should be initiated through Hudson.

Sir Orme Sargent, the Under Secretary of State at the Foreign Office, who had long favoured positive acceptance of the existence of Tito's forces, urged early assistance to the Partisans, while continuing the present scale of support to Mihailović.

The War Office commented more critically on Bailey's proposals. They did not consider that he was accurately informed on conditions in the 'Bihać republic' and Partisan-held territory in Bosnia and Croatia, nor on the strength of pro-Partisan and anti-Mihailović feeling, which existed throughout most of the country except among the Orthodox clericals and the extreme Right.

The War Office did not therefore consider that Bailey's reports could be taken as a basis on which to frame British policy towards Yugoslavia.

During February 1943 Bailey had toured in Montenegro and reviewed Djurišić's troops in Kolašin where he met Četnik representatives from Split.

At a christening in the house of the Mayor of Lipovo on 28 February, Mihailović burst out to Bailey in an anti-British tirade, announcing that the Italians were his 'sole source of benefits and assistance generally'. British material assistance to him was so small as to be negligible, while 'the B.B.C.'s new policy of advertisement for Tito' merely infuriated Mihailović without coercing him.

Behind this explosion of temper lay the roots of Mihailović's fears and frustrations. His bases in Bosnia, Hercegovina, and Montenegro had been overrun by the Partisans, and the centre of his movement lay exposed to their push into Serbia. His only hope of regaining the initiative in this civil conflict was to retain the exclusive aid of the British, firstly in the form of material supplies of arms and equipment by air, and secondly by a monopoly of propaganda support through the channels of the B.B.C. Since October 1942 he had received only two British air sorties, and after Bailey's arrival, three tons of supplies.* He was aware of the massive commitment of the Royal Air Force in raids over Germany and the battle for superiority in Africa, and the effect of limiting to vanishing point the dropping of supplies in Serbia, and this provided him with the main pretext for collaboration with the Italians as an urgent alternative source of military aid against the Communists.

Even the timid and unheralded beginnings of B.B.C. references to the fighting by the Partisans against the Axis were a threat to his claim to be the resistance leader. Indeed, the value which he attached to exclusive B.B.C. support seemed to indicate the weakness of his internal position.

For six weeks – a period during which decisive changes were debated and agreed in London on British policy towards Yugoslavia – Bailey had no effective contact with Mihailović. First, Bailey himself decided to withdraw to his mission headquarters, leaving his staff officer, Major Kenneth Greenlees, who had been dropped to him in mid-February, to maintain routine contact with Mihailović. This demonstration of displeasure over the christening incident would, Bailey hoped, bring Mihailović to a more reasonable frame of mind, for fear of losing British support, which could be turned to good account in securing Mihailović's more active collaboration in anti-Axis activities. Unfortunately, the end of this first period of what might be loosely termed rupture of

---

* These included 30 million occupation lire printed by the British occupation forces in Ethiopia and a large supply of anti-snake-bite serum from the same source. Both items were without any value whatsoever in Yugoslavia. The author is indebted to Colonel Bailey for these whimsical details.

diplomatic relations coincided with the Partisan return, in strength, into Hercegovina and Montenegro, across the Neretva River. For about another week Mihailović was preoccupied with the organization of Četnik operations to halt this advance. He left his headquarters to take personal charge of these operations, and did not return to Lipovo until 15 April.

In accordance with an agreement made by Bailey with Mihailović, nine British missions with independent radio links to Cairo were now dropped into Serbia, starting in April 1943, with the intention of obtaining a more integrated picture of the military value of Mihailović's movement in Serbian territory as a whole. Almost without exception their reports were unfavourable to the Četniks as a fighting force and, as their wireless communications with Cairo were direct, and uninfluenced by any contact with Mihailović's headquarters or by Bailey's and Hudson's appreciations, these messages completed the critical impressions being formed both by S.O.E. and the British G.H.Q. Middle East of the Mihailović movement even in Serbia.*

These British sub-missions were sent to selected strategic points in Serbia, both to collect evidence of the local Četnik organization and strength, and to conduct, if necessary, independent sabotage operations, against lines of communications and valuable mining installations.

The main Mihailović-controlled regions were the wooded heights of Šumadija in Old Serbia, where his own headquarters was again at Ravna Gora after April 1943, and the mountain bases of Homolje and Kapaonik. The situation in South Serbia and Macedonia, areas occupied by the Bulgars, was as yet unexplored by British parties.

Against Bailey's advice a mission under Captain Morgan was dropped 'blind' on 15 April 1943 to Porec in Macedonia, and the group were promptly rounded up by Bulgar troops.

On 18 April Major Erik Greenwood and a British party were parachuted to Homolje in North Eastern Serbia, and on 21 May a second group with two British officers, Captain Jasper Rootham †

---

* Many of these files were destroyed after the war, but brief notes remain of conversations of the author with the officers concerned.

† Jasper Rootham has written a remarkable and fair account of his frustrating experiences in *Miss-Fire* (Chatto and Windus, 1946), which conveys with style and sad reflection the climate of a typical British sub-mission in Serbia at this time, and which applies in general terms to the others.

and a New Zealander, Lieutenant E. ('Micky') Hargreaves, joined him. This base was chosen as a point from which to attack enemy shipping on the Danube and to reconnoitre the possibilities of sabotaging the largest copper mine in Europe at Bor.

Greenwood led a gallant independent operation which temporarily disrupted the river traffic (on 25 October 1943). The Bor mines were heavily guarded, largely by White Russian troops under German command, and the local Četnik commander did not feel able to co-operate in this enterprise.

On 20 April two British officers, Captain Wade and Lieutenant More, were dropped with a party to Kapaonik, a mountain base on the border of Western Serbia, the fief of a dubious Četnik commander, Keserović, and were joined on 23 May by Major Neil Selby.

The frustrations of this mission, which divided into separate groups in the hopes of rallying the local Četnik units to attack the railway line on the Morava valley, is illustrated by the fate of Selby.

At the end of August he signalled to Cairo that Mihailović's forces in the region were more 'pro-Fascist than pro-Allied'. Keserović had been promised by Mihailović the command of Serbia after the liberation. On 23 August Selby sent the following message: 'I am prepared to go deeper into enemy-occupied territory with a W/T set and one man if you so direct, and do more in one week than all I have done in months on Kapaonik.' He did not wait for an answer, and set out on the same day to join the nearest main Partisan group on the mountain of Jastrebac.

He was captured in the village of Kulina by Serb collaborationist troops, and handed over to the Germans. After the war, an inquiry revealed that Selby had been taken to prison in Belgrade, and after punctual and daily interrogations by the Gestapo planned an escape. In the incident he killed two SS guards and was himself shot down in the courtyard of the prison.*

On 19 April a further British mission under Captain John Sehmer was parachuted near Priština on Kosovo Polje with the main task of organizing the sabotage of the Allatini chrome mines which lay under the north-eastern slopes of Šar Planina some 35 miles away. He was joined by a second British party under Captain Hawksworth on 20 May, and shortly afterwards the

---

* This information was pieced together in an inquiry conducted by the author after the war.

main group of the mission were ambushed by Bulgar forces and five British members of the mission were shot out of hand.

Sehmer himself was not present, and later headed a British liaison mission to the Slovak rising in August 1944. He was captured by the Germans together with the Slovak leaders, and executed in Mauthausen concentration camp.

The frustrating and at times tragic experience of these missions showed that there was no prospect of organizing local Četnik commanders in Serbia to undertake attacks on enemy bases, mines, or communications, and that it was impossible to operate in Bulgar-controlled territory in South Serbia and Macedonia where no safely-held Četnik areas existed, except those under the 'official' control of Kosta Pećanac, who was working under German directives.*

These reports from British sources in Serbia were now studied by British General Headquarters in Cairo – and not only by Special Operations, but also by the operational and intelligence authorities of that Command, in further relation to evidence regarding the troop movements of the enemy as established by examining the Italian and German order of battle in Yugoslav territory. The picture presented by these latter intercepted messages – the only sources available to the British at that time for areas outside Serbia – revealed the general concentration of Axis units in Croatia, Bosnia, Montenegro, and Dalmatia. Little or no significant enemy activity or movement could be traced either on the main railway lines and economic targets in Serbia, or in areas claimed to be directly and 'illegally' under Mihailović's control. It was on the initiative of Cairo, and in strictly military terms, that the case was now pressed in London to promote the dispatch of probing military parties into areas outside Serbia and unconnected with the official Bailey mission to Mihailović.

These plans followed by coincidence Mihailović's anti-British outburst to Bailey on 28 February.

The proposals from Cairo were received in London with mixed feelings. A genuine and sincere division of opinion emerged, cutting across not only S.O.E., but also the Foreign Office and the Service ministries.

The policy of the British government was still the reconciliation – if possible with Russian diplomatic aid – of the two rival

* Pećanac was later caught and shot by Mihailović Četniks.

guerrilla parties inside the country. Any departure from this hopeful formula must inevitably affect and disturb the political balance of power within post-war Yugoslavia. On the other hand, the military needs of the Allies were pressing, and on their fulfil-ment depended the issue of the war. These were increasingly at variance with the official policy of exclusive support to Mihailo-vić. Bailey's proposal of 'spheres of influence' of supporting both sides in separate defined areas, and attempting to get agreement, at this stage not on joint action but on at least a demarcation of areas of operation, was doomed to failure from the start. Any suggestion also that local non-aggression agreement could be made between Tito and Mihailović was equally fated. After two years of isolation and uncertainty as to ultimate Allied intentions, Mihailović was opposed to any compromise, and progressively – if reluctantly – driven into varying limited stages of collaboration with the Axis.

Bailey himself sadly expressed the claustrophobic frustrations prevailing at Mihailović's headquarters:

'The fact that he is willing to compromise himself in order to defeat the Partisans is a salient demonstration of the fear and hatred felt for them. He trusts that the general joy and relief at the end of the war will conceal and pardon his misdeeds.'

The Partisan movement, in spite of savage pressure from the Germans and Italians, was now established in several key areas of the country outside Serbia, and the memories of the Četnik 'stab in the back' in Serbia in November 1941 and the mounting participation of Četnik bands in Bosnia, Croatia, and Dalmatia, armed by the Italians, and in some cases by the Germans, to fight against them, made equally on their side any such arrangement impossible. Both were committed to a policy of tragic and mutual destruction. Bailey's proposals – admirable though they might have been in 1941 – could not have any effect on the situation in 1943.

But his suggestion opened the immediate military possibility of attempting to make contact with the Partisans in Croatia, and this, combined with Hudson's reports, convinced the British Command in Cairo that they should initiate planning on these lines.

On 3 March a major decision was made in London, which was henceforward for the next months to govern British policy. Mihailović was to be supported: British officers were to be infiltrated to other resistance groups, and, if information from

these officers justified it, all possible support was to be sent to such
groups. This was the directive which authorized the planning in
Cairo of making contact with 'the Croat guerrillas'.

S.O.E. Cairo had already signalled to Bailey, at the end of
January, without consulting London, that G.H.Q. Middle East
would favour supporting 'Croat guerrillas' – otherwise the latter
would turn automatically to the Russians. It was also the intention
of Cairo to support the Partisans in Croatia as a means of pressure
on Mihailović.

British General Headquarters Middle East had been convinced
for some months* that Partisan units, reported on 18 May to be
moving south of Mihailović's units in the Sandžak towards the
frontier between Montenegro and Albania, represented the largest
anti-Axis force at least in the area between the line of the Neretva
river and the Albanian border.

It was now clear that the military organization of the Partisan
movement must be regarded as a territorial whole, and the
decision was taken in Cairo to contact the central headquarters of
the Partisan movement and to propose joint military co-operation.
At the same time, an attempt was made to avoid delays which
would be involved in facing the inevitable political complications
and further protracted discussions in London on this aspect of
our relations with Yugoslavia.

The latest intelligence, however, showed that Mihailović was
retreating into Serbia, and that whatever his future military
strength and significance might be, it would be unlikely to extend
beyond the historical frontiers of old Serbia.

On 25 May Cairo informed London that the Commander-in-
Chief Mediterranean had the impression that the Ibar river in
Western Serbia represented a real dividing line between the
retreating Četniks and the advancing Partisans.

'The Partisan movement must be regarded as a whole. Only
1–2,000 Četniks were moving with Mihailović into Central and
Eastern Serbia.'

S.O.E. Cairo was fully supported by the Middle East Defence
Committee in its interpretation of these events.

On 12 May the British government had dispatched an ultimatum to Mihailović which marked for the first time the change in
emphasis in policy towards the Četnik movement. Unless he
accepted the following conditions, the British would be compelled

* Presumably from intercepts of Axis military signals.

to withdraw further support: his exclusive object must be resistance to the Axis; he must accept the strategic directives from the Commander-in-Chief Middle East, and work closely with our liaison officers; all collaboration with the Italians and with Nedić must cease, '*except* with the express approval of the British and Yugoslav governments'; and finally, he must make special efforts to co-operate with all other guerrillas and refrain from attacking the Partisans. 'The difficulty of suddenly interrupting the struggle against the Partisans as distinct from Croat and Slovene guerrillas is appreciated.'

This directive from the British government to Mihailović was drafted in London on 12 May, and intended to impose conditions on further aid to him. The document was sent to Cairo on the same day, but not passed on to Bailey to deliver to Mihailović until 28 May.*

On the following day, 29 May, the British General Headquarters in Cairo, on the authority of the Commander-in-Chief Mediterranean, without consultation with London or regard for any later political implications and on strictly military grounds, took an immediate and double decision.†

The first was to instruct Colonel Bailey to convey to Mihailović the substance of the following telegram:

The war in the Mediterranean has come to a phase in which the Allied offensive can be considered imminent. It is absolutely necessary that General Mihailović now carries out the obligations which he accepted earlier, and that he co-operates totally at this time. . . . Mihailović does not represent a fighting force of any importance west of Kapaonik. His units in Montenegro, Hercegovina and Bosnia are already annihilated or else in close co-operation with the Axis; it is also difficult to say that his units exist in Croatia, Slovenia and Slavonia. . . . The Partisans represent a good and effective fighting force in all parts where only the quislings represent General Mihailović.

The decisions are:

You will advise Mihailović that the British General Headquarters in the Middle East requests that he, as an Ally, stops all co-operation with

---

* Bailey had not been informed by Cairo of our landing in Montenegro on that same night. Mihailović, however, received a signal on his internal W/T network that a mission had landed and joined the Partisans in East Bosnia on or about 23 April. This was the Croat–Canadian party headed by Serdar. See p. 213.

† This decision was of course in general accordance with the Foreign Office directive sent to Cairo at the beginning of March.

the Axis and that he goes towards the east into Serbia. There he is to establish full authority and personal influence in order to continue the attacks on enemy communication lines.

You will advise Mihailović that he immediately go to Kapaonik with all his faithful officers and men; if necessary he is to force through with armed forces.

In the future the British General Headquarters will consider the district under his command and influence bordered on the west by the fighting elements already existing on the right bank of Ibar river and towards the south to Skoplje. To this territory the British General Headquarters will send great aid by air. . . .

We want you therefore to explain this to Mihailović and to represent these decisions to him as forcefully as may be necessary, and attempt to obtain his immediate and unequivocal action in their favour. You and the whole British mission will accompany Mihailović to Kapaonik and ensure that his co-operation remains genuine and effective. . . . We are asking London to try to arrange for King Peter and Jovanović to send instructions to Mihailović informing him that the closest possible co-ordination of action with the Allied powers is necessary in view of future operations in Southern Europe.*

The second decision now made was to make immediate preparations to send an official liaison mission to the headquarters of the Partisan leadership, whose whereabouts had just been located for the first time.

Such an empirical step was to be taken on strictly military grounds and, if successful, would inevitably bring into sharp relief the consequences of possible British aid to two rival and hostile resistance movements in Yugoslavia, with long-lasting implications which the future would unfold.

In the meantime, fragmentary reports of the collapse of the Četnik organization, deeply committed as Axis satellite allies in the recent enemy operations under the code name 'Weiss' against Tito in Croatia and Bosnia, began to filter through to Bailey,

---

* This text is to be found in *Why the Allies abandoned the Yugoslav Army of General Mihailović* by Lt. Col. Živan L. Knezević (Washington D.C., 1945). This so-called 'Ibar telegram' had been drafted and previously agreed in London, and a copy sent to the Royal Yugoslav government (the above is a re-translation of the Serbo-Croat text). Mihailović was informed of this telegram by Bailey on 29 May. The former reacted with a natural explosion of temper and announced that 'he would go into exile on Kapaonik'.

o

and from him to Cairo and London. Owing to the sullen reluctance of Mihailović and his staff officers at Lipovo to pass on fragments of news their significance was not fully clear to the British planning staffs in Cairo, nor to London.

In a signal of 14 March, Bailey warned Cairo in these terms: 'Fighting on the Neretva continues, but at the moment I am cut off from the normal sources, but will endeavour to obtain Mihailović's version soonest. Italian material is definitely being employed against the Partisans.'

Bailey's inevitable dependence on Mihailović and his staff obscured the whole intelligence picture, as presented to the British, of the critical events arising out of the large-scale Axis offensive now developing from the borders of Croatia and Bosnia to the line of the river Neretva, which controlled the approaches to the main Četnik bases in Hercegovina and Montenegro.

The total mobilization of Mihailović's main forces, with direct and active Italian aid, to resist the penetration of Tito's central military group back into these regions was thus concealed with elusive deliberation from the British mission.

Bailey was obliged to piece together and report as best he could on the development of large-scale fighting to the west. The extent of the crisis could be dimly perceived.

Unless the Partisan move into Hercegovina and Montenegro, the regions which now formed the present base of the Mihailović movement, could be halted by combined Axis-Četnik operations, the issue of civil war in Yugoslavia would be settled by the disintegration of the main Četnik organization. The ultimate menace of a return of Tito's forces to Serbia would, if fulfilled, complete the disaster.

Tito would be in control of the vital strategic hinterland of the Adriatic coast from the Neretva to the borders of the Sandžak in calculated anticipation of a British seaborne landing, an assumption which was haunting the planning of all parties – Germans, Italians, Tito, and Mihailović.

On 15 March the latter had a two-hour talk with Bailey. He had already decided to take over direct command of the Četnik forces opposing the move of the Partisan columns eastwards into Hercegovina and Montenegro, but gave orders to his staff that this move should be kept secret from Bailey.

At dusk on 17 March Mihailović left Lipovo with his escort and W/T station to set up headquarters at Kalinovik.

His main staff, headed by Hudson's former companion Lala-tović, had informed Bailey, two days previously, that the Partisan forces had been completely broken with four thousand casualties. But, six days later, on 21 March, Bailey confirmed to Cairo that the fighting in Bosnia and Hercegovina was going against the Četniks and that Mihailović might bolt and abandon the British mission as had happened to Hudson in the previous year. Bailey added that, in the present position, there was no *de facto* difference between Milhailović 'in these parts' and Nedić in Serbia. 'Both are policing the country for the Axis, and conserving Serbian blood.'

On 26 March it was admitted by Mihailović's staff at Lipovo that the Partisans had broken across the Neretva through the Četnik defences, but the full extent of the spreading crisis of the movement was not yet revealed to Bailey, and therefore neither to Cairo nor London.

While the Mihailović organization was fast disintegrating in Montenegro and the Sandžak under Partisan assault, British policy towards him was under critical review.

On 23 March Sir Alexander Cadogan, the head of the Foreign Office, informed the Prime Minister of the results of Bailey's mission and the mounting evidence of Mihailović's collaboration for which, as it began to be seen in London, he was being called to savage account by Tito in the field.

A formal decision had now been taken in London to establish experimental contact, through S.O.E., with Partisan elements in Croatia and Slovenia.

The Prime Minister agreed that the attitude of Mihailović was 'intolerable', but so was his position, and little had been done for him.

On 6 April Bailey reported that Mihailović had moved to Foča, and that the Četniks were openly collaborating with the Italians in that area. He had refused all access to the British mission.*

* Mihailović was away for three weeks, and somewhat naturally did not tell Bailey why or where he was going. Hudson seems to have found out certain information about Mihailović's movements; he moved from Kalinovik to an advanced headquarters at the small town of Konjic on the Neretva in order to take direct charge of Četnik operations. His silence was not only for 'security' reasons, but also due to the breakdown of his internal W/T network. His only communications with his staff at Lipovo during these critical days was by courier. (Information from Colonel Bailey to the author.)

Panic seized Royal Yugoslav government circles in London. On 29 March Mr. Churchill had sent a personal note to Professor Jovanović, the Yugoslav Prime Minister, expressing dismay at the internal discord in Yugoslavia, at the evidence of Četnik–Italian collaboration, and asking him to warn General Mihailović of the British view. The Prime Minister, Jovanović, signalled to Mihailović on 7 April: 'It is absolutely necessary as soon as possible to meet Bailey at Foča or elsewhere as Bailey has most urgent and important messages from the Yugoslav government to discuss with you.'

On 9 April a direct message to this effect was sent by Jovanović to Mihailović's headquarters. The latter was in Foča, and his staff at Lipovo considered this signal without awaiting his return. It read as follows:

The British Foreign Office has transmitted to me the text of a speech which you made at a gathering on 28 February. In this speech, which is full of complaints against the British government, is a passage which has aroused the particular attention of the British . . . in which you say that the Italians are your only source of support and help.

The British government takes a serious view of this remark, and, on these grounds, has delivered to me a sharp protest.*

The message from Jovanović must have been passed on Mihailović's internal radio links to Foča, as on 10 April the latter replied to London:

I do not know what Colonel Bailey reported to his government in London. But in the course of this speech I told him many sad truths. I explained to him that, with the weapons so far received by air, I could not even equip 200 men, and I had still not been sent any explosives. Yet we were being requested to destroy public objects which, however much they were willing, units of the Yugoslav army could not carry out.

I deny the suggestion that I have any kind of connection with the Italians. Some of our units have simply succeeded in fooling the Italians, and in this way extracting a greater quantity of weapons from them. I said in my speech to Colonel Bailey that he would do well, in his report to London, to stress that we were ourselves using these weapons against the Italians.

I would ask for steps to be taken so that my words should not be misinterpreted for I know what I say. I do not permit the slightest suspicion that I have any contact whatsoever with the enemy. The best

* Washington National Archives, Italian Collection T 821 Reel 356. Mihailović messages intercepted by the Italian intelligence (SIM).

proof is that I am being uninterruptedly chased by them. They would gain a great success if they caught me.

On 12 April Jovanović sent a second signal:

The British government has further taken amiss the passage in your speech where you say that you regard the Communists, the Ustaša, the Moslems, and the Croats as your main enemies, and that you will first use your forces to deal with them before taking on the Italians and the Germans. . . .

Since you are a member of the Yugoslav government, the British government requests that you should be instructed to change your attitude both towards the Italians and the Yugoslavs, otherwise the British government will feel obliged to revise its policy which is to give exclusive support to your movement in Yugoslavia.

Even if this support appears to be insufficient the British government is not lacking in good will in helping you. The reasons why your requests have not been met are the great distance between you and the British bases; the shortage of means of transport; and the need to concentrate their strength in the Middle East. The British government assures that the military situation in the Middle East will shortly permit the sending of extensive support; but only on condition that your attitude to your internal enemies is in accord with the view of the British government and that in future you collaborate loyally with them (the internal enemies) and with the best understanding.

On receiving this note, I informed the British government of your latest reports in which you deny any collaboration with the Italians and blame the Communists as the aggressors against the Serb population. In regard to the Ustaša, I quoted that they represent a part of the armed forces of the enemy, and that thus conflict with them is un-avoidable.

In spite of all these excuses I must say that your speech of 28 February represents neither the view of the British nor the Yugoslav governments.

The Germans and Italians, who have dismembered Yugoslavia, and robbed her people of their freedom, are to be regarded as our main enemies, against whom, leaving out the question of internal strife, the combined military forces of Yugoslavia should be united.

As to the delivery of arms by the Italians, which may appear to you to be useful and in conformity with a loyal attitude, this would be dearly bought if it calls into question the much more important and valuable help of Great Britain.

As Prime Minister of the Yugoslav government I entreat you, in dealing with the British officers on the spot, to adopt an attitude which will not give cause for criticism by the British or the Yugoslav government.

On 14 April Mihailović signalled:

In my speech of 28 February, I described the Italians as the source of supply for our future armament. This was intended to convery that, at a given moment, in a general assault on the Italians we would collect their weapons. This passage in my speech has been misinterpreted. In addition I have taken to heart the warnings of the [Yugoslav] Prime Minister and will work, to the best of my ability, in the direction desired by the government.

This exchange of messages must have contributed to the abrupt departure of Mihailović from Foča and to renewed relations with the British mission at his headquarters.

The extent of the Četnik disaster on the Neretva, and the presence of strong Partisan forces on the Drina and spreading in advanced columns through Montenegro and towards the Sandžac, could no longer be concealed from the British.

Bailey signalled that Mihailović had returned to Lipovo on 13 April and was 'on the run'. The advance Partisan units had reached Savnik about twenty miles away, which explained this move. Mihailović evacuated Lipovo, under Partisan pressure, on the evening of 19 April, and ordered general mobilization of his forces in Serbia against the threat of Partisan penetration to the east.

There could have been little time for discussion between the two men, but one message from Bailey revealed the extent of Mihailović's obsessive fears and interpretation of Tito's intentions: 'Opinion in better-informed circles here is that the Partisan leadership will endeavour to make its way into Macedonia or Greece to join up with the Communists there, and thence to make contact with comrades in Albania. This I consider possible.' *

The British mission divided into two groups: one under Bailey together with Mihailović's staff; the second to follow on its own.†

Two days after Mihailović's flight from Lipovo, his village headquarters near Kolašin in Montenegro, the first S.O.E. parties were dropped 'blind' on a mission to locate 'guerrilla' forces in Croatia.‡

* Bailey also referred to a desperate plan of Mihailović's to make political contact 'with the Croats'.

† Bailey and part of the British mission left Lipovo at 10 p.m. on 19 April, passing through Mojkovac and crossing the Morača river near Bijelo Polje. The mission established new headquarters in the village of Milanovići on the Jahorina range on 15 May.

‡ See p. 211.

The reports of Bailey and Hudson from the headquarters of Mihailović in Serbia in January and February 1943 provided the British military authorities in the Middle East, the British government, and Chiefs of Staff in London for the first time with an ordered, if fragmentary, picture of the state of affairs on the spot in those districts of Serbia, the Sandžak, and Montenegro which these British officers had been able to tour.

After the arrival of Bailey as commander of the British mission to Mihailović with improved radio communications, Hudson began to report, in a series of 240 telegrams, his analysis of the Četnik movement since his arrival in early October 1941, at Ravna Gora.

S.O.E. Cairo and the British authorities in London were now able to form a belated but direct and vivid impression of the critical months of Hudson's mission.

This series of telegrams, beginning in February 1943, is of considerable historical importance, and was, in great part, instrumental in the re-examination of British policy towards the situation within Yugoslavia. The telegrams formed an antidote to the previous flow of Mihailović signals, which had hitherto provided the exclusive picture of the development of resistance in Yugoslavia, and demolished, point by point, the creation of the Četnik 'myth', without replacing it with a Partisan legend. Hudson had witnessed events at the end of 1941 both with Tito and Mihailović. He had arrived on Ravna Gora at the end of October to find a situation of incipient civil war between Partisans and Četniks, and not the idyllic common resistance front dreamt up in London and Cairo. For 'technical' reasons, Hudson had not been able to transmit a record of these confused events at the time.

Mihailović already knew by telegram from London that he would get British support. 'He felt rightly that nobody outside the country knew about the Partisans or that he alone was not responsible for revolt.' As Hudson pointed out, 'It was the Communists who united the Serbs, not Mihailović. His job is to change this unity against the Communists to a unity against the Axis. Mihailović and company have done precisely nothing in this line in Italian-occupied territory. They have merely increased the emphasis against the Communists.'

The Partisan leaders had been, according to Hudson, anxious to avoid hostilities with Mihailović, who was, together with Nedić, unable to break the Communist hold on the youth and the peasantry. 'In towns held jointly, notably Čačak and Požega, the Partisans showed an enthusiasm and initiative that kept the Četniks in the shade.'

'When the Partisans, with the great advantage of the Užice rifle factory left intact by the Germans, were about to push Mihailović off Ravna Gora, he, despite indirect help from Nedić, was obliged to ask for a truce (on 20 November 1941).'

Hudson had attended one of these peace parleys, despite opposition from Mihailović, at which the Partisans demanded a joint headquarters.

Mihailović took the first step in attacking the Partisans, and British promises of support to him had directly contributed to the worsening of Četnik-Partisan relations.

When Hudson returned to Ravna Gora after leaving Tito's forces following their retreat from Serbia, he found no remains of Mihailović's men except himself and a few officers.*

The Četnik movement was out to protect the future of the Serbs, and destroy the main competitors – the Croats. 'Zagreb must be destroyed; and he [Mihailović] would like to hang Maček [in a speech to a Serb youth delegation].'

The Partisan solution was the 'internationalization' [sic] of Yugoslavia. Hudson had 'a high opinion of Tito, Arso Jovanović, and Djilas. They are practical fighters for sweeping social revolution with themselves on top. I met Moša Pijade for a few minutes.' In the ranks were young enthusiasts and peasants. Their appeal cut across religion and national background. Most of the youth of Serbia were with the Partisans.

By the beginning of 1942 'the Ravna Gora movement melted away into the ranks of Nedić's militia, and finally reappears, chastened, in Montenegro. Had it not been for the German punitive expedition, the Communists might have had both Nedić and Mihailović out.'

Outside Serbia, Hudson had noted certain realistic points. In Montenegro, the Partisans had stuck to a policy of reconciliation even in the autumn of 1941. Communist atrocities there had been exaggerated. 216 Četniks had been liquidated; 40 had been killed by Italian bombing.

'Mihailović is still co-operating with the Axis in Montenegro and the Sandžak, and standing still in Serbia.'

* See p. 146.

In Dalmatia, Trifunović's Četniks* were 'legalized' and, inspired by the Italians, dreamt of a 'Serbo-Slovenia and Dalmatia'. The Četnik Dinara Division, operating on Croat territory, had killed 700 and wounded 1,000 Partisans.

In Bosnia, the Partisans held a 'free zone' which must not be attacked by Mihailović.

The Četnik–Partisan conflict 'is primarily the result of two separate groups fighting for leadership of the peasants. On the whole the peasants "bow before prevailing wind". The effect o ambitious leaders on both sides is to precipitate a minor civil war in each new territory. The Communists wish to liquidate Mihailović by absorbing his followers by co-operation. Several Četnik units asked to be relieved of duty of fighting the Partisans.'

At the moment when Mihailović played quisling on a large scale he was rewarded by the most powerful British propaganda possible.

Except for some extra organization in Serbia, he has done little more than get elected as head of Nedić's and Trifunović's organizations on insistence of the B.B.C. . . . Mihailović should be told definitely that British prefer Communists to quislings.

We must draw the line at B.B.C. encouragement of co-operation with the Axis. Sabotage and threat to the Axis will remain at their present minimum while [the Četnik leaders in Montenegro, Hercegovina, and Dalmatia] cry 'Viva il Duce' with Mihailović's blessings and while he is content with telling us that nine-tenths of Nedić's and Pećanac's men are loyal to him. . . . His adherence to the old Belgrade clique policy, aggravated by the opportunity of liquidating the Croat question on the strength of their atrocities and pro-Axis behaviour, will be exploited to full by the Partisan leaders among Croats and Moslems.

The reactions in London and Cairo to Hudson's messages were mixed. S.O.E. Cairo pressed for supporting 'other resistance groups' in Slovenia and Croatia; S.O.E. London accepted that the British should refrain from backing Mihailović exclusively, 'except in Serbian lands', and be free to establish relations in other areas. The Foreign Office displayed a more precise sense of history and geography. Mihailović interpreted Serbia as including Bosnia, and to admit this on the British side would be a betrayal of ultimate Croat interests. Mihailović was a thoroughly bad choice

---

* Trifunović-Birćanin was the veteran head of the pre-war nationalist association 'Narodna Odbrana', and closely associated with the 'official' Četnik organization.

for the leadership of Yugoslavia, but, at the same time, represented 'the only stable element in the country'. No immediate action or change in policy was recommended.

The reports from Bailey presented an objective picture of the structure of the Mihailović organization, in particular in Western Serbia, and an analysis of his general attitude towards the British in regard to the promotion of any joint plans for immediate resistance against the enemy in those territories under his control. The study of this new evidence from the British mission in Serbia, however controversial some of the conclusions transmitted by these two officers might be considered in Cairo and London, meant that at last the British were more firmly placed to construct a picture of the events of the last two years in certain regions of Yugoslavia, and of the present aims, intentions, and nature of the Četnik movement. The British authorities had no reliable intelligence regarding the existence of other resistance groups. Apart from the sparse telegrams from Hudson from Montenegro just after his landing in September 1941, the radio messages of Mihailović, and courier reports 'loaded' and compiled under his influence, no evidence of any significance had reached either Cairo or London as to the activities or strength of any such movements. The only other British mission which might have been able to transmit some evidence in this direction, that of Atherton in February 1942, had vanished without trace.

The reports of Bailey and Hudson could be summarized in the following terms: the military structure of the Četnik movement in Western, Central, and Eastern Serbia existed in the traditional Četnik territorial form, with a conventional military headquarters, and a series of regional commands on a skeleton basis. The attitude of Mihailović to any immediate action, either in terms of sabotage against the lines of communication and the mining areas essential to the German war effort, or attacks on the German occupying forces, was not only passive, but hostile. Many of his officers were, on his instructions, concealed as members of the various para-military organizations of the German-controlled government of General Nedić in Belgrade.

The mass of the local Serb peasant population were dispersed in their villages and engaged in the peaceful tasks of tilling their fields and tending their pigs and cattle, but, according to the assurances of Mihailović, impressive mobilization lists had been drawn up and the majority of the peasantry in these areas could be called up at short notice. Secret lists had already been prepared, and 'the Royal Yugoslav Army in the Fatherland' would be an effective force at the disposal of the Allies in the event of a major landing in the Balkans.

The savage reprisals of the Germans in suppressing the rising in Serbia in the autumn and winter of 1941, the memories of similar Austrian and Bulgarian punitive expeditions in Serbia and Macedonia during the First World War, and the derisory trickle of British air sorties to Mihailović since November 1941, provided him with the arguments for his present attitude of total passivity, and calculated collaboration with the Nedić authorities. Any form of immediate resistance would bring down on the Serb population, especially in the plains and valleys, renewed and massive enemy reprisals, decimating them, and rendering impossible any effective future rising in collaboration with a British or American landing.

Mihailović stated that he had links with Četnik groups outside Serbia, in particular in the Sandžak, Montenegro, and Bosnia, but also in Dalmatia and Slovenia. These were primarily the remains of the official 'pre-war Četnik organization' led by former Royal Yugoslav officers and N.C.O.s, strengthened by the spontaneous assembly of the local Serb population in these areas round these small bands, in protective flight from the Ustaša massacres of 1941, and the imposition of the authority of the Independent State of Croatia of Pavelić in those regions not under direct Italian military occupation.

The British government and military authorities were now confronted with a picture which, beyond any doubt, conflicted with their official policy of political and military support to the Četnik movement of Mihailović. This policy had been conceived not only on the basis of formal treaty obligations to the Royal Yugoslav government in London but also in the hope that, following on the news of the existence of Mihailović in Serbia in the autumn of 1941, by British mediation a joint resistance movement could be created as a national front against the Axis – which was also the professed intention of the Soviet government – and that the warning signs of civil war reported by Hudson between Communist-led Partisan bands and the units of Mihailović could be avoided.

The present messages from the British mission at Mihailović's headquarters confirmed the existence of a state of civil war, and stressed that there could be no question of persuading him to have any dealings or co-operation with his Communist rivals. Evidence pointed to the disappearance of the early Partisan bands in Serbia after the German punitive expedition of December 1941 in the Western Morava valley and the surrounding areas, but little if anything was still known of their fate or location. From enemy sources, however, it was clear that unidentified guerrilla bands were operating in force against them, particularly in Slovenia, Croatia, Bosnia, and Dalmatia. These areas were of at least equal strategic and economic importance to the Allies in terms of cutting German rail communications to Greece and to the Roumanian oilfields, and of the bauxite mines, vital to the German aircraft industry and the Goering Four Year Plan.

British relations with Mihailović had reached a deadlock. But it was of military importance to explore the situation in regard to the 'Slovene and Croat guerrillas', and the extent and value of their activities as a resistance element against the Germans and Italians in key territories, blank on British maps. The telegrams of Bailey and Hudson showed that, whatever might result from future attempts to press or cajole Mihailović into active resistance, any such action would be confined to precise districts in Serbia. It should therefore be possible to plan contacting resistance groups in other regions without the risk of merely adding to the dangers of promoting an extension of civil war throughout Yugoslavia. Any such contacts, if successfully established, could be kept quite distinct from events in Serbia.

Both Hudson and Bailey had also hinted that the so-called Partisans were not necessarily under the firm control of the Yugoslav Communist Party, an organization with which the British had never been in touch and of which they had little evidence. By sending British missions to contact these unidentified guerrilla bands, it might turn out that these forces in many cases could be induced to join some form of united resistance organization under British leadership. This illusion was not only derived from the analysis of events within the country by Bailey and Hudson, but, in more realistic military planning terms, it also gave an added pretext, on the part of the British General Headquarters in Cairo, which was responsible for special operations into the Balkans, to seek authority from London to undertake planning on these lines, on exclusively military grounds, and to leave aside the political dangers and implications of such action.

There had been an overriding technical difficulty in attempting to parachute missions farther north than Serbia and Montenegro, because of the range of the small bomber group of four Liberators now operating as a special squadron from the former Italian airfield at Derna in North Africa. This situation had been remedied in a limited but effective way when, after a visit to Cairo in February 1943 on his return from the Adana Conference with the Turkish government, the British Prime Minister, Mr. Winston Churchill, had instructed the Chiefs of Staff to place a squadron of six Halifax bombers with a longer range at the disposal of the S.O.E. authorities in the Middle East. The use of submarines in the Adriatic was precluded by the priorities of the Royal Navy in the Mediterranean in concentrating on the Axis convoys to North Africa.

S.O.E. Cairo had already, in the last weeks of 1942, begun to construct, as far as the information at its disposal permitted, the following very general picture. The main enemy troop concentrations were in the areas where no Četnik bands existed and engaged in large-scale operations against unidentified 'guerrilla forces'. It was known that in Montenegro and the Sandžak there was active collaboration by certain local Četnik commanders with the Italians. There was some evidence that strong forces under their command had been sent into action along the line of the Neretva river on the western edge of Hercegovina where they had suffered heavy defeat from the Partisan forces moving southeastwards from Bosnia and Croatia under heavy Axis pressure. It also looked from the map, as drawn in Cairo, as if these Četnik units were at least in parallel action alongside the Germans and Italians.

On 23 March it was decided by British General Headquarters in Cairo to make contacts in Partisan territory. It was not even known where the main headquarters of the Partisan movement were situated.

The lack of information on the British side regarding the Partisan movement was not surprising in view of a series of peculiar accidents. At the time of the *coup d'état* of March 1941, the British officials in Belgrade had no contact with the underground Yugoslav Communist Party. No reports existed of its strength, organization, or activities. It was logical that there should be no reference to Communist activities immediately after the Axis invasion of 1941, since the orders of the Central Committee of the Party for a general rising based on Serbia were not given until after the German attack on the Soviet Union on 22 June. News bulletins from the German radio referred to the existence of Communist bands attacking German troops in Serbia. Goebbels and his propaganda machine deliberately, in the first stages, referred to all such acts of sabotage and resistance as being Communist-organized, in an attempt to conceal the existence of any nationalist bands similarly engaged against the German occupying forces in Serbia. The first direct links with the country were the chance radio signals from Mihailović which were picked up in Malta in the middle of September. From the outset, Mihailović adopted a policy of contrived concealment of any details regarding resistance in Serbia, from whatever quarter, which he could not claim to be under his direct control.

The arrival of Bill Hudson in Montenegro at the end of the same month revealed in a few brief messages the existence of 'patriot forces' which were prepared, if supplied with British aid, to fight against the Italian occupation troops. The body with which Hudson found himself was referred to in telegrams as 'the Montenegrin Freedom Force'. The impression given to Cairo, at the time correct, was that these bands consisted of loosely-knit nationalist and Partisan elements, and at no point was there any indication of the existence of a local Communist leadership. Indeed, a confusion set in from the beginning as to the designation of the word 'Partisan' itself. Hudson referred to the leaders whom he met as Arso Jovanović and a certain 'professor', identified in a subsequent message as Djilas. There was no further evidence as to the functions of these two men, their connections with the Yugoslav Communist Party, nor any indication from this source that there was any similar Partisan resistance in Serbia, except the group of Mihailović, whom Hudson was ordered by Cairo to contact. Although Hudson met Tito in Užice, he had no means of radio communications and could not report from Tito's headquarters to Malta.

On his arrival at Mihailović's headquarters at the end of October 1941, Hudson was obliged to use the latter's radio set to re-establish communications with the British, but in his own ciphers. It is, however, strange that in none of his surviving messages does the name 'Tito' occur. The existence and strength of 'Communist-led Partisans' in superior numbers to the skeleton forces of Mihailović came to the knowledge of the British in a few brief signals from Hudson.

The first mention of Tito occurs in a Mihailović telegram dated 5 November 1941: 'The Communist leader in Serbia, under the false name "Tito", cannot be considered as the leader of resistance. The Communist fight against the Germans is a sham.' There is also some evidence to show that, on the two occasions when Mihailović and Tito met, the Četnik commander formed the conviction that he was dealing with a Comintern agent who was probably of Soviet nationality. But all subsequent messages of Mihailović reaching the British and the Royal Yugoslav government in London were carefully worded to give the impression that there was no central Communist leadership of a Yugoslav resistance movement. There were merely bands, which were temporarily active in Western Serbia and would either be driven to accept Mihailović's own command or be liquidated by the Germans.

The first two significant reports to reach Cairo and London by courier were brought out by Dr. Miloš Sekulić * to Istanbul and by Gradomir Bajloni † to Lisbon about this time. The latter merely refers to 'guerrilla action being undertaken by Mihailović and by the Communists', and the former mentions in passing that 'a group of Serb patriots originally formed of Communists existed in Serbia and one group was in the Šabac area, headed by a certain Lebedev'.

The intrusion of this name into the confusion of identities is of some historical importance. Such a man did exist. He was a Soviet diplomat, who had been sent to Belgrade, ostensibly as Commercial Secretary, to re-open the Soviet legation when relations with the Royal Yugoslav government were restored after the *coup d'état* of March 1941.

After the Axis invasion of the country, Lebedev reappeared in the Soviet legation in Sofia. The courier link between Tito's headquarters and the Comintern in Moscow seems to have passed through this channel. But, whether deliberately or not, an impression had been given in London that these loosely-defined Communist groups in Serbia were under direct Soviet control.

* A senior member of the Committee of the Serb Agrarian Party with whom the British had been in contact during the events leading up to the *coup d'état* of 1941.
† A member of a well-known industrial family in Belgrade.

When all contact between Mihailović and Hudson had been lost in December 1941, the three ill-fated probing missions sent in February 1942 failed to re-establish contact. By the end of the year it was merely known in Cairo that the Germans had dispersed all resistance groups in Serbia at the end of the previous December. There are no reports as to the whereabouts, or survival, of the early Communist groups in that region.

In British diplomatic contacts with the Soviet government from June 1941 and through 1942, the problem of creating a united resistance front in Yugoslavia was under constant discussion and review. It was an urgent consideration of British policy to persuade the Russians to use their influence on the Communist bands reported in Serbia to unite under the command of Mihailović. It was not in the Russian interest to disclose to the British any evidence of the structure or leadership of these bands, nor did they admit at any stage that they had any contact with them. The British had vaguely supposed that some such individual as Lebedev might be the leading personality, whereas the Russians had every interest to conceal the identity of Tito as a former Comintern official, and not to reveal to the British any information regarding the activities of the Yugoslav Communist Party as a resistance organization within that country.

British circles did note that as from November 1941 a radio station under the name of 'Free Yugoslavia' was operating from Russian territory and broadcasting increasingly numerous bulletins of the operations of a so-called National Liberation Army. These early announcements were signed 'T.J.', later 'T.T.', and by the end of 1942, 'Tito'. It was reasonably assumed by the British that this radio station was under direct Soviet control, and a study of its broadcasts, although drawing attention to the existence of Partisan forces scattered throughout Yugoslavia, could be interpreted, at least in part, as a propaganda operation of the Russians and, as such, lacking in a certain objectivity and accuracy. The latter were, perhaps, building up, for tactical reasons of diplomacy, an inflated and imaginative picture of an alternative resistance organization, in order to justify to the British their own refusal to act as mediators between these Partisans and Mihailović. The Soviet government continued to impress on the British that they regarded by now (mid-1942) the whole question of either a united front or civil strife within Yugoslavia as an internal matter.

The ablutions of Slim Farish

Glamoč

General Arthur Phleps, Commander of the S.S. Mountain Division Prinz Eugen, and his staff

On 27 April 1942 Eden had written to Maisky that Mihailović was complaining 'that he is being constantly disturbed in his work by the "Communists" who, he has proof, are being helped by the occupying powers, who are anxious that both sides should be kept busy this spring fighting each other. . . . I realize that it is difficult for the Soviet government to maintain any control over these "Communists"; it seems to me, however, that a word of authority broadcast from Moscow would probably carry influence over them.'

Direct representations from the new Royal Yugoslav government of Slobodan Jovanović seem, however, to have met with an increasingly adverse reception.

On 14 May Jovanović sent the following message to Mihailović: 'We have done all we can to prevent the Partisans attacking you. All efforts without success.'

In July Maisky refused, in a conversation with Eden, to recommend any joint Anglo-Soviet action to avoid civil war in Yugoslavia on the grounds of firm evidence that Mihailović was collaborating with Nedić and at the end of the month the Royal Yugoslav Ambassador in Moscow received a Soviet memorandum accusing Mihailović of treason.

Diplomatic contacts on Yugoslav affairs between the British and Soviet governments now lapsed. Both sides, without consulting each other, seemed to be considering the dispatch of missions to Partisan territory.

One attempt was made by S.O.E. to elicit from Mihailović some information about his rivals, and a signal to this effect was sent on 21 April 1942. 'To help us secure the co-operation of Moscow please advise who are Partisan leaders disturbing you. Where is their headquarters that is the cause of conflict? What are your relations with Partisan movement in general? Please advise whether you think Russians are in contact Partisans.'

Mihailović was, by this time, 'off the air'.*

In July 1942 Lieutenant Rapotec, the leader of the party landed by submarine on Mljet at the beginning of the year, arrived in Istanbul. He had made contact with both the Mihailović organization in Dalmatia and also, it seems, in Belgrade and at Mihailović's headquarters. His report added to the confusion. He not only repeated, presumably on Mihailović's instuctions, that Atherton had been killed by the Partisans, but that, as a direct

* The last message received from him was dated 11 March 1942.

P

result of this crime, Mihailović was engaged in their final extermination and that their resistance was practically at an end.*

According to Rapotec, the head of the Partisan movement in
Montenegro was a 'former Belgrade photographer of Jewish
extraction, Moša Pijade', and in Serbia the Partisan organization
was led by Lebedev.

In November 1942, 'Radio Free Yugoslavia' reported the
deliberations of a provisional Partisan administration set up in a
'free territory' held by their forces, with a capital at the small
town of Bihać on the borders of Croatia and Western Bosnia. This
assembly had assumed the functions of a temporary political
administration in direct opposition to the Royal Yugoslav
government in exile in London. The proclamation of these
decisions over 'Free Yugoslavia' was signed for the first time
under the real name of 'Tito' – Josip Broz.

This identification meant nothing to the British, nor does it
seem to have been regarded by them as of any significance. A
message was sent to Hudson to ask him if he could provide any
details of these Bihać proceedings. It was not surprising that he
could elicit no information whatever from Mihailović, who was
his only source.†

A surviving telegram from Mihailović, dated 3 April 1943 and
marked 'private cipher' reads as follows: 'Shall the jailbird who
is registered as No. 10434‡ and under the name of Josip Broz –
otherwise the leader of the Communists under the assumed name
of Tito – be compared with us as a national fighter?'

As it is now clear that Mihailović had at least two W/T communications with the outside world, unknown and uncontrolled
by the British, it is possible that this signal was never seen by the
latter authorities.

Apart from these scraps of evidence as to the identity of Tito,
ingenious experts sifted information which was intermittently
reaching the British from Yugoslavia, from the enemy and neutral
press and radio, and even put forward a theory that Tito repre-

* See p. 174.
† Hudson's long series of telegrams which began to be picked up in Cairo in
   February 1943 contain several references to Tito by name as the leader of
   the Partisans in Serbia in the autumn and winter of 1941, but give no clue as
   to his identity or background.
‡ The Pavelić authorities in Zagreb had identified Josip Broz as Tito, after the
   release of his real name at Bihać, and certain details of his police file were
   released at this time to the Axis press.

sented not an individual, but was in fact the initials of a revolutionary organization. By translating from Serbian the word 'Tito' can mean 'Secret International Terrorist Organization'.

Such was, in essence, the state of information as to the identity of the Partisan leadership at the moment when the British authorities were formulating their plans to contact the 'Croat and Slovene guerrillas'.

The planning of infiltrating missions into Croatia began in the autumn of 1942, before high-level decisions had been taken.

The British officers at S.O.E. studied in particular the failures of the previous year when three British parties had been sent in 'blind'.

The essential purpose of the Croat 'project' was to explore the chances of supporting resistance groups in territories where it was known that the Mihailović organization had few links; the existence of Trifunović-Birćanin and a group of his adherents, inactive and hiding in Split, was known. The personal and obsessive hatred of Mihailović for the Croats, whose 'treason' he held mainly responsible for the collapse of the Royal Yugoslav Army in April 1941, had to be taken into consideration. The wrangling of Serb, Croat, and Slovene members of the Royal Yugoslav government of Professor Slobodan Jovanović in London, dominated by pan-Serb tendencies,* and especially through the influence of Major Živan Knezević, the main backer of Mihailović in London circles, and now head of the military cabinet of the Prime Minister, precluded, both for political and practical reasons, any thought of repeating in Croat regions the bleak experiences of previous joint British-Royal Yugoslav missions to Serbia and adjacent territories.

The Slovene and Croat members of the exiled Yugoslav government would have welcomed the experiment of sending missions to their own districts, but only if organized without the knowledge of their Serb colleagues. But quiet and conspiratorial feelers were made.

In political terms, implications of any such projects were delicate in the extreme. The Slovene 'bourgeois' parties had possessed a well-organized structure in the pre-war years, but

---

* This administration had replaced in January 1942 the first Royal Yugoslav government-in-exile under General Simović, which had been evacuated from the country through Greece in April 1941.

their representatives in London, Miha Krek and Alojz Kuhar, had scant intelligence of developments since the division of Slovenia into Italian and German occupation zones. But, as in the case of their Croat colleagues, they nursed the hope of re-establishing direct links with their supporters in the country.

In Croatia, the political life of these areas had been exclusively dominated up to April 1941 by the powerful Peasant Party (H.S.S.) of Dr. Vladko Maček, now interned and controlled by the Pavelić authorities, but whose close and designated representative collaborator, Juraj Krnjević, supported by a loyal and close-knit group of party colleagues, stubbornly sought every means to create from London private links with occupied Zagreb.*

At the end of March 1943 an astute and encouraging letter from August Košutić, a senior member of the H.S.S. leadership, who had stayed in Zagreb, was smuggled out to Istanbul. This party was well organized and working underground. They were in contact with the Domobran, the forcibly mobilized armed forces of Pavelić (as distinct from the fanatical S.S. type Ustaša paramilitary brigades).

A group of senior leaders in Croatia, under party instructions, were associated in anti-German operations with the Partisans, who were, however, not dangerous or numerous. Mihailović propaganda as put out by the B.B.C. was not suitable for Croat circles, and the H.S.S. was the only organization which could take over control throughout Croatia when the Germans withdrew.

This letter of Košutic caused a moment of excitement. Plans were made, with the apparent connivance of certain British officials, to infiltrate a courier to Zagreb, and to seek a clandestine interview with Maček.

The illusion was brief. The British Foreign Office was firmly committed to the post-war restoration of a united Yugoslavia. The prospect of encouraging Croat separatism under British auspices to replace Pavelić, now in nominal control of an Independent Croat State under Axis supervision, could not be considered on any terms.

It was conceivable, and anticipated with a muted note of expectant approbation in some British quarters, that the dim and indeed contrived image of non-Communist 'Croat and Slovene guerrillas' might be proved to have some substance.

* Krnjević, under British persuasion, remained as Vice-Premier in the new Royal Yugoslav government.

But more precise reasoning and interpretation prevailed. The British authorities responsible for Yugoslav affairs, and in particular certain of those dealing with special operations, were not prepared to accept the strident dissensions and conspiracies among the members of the Royal Yugoslav government in London, further intensified in their missions in Istanbul and Cairo, nor the passive non-co-operation of their Minister of War, General Mihailović, in Serbia and his pan-Serb dream.

The vague proposal to send a Maček courier to Zagreb, emanating from Istanbul, may have raised a convenient cover and blind to conceal a more realistic plan, both in technical operational terms, and its politico-military implications.

The Croat 'project' was to be put up by S.O.E. in a novel form.

Croat immigrants had already been recruited in Canada, with the co-operation of the Canadian intelligence authorities, by the S.O.E. section in New York, where an office functioned in agreement with the American authorities.* This preliminary operation was conducted with every precaution by Bailey. A small group of volunteers was recruited and selected, according to chosen areas in Croatia where it was intended to drop parties 'blind' and where it was now believed, from an accumulated study of available intelligence, that Partisan forces were operating.

These men were to be trained and dispatched to Croatia. These plans were conceived without the knowledge of the Royal Yugoslav authorities,† or of the Croat members of the exiled government in London. The success of the experiment depended on the accuracy of the intelligence, upon the basis of which the missions would be parachuted to a given area; upon their training in radio communications; and on the basic assumption of the whole scheme that the Croat 'guerrillas' were Communist-led.

All the recruits selected, who had arrived in Canada from Yugoslavia during the lean years of the 1930s, were members of the Canadian Communist Party. Some of these men were unskilled labourers; others small tradesmen; and a group were

* The author is much indebted for certain details regarding this group of Canadian Croats to Dr. G. R. Maclean of Dalhousie University, Halifax, Nova Scotia, who is compiling a study of Canadian participation in Yugoslavia during the war, and has generously placed certain notes at his disposal.

† It appears, however, that the Royal Yugoslav Consul-General in Montreal got wind of the recruitment of this group, but not the underlying purpose of the move.

miners, whose experience of explosives was to be put to useful purposes. They were informed that they would be returning, by unspecified means, to their home villages to join the 'Partisans'.

One of them subsequently wrote a brief account of his experiences.[31]

In August 1942 a meeting of the Croat section of the Canadian Party was held in the Workers' Club in Vancouver. A select group, who had already been quietly approached by the Canadian Mounted Police and British representatives, held a farewell party.

They were escorted to Toronto where, outside the city, other recruits joined them at a training camp, under British control, where they underwent a commando course.*

Disguised as civilian 'technicians', they were embarked in two groups in merchant ships sailing from Montreal round the Cape to the Middle East. One party was torpedoed in the Caribbean, but without loss of life, and the whole group reached Cairo safely at the end of February 1943.

After completing a parachute course at the British school at Haifa, and undergoing training in the latest W/T equipment, these Croats were housed in a heavily guarded villa outside Cairo.

The detailed planning of the first experimental mission had just been completed.† It was based essentially on the latest intercepted material from the German and Italian military intelligence. The course of the Fourth enemy offensive (operation 'Weiss'), designed to liquidate the central leadership and forces of the Partisan movement holding the 'free territory' of the Bihać Republic, were known in very general outline by the British General Headquarters in Cairo. There was also more detailed evidence that the Croat regions of Gorski Kotar and the Lika and in part of the coastal districts of Hrvatsko Primorje were clear of Axis forces, now engaged in pressing the main Partisan group through Bosnia to the south-east. There were also signs of sufficient precision to assume that local Partisan units had infiltrated back into these areas.

* The total party was thirty-eight, some of them having been picked in New York.

† Bailey and Stuart had arrived from New York in Cairo at the end of 1942. The latter was originally designated, by an irony of fate, to be sent to Mihailović in Serbia. Bailey was sent to Cairo for briefing and training to take over from Hudson at the Četnik headquarters, and his rôle in the first stages of the Croat 'project' was completed. The final stages of planning were worked out by the Yugoslav section of S.O.E. Cairo which I had joined from headquarters in London in December 1942.

The final stage was to select the first mission by relating this intelligence to the personal background of each man and the location of a pinpoint where there was a reasonable chance that, on landing, members of the party would be able to identify themselves to their families or friends whom they had left behind when emigrating to Canada.

One evening in late April 1943, I went to the villa outside Cairo where the Croat group were isolated and tense. After briefing them on the details of our planning and on the latest local picture which had been pieced together, I gave them a firm assurance that our headquarters would only issue final technical instructions if it was considered that the realistic chances of success were high.*

Three men were selected, and sent to the special operations airfield at Derna. The mission was allotted the code name 'Fungus'. The appointed target had been fixed, in discussion with them, on Crnacko Polje near Drežnica in the region of the Lika.

On the night of 20/21 April 1943 the party left on their perilous task.†

After a safe landing in a familiar countryside, they were picked up by peasants, and taken to the nearby village of Brinje, which turned out to be the headquarters of the Partisan General Staff for Croatia. The commander recounted to me after the war that his first reaction was to shoot the party out of hand as disguised German agents. They carried two W/T sets, and no written instructions. But, as we had gambled, they succeeded in confirming their identity and local connections.

Two delegates of the Supreme Staff, Arso Jovanović and Lola Ribar, were touring the territory at this moment and reported to Tito by the W/T set of the Croat Partisan headquarters that a 'British–American' mission had parachuted near Brinje, allegedly with full powers to investigate this [sic] situation in the Balkans. 'We are awaiting firm reports about this . . . whether they sincerely, and with good intentions, are associated with us or whether again they are some "dražinovci" ‡ who have come to us by accident.'[32]

* I remember using the phrase '60 – 40'.

† They were Petar Erdeljac, Pavle Pavić (or Pavicić), and Alexander Simić, who had been recruited separately from the main group from Canada. He was of mixed Serbian–British parentage. Erdeljac had fought in the Dimitrov battalion in the Spanish Civil War; Pavić had worked in a Vancouver shipyard. Both men settled in Yugoslavia after the war.

‡ Supporters of Mihailović.

There was a pause of suspicion, and the party pressed in vain to transmit a signal to Cairo announcing their safe arrival.

But on 28 April Tito sent a message to the General Staff in Croatia.* 'Radio set must not be taken away from mission. You can ask them, if they do not need two sets, to lend us one. But I underline – only if they give it to you freely and without pressure. You can let them contact England [*sic*]. Give them necessary information about Četnik treachery and/or enemy forces but no information about our forces or armament until we give you the details.'

The first message from this party was picked up in the next days, informing Cairo of their safe landing, and presence at Partisan headquarters in Croatia.

On 7 May Cairo signalled with greetings to the 'Partisan war effort' and asked that agreement should be obtained for the immediate dispatch of a British party to discuss the sending of a mission to the central Partisan command, whose whereabouts were as yet unknown.

The prompt establishment of radio contact between this Croat party and its British base, in contrast to the failure of Atherton's operator to work his set and the consequent suspicions aroused, on that occasion, in the minds of the Partisan leadership, was of marked psychological importance. There was cause to accept the fact that at last the British, whatever their motives, were deliberately seeking to establish exploratory relations with the Partisan command.

The next W/T message received from Cairo was more precise, and encouraging.

On 12 May the Partisan headquarters in Croatia signalled to Tito that the group of British emissaries had informed them that a message had been received from their General Staff in Cairo proposing talks with a view to attacking the railway Ogulin–Rijeka–Sisak–Brod; Zagreb–Ljubljana; Koprivnica–Zagreb–Zidani Most . . .

to disrupt the transport of petrol from Roumania to Italy and of war material in both directions. . . . We [British headquarters] think it a logical step to work out a treaty [*sic*] with the Partisans. The destruction of the railways is now of great importance to the North African front, *and its possible extension*.† . . . We are awaiting impatiently to make

---

* Zbornik II, 9, p. 176. The spare W/T set, Tito hoped, could be sent urgently to the Bosnian Corps with whose commander he had no radio link.

† The author's italics.

contact with the Partisan Staff in the southern sector. Call us up daily. The above plans are very urgent. Answer us soon as you can. Our direct proposals could form a firm basis for our future co-operation.'[33]

On 17 May, Cairo received confirmation of their proposal to send British officers to the Croat mission, and stating that concrete proposals would follow. Two British officers, Major William Jones, M.C., a one-eyed Canadian with a gallant record in the First World War, and Captain Anthony Hunter, who were standing by at Derna, were successfully parachuted, on the night of 18–19 May, to an agreed pinpoint near the Partisan headquarters in Croatia.*

On 17 May Tito replied to the Croat Partisan Staff:

Communicate to the British mission in our name the following: We consider co-operation with the Allies as logical. Let them send a liaison officer to our staff. He must land at once in Montenegro, near Durmitor. We ask the British air force to bomb Berane, Bijelo Polje, Plevlja, Andrijevica, Mostar, Podgorica, and Nikšić.† Further details follow.[34]

As yet, the British had no conception of the structure of the Partisan command, and these messages assume the existence of a separate organization in Croatia, and 'a staff in the southern sector'.

On the same night as the 'Fungus' party had been parachuted to Croatia, on 20–21 April, a second group of Canadian Yugoslavs had been dropped 'blind' near the village of Šekovici and the heights of Javornik in Eastern Bosnia.

This was a probing mission sent on summary evidence, which proved accurate, that in this region also Partisan forces were active. In fact, the Partisan Bosnian Corps was in the area. In event of the loss of the mission to Croatia, this second operation was a supplementary attempt to contact the Partisan forces.‡

The first signal from this party was picked up in Cairo on 11 May, reporting their safe landing but that they were on the run.

---

* Major Jones died in Canada in August 1969 before completing his memoirs. Extracts of conversations with him have been published in *4 July*, the organ of the Yugoslav war veterans association, in October 1969. A pamphlet written by him, was published in Canada in 1946, entitled *Twelve Months with Tito*.

† These were the bases and garrison towns from which the concentric Axis assault was mounting against the Partisan main group.

‡ This mission, 'Hoathley I', headed by Stevan Serdar, a Spanish Civil War veteran, a miner from Quebec province, Milan Druzić, and 'George' Diklić.

As Tito's headquarters had no radio contact with his Bosnian Corps, news of the arrival of this party was not immediately reported to him.

The message of 17 May from Tito was relayed to Cairo by our mission at Partisan Croat headquarters, probably before the landing of Major Jones and Captain Hunter on the night of 19 May.

Events had moved with such speed, and the first stages of the operation, mounted in Cairo, had evolved so smoothly, that the S.O.E. section there had not either briefed or selected the mission proposed to be sent to the 'Partisan Staff in the southern sector'.

The party, now hastily assembled, was to be a joint mission, in two equal-ranking sections, Special Operations and Military Intelligence, and under the direct orders of British General Headquarters, Middle East.

After some friendly argument and rivalry in the office of the Balkan section of S.O.E. in Cairo, where I had been working since December 1942, my immediate commanding officer decided that I should go. My qualifications were adequate although in no special degree different from those of my brother officers engaged on the same duties. I had been trained to parachute in England and, after attachment to S.O.E. headquarters in London, I had been involved by an element of chance in the affairs of the Balkans. As trained officers to be held in readiness for operations in these regions seemed scarce, and as a reproof for a certain indiscipline, I was dispatched by sea instead of by air, in a Free French tramp steamer to my new assignment in Cairo, travelling by way of the Brazilian coast – the captain of the ship having lost our convoy on the first night out of the Clyde – to Lagos, and thence across Africa in a Belgian civilian aircraft through the Congo and up the Nile to Egypt.

I was not an outstanding specialist on Yugoslav affairs, but had been directly engaged in studying the situation in the country for some time, and, now in Cairo, had been closely connected with the recent operations.

Shortly after my arrival, Colonel S. W. Bailey was parachuted, on Christmas Day, to head the senior mission to the headquarters of Mihailović. Bill Bailey and I had already worked together on Yugoslav affairs, and were close colleagues. We had at one time a private scheme of our own that, as he was destined to be sent to

Serbia on a mission to instil some reality into the legendary and mythical figure of Mihailović as the sole organizer of Yugoslav resistance – indeed, the only symbol of such a leader in the enemy-occupied Balkans – I would eventually parachute to Bailey as his second-in-command.

Fate, however, played the game in another fashion.

At the moment when, without a hitch and with unforeseen and model promptitude, the first stages of the Croat 'project' reached the point of requiring the urgent and unexpected dispatch of a British mission to a central headquarters of the 'guerrillas', I was selected in a matter of hours to head the S.O.E. component of the party, which was allotted the code name of 'Typical'.

Captain W. F. Stuart of the military intelligence branch of the British General Headquarters, Middle East, was instructed to lead the mission jointly with me, but with a separate chain of command. Since December 1942 we had also worked in close association in Cairo. One of his recent duties had been to assist Bailey in the recruiting of the Croat group in Canada. Stuart possessed very specialist qualifications for the task ahead of us. He was a pre-war expert on Serbo-Croat matters, having served both in the Canadian Department of Immigration, selecting South Slav immigrants to Canada, and also in the British Consulate in Zagreb up to April 1941. He spoke the language fluently and, as a military intelligence officer after 1941, had been dealing with such reports as reached the British military authorities from the occupied regions of the country.

Neither of us had expected to be selected for the present probing mission into Partisan territory, although we had, as staff officers, been engaged in planning this series of operations.

It was therefore his task to assess and report on the military situation both on the Partisan and enemy sides, whereas it was for me to consult with the Partisan leadership on joint operational tasks, and also to convey general impressions of the strength and structure of the movement. We each had a separate radio set and W/T operator linking us with our respective stations in Cairo.

On 20 May I received my directives in the Cairo office of the Yugoslav section of S.O.E. and was instructed to commit them to memory. I was appointed 'liaison officer with Partisan G.H.Q. for Yugoslavia. You will represent yourself as the nominee of G.H.Q. Middle East, under whose orders you have been placed.'

I was to 'proceed by parachute' to a prearranged area at

present occupied by the 'Partisan G.H.Q. for Yugoslavia', and would be accompanied by Captain W. F. Stuart, with two radio operators, and a Yugoslav from Canada.

One of the W/T operators and the Canadian Croat would be under my orders. The former, Corporal Walter Wroughton of the Royal Air Force, had been attached to British G.H.Q., Middle East, since the end of March. I had never seen him before.

Wroughton was twenty years old, a cussid Lancashire lad who had volunteered for 'special duties' out of the boredom of a W/T training school where he had been an instructor, and had glumly undergone a parachute course.

His conception of 'bullshit' was refreshing. His particular technical skill and stubbornness, together with natural powers of acute observation and ability to work on his own, made his random choice as a member of the party my personal good fortune.

Ivan ('John') Starčević, the Canadian Yugoslav, was already known to me, and had been selected from the remaining members of the group housed in the villa near Mena House outside Cairo. I was ill-qualified in Serbo-Croat, and he was nominally allotted to me as an interpreter.

If he had any other duties, I never discovered them. There were many times during the coming months when I was grateful for his presence.

Bill Stuart's operator joined us also at the last minute, and reported to him as Sergeant 'Rose'.

It is, perhaps, the irony of such enterprises to be unaware of the secrets of companions. Sergeant 'Rose' was a Palestine Jew of German origin, from one of the early founding settlements in that mandated territory. He revealed this to me later in his own time. He had been pressed into the British Army by the Jewish Agency under the illusion that, as a radio technician of special quality, he was being posted to Egypt in February 1943 as an instructor at a British W/T training school.*

'Rose' had recently and inexplicably been dispatched on a parachute course, unbriefed on the wise calculations of his superiors but with the natural fatalism of generations of his race. He now found himself attached to our party.

On a visit to Israel twenty years later, I learned by chance his

* 'Rose' was told by the head of the Jewish Agency in Cairo, that he was to 'try to get information about what happened to the Jewish communities in Yugoslavia and to report'. (Letter of Rosenberg to the author.)

real name – Peretz Rosenberg. In the meantime, he had served as
the chief radio specialist of the Hagana. We met on his settlement
near Haifa and continued where we had left off.

He was a quiet small man, with smiling eyes, short of speech,
alert and imaginative. Nothing surprised him. This was just as
well.

Wroughton and 'Rose' between them made possible the survival
of our mission.

Bill Stuart also received a further attachment to his section of
the mission. Sergeant John Campbell, Royal Marines, had been
detailed by the appropriate authorities on the morning of our
departure. He was to act as a cipher clerk, and bodyguard. It was
not his fault that his services, in both capacities, were not often
to be called to account.

The detailing of 'Typical' mission was now complete.

My own duties, as distinct from those of Bill Stuart (we both
had separate ciphers), were set out in the directive which I had
received and committed to memory on the evening of 20 May.

I was to explain to the Partisan leadership

the point of view maintained by G.H.Q., Middle East, namely, that the
war in the Mediterranean has reached a stage in which Allied offensives
may be considered imminent and the synchronization of the Partisan
effort therefore becomes desirable.

My further instructions were

to arrange for the Partisan forces to attack specific targets on enemy
lines of communication with supplies and, if necessary, British per-
sonnel provided by us; to report on the military situation in the country
and advise us on the selection of targets; and to convey the wishes of
G.H.Q., Middle East, to the Partisan G.H.Q. and to report the point of
view maintained by them.

In dealing with British relations with General Mihailović you will be
guided by the following considerations, which you will make clear to
the Partisan G.H.Q. in suitable form. Her Majesty's government was not
until recently aware of the fact that certain of Mihailović's commanders
had compounded with the enemy. As soon as this information became
available Her Majesty's government had taken steps to express its
complete disagreement with General Mihailović in continuing to
maintain relations with these commanders.

Meanwhile G.H.Q., Middle East, is of the opinion that certain of
Mihailović's units in East and South Serbia are in a position to render
service to the Allied cause by planned attacks on enemy lines of
communication. It is the wish of G.H.Q., Middle East, that nothing be

done to interfere with these plans, and they will continue to support all elements in Yugoslavia who offer resistance to the Axis. G.H.Q., Middle East, therefore welcome this opportunity of co-operating with the Partisans.

Bill Stuart had received similar instructions with special emphasis on procuring military intelligence on the enemy order of battle in Yugoslavia.

The British intentions expressed in these directives were more precise than those given to Hudson and later to Atherton, or to 'Fungus'.

The dispatch of our mission was an indication of the changes in the strategic position of the Western Allies in the Mediterranean theatre, which could be interpreted by implication to mean that an Allied landing in Yugoslavia was being considered.

We were to seek the co-operation of Partisan G.H.Q. in sabotage operations, and to offer explosives, and if necessary British demolition experts, for this purpose.

Such operations could be aimed not only at the German lines of communications from Central Europe to Greece to disrupt supplies to North Africa, and the shipment of Roumanian oil and Yugoslav minerals to Germany, but could also be interpreted as a prelude to a British landing in the Balkans.

Stuart and I were being sent to a central headquarters of a Partisan army as liaison officers under the direct orders of British General Headquarters, Middle East.

The intention expressed in the directive that the British Middle East Command were sending the present mission was confined to the working out of co-operation with the Partisan Headquarters, and there was no hint that such a proposal implied the recognition of the Partisan forces as formal allies.

Our mission was a probing operation and, while the instructions were categorical that I should in no way come 'under Bailey's orders', there was also no explicit instruction that I should attempt to secure Partisan agreement to co-operate with Mihailović.

Our superiors left to our judgement the manner, extent, and stages in which Stuart and I would communicate the substance of our directives to Partisan Headquarters.

But, as with our predecessors, we carried no written authority.

Our sole credentials were the acceptance by the Partisans of the authenticity of the radio signals being exchanged for the planning of our reception.

These W/T communications, upon which the safe arrival of our mission depended, worked smoothly.

On 21 May a message was passed on through the British mission at Croat headquarters to Cairo:

Inform the British that the Germans are concentrating great number of troops in Sarajevo and three hundred aircraft. Further concentrations at Plevlja, Kolašin, Peč, Trebinje, and Mostar. They are engaged in hostilities against Montenegro and the Sandžak in the direction of Golija, Maglić, and Volujak; from Plevlja in the direction of Djurdevića Tara; from Foča, along both banks of Drina towards the Piva; from Trebinje and Bijelo Polje towards Nikšić, Šavnik and Žabljak.

Our troops are engaged in heavy fighting and bloody clashes with the Germans who intend to clean up the region and organize their defence, in Montenegro and Hercegovina, against Allied invasion.

We request that the airfield at Sarajevo is bombed and the garrisons in the towns mentioned above. We consider this to be in the Allied interest. Send urgently representatives, and explosives to destroy targets, railway tracks and tunnels. Call for this in our name. Tito.[35]

On the same day, a further signal indicated times and map references. 'We agree about the date. Everything will be ready. [Details of the map co-ordinates giving the precise landing point near Mount Durmitor.] Hour for parachuting at night between 10 p.m. and 2 a.m.'[36]

Members of the mission, now being hastily assembled for this operation, were still in Cairo when the signals were received.

Tito had revealed his pseudonym as commander of the Partisan forces in Montenegro and the detailed place names indicated that, in the mountains grouped round the peaks of Durmitor rising to seven thousand feet, his troops were encircled by strong enemy forces moving from a ring of bases and their main airfield at Sarajevo, which the Royal Air Force was requested to bomb without delay. Tito had accepted the proposal made in the Cairo message of 12 May to undertake joint actions of sabotage, and called for explosives.

On 23 May, Major Jones sent the first of a series of messages reporting on the existence of a strong Partisan organization in Croatia. One of these signals, dated 26 May, asked when British G.H.Q. Cairo would reorganize the Partisans as a Second Front. 'What could be done to equip four Partisan divisions?'

A further suggestion seems to have been made that the Partisan headquarters in Croatia would be prepared to send out at once a delegate for talks in Cairo.

These 'Fungus' telegrams were disturbing in their wild and irresponsible enthusiasm, and indirectly had unfortunate consequences.

The development of these 'Croat' operations had gathered such speed that London was only aware of the barest details, and not even that the first 'Fungus' operation had been successful.* They were as yet unaware that our own mission was on its way. But the British General Headquarters in Cairo were acting, through S.O.E., on the general instructions of the previous March instructing them 'to infiltrate British officers to other resistance groups'.

But a reception of Partisan delegates in Cairo, proposed by Jones within three days of landing, and requests for material aid for four divisions, coupled with Tito's request for explosives, which was practical and in accord with Cairo's own signal of 12 May via 'Fungus' to the Partisan Staff 'in the southern sector', went beyond any instructions or authority upon which British military command in the Middle East, could act.

Even appreciating the gallant eccentricity of Jones, the S.O.E. Staff in Cairo realized that the sending of explosives would be an admission of future support, which they were ordered not to send until the British mission now on the point of departure to the Partisan command in Montenegro had arrived and been able to report reliable evidence.

The Chiefs of Staff Committee, Middle East, turned down the proposal to send explosives, but Stuart and myself successfully pleaded that we could hardly arrive empty-handed as a burden of neutral observers in the midst of fierce fighting as described in Tito's measured but dramatic signal of 21 May. We should be permitted to bring at least medical supplies with us. This was accepted.

On the following day, 22 May 1943, we left Cairo, somewhat inexplicably, by train instead of plane, for the terminus of the Egyptian railway at Mersa Matruh and on by lorry to Derna. Perhaps things were going too well, and everyone concerned had lost their breath – and nerve.

---

* In April 1943 the British Ambassador in Moscow was informed by the Foreign Office that the British had no contact with the Partisans, presumably before news from Cairo regarding our first missions to Croatia had reached London.

Near the
summit

German
mountain
troops
on Maglić

The enemy ring

Killing the wounded

The optimism of Major Jones seems to have reflected in some degree the excitement, and ambitions, of the Croat Partisan leadership. Tito, on learning the substance of Jones' requests, sent to the G.H.Q. Croatia, on 23 May, a signal which indicated a lurking anxiety at the independence being shown by a subordinate headquarters:

Ask help from the British, but with our knowledge and approval. Don't communicate to them our internal affairs and plans. We will appoint a delegate to Cairo when it may be possible. You are not to send a special representative. Without our knowledge you are not to make any arrangements. Inform the British that here we are engaged in heavy fighting for ten days against the Germans, Italians and Ustaša, who hope to occupy Montenegro, the Sandžak, and Hercegovina. Germans have thrown in eight divisions against us . . .[37]

Our mission reached Derna airfield on 23 May 1943, and awaited the final confirmatory technical signal from Montenegro.

On 24 May Cairo had signalled 'Fungus' to pass to Tito's headquarters a message that a military mission would parachute on the same night (24/5 May) to the appointed place with 1500 kilograms of medical supplies.[38]

That morning a message was received from Montenegro.

We are awaiting the British and material on the night of 25 May on Negobudjo Polje, where they asked.* They must not start later, because the Germans, with strong forces, are trying to press forward from Kolašin towards Sinjajevina and it is not excluded that in a few days fighting will flare up. In event of bad weather we will wait another night.[39]

The members of the 'Typical' mission now knew what to expect. The previous Cairo signal referring to medical supplies had however not been repeated to Derna. That evening, Tuesday 25 May, after a briefing with the R.A.F. squadron commander at the airfield, and the young New Zealand air crew of the Halifax bomber which was to take us on our journey, a signal came in from Cairo ordering us to leave behind the medical supplies. The aircraft was already loaded.

* The Partisans had proposed a landing ground which appeared to the British Air Force experts to be too close to Mount Durmitor, and the latter signaled that the field at Negobudjo – the region had been studied on large-scale Austro-Hungarian military maps dating from the First World war – was more suitable. The above signal contains a note in Tito's hand-writing: 'We are awaiting the British today (24 May) at our and their place, and tomorrow (25/6 May).'

Q

Stuart and I obeyed these orders. Somebody had decided that the dispatch, even of drugs, bandages, and surgical equipment, as a merest token of good will, and replacing the explosives requested by Partisan command for immediate sabotage action which Cairo headquarters themselves had proposed to them, represented an infringement of the formal British obligations to the Royal Yugoslav government. Enraged by this note of inhumanity and breach of faith, Stuart and I, with the connivance of the R.A.F. Staff at Derna, looted the sheds and hangars of every item of military boots and clothing, guns and ammunition, which we could seize, and re-loaded the bomber. Perhaps this could be regarded as an act of military indiscipline. But, in our anger, our minds bright with the fragments of the scene awaiting us as transmuted through the terse messages from our appointed destination, we wondered, in a fleeting moment of frustrated wrath, whether, in certain British quarters, there was a faint indication that the failure of this mission would save many complications.*

In this manner, an hour behind flight schedule, operation 'Typical' boarded the waiting aircraft, which bore us in the dusk over the bluffs at the end of the runway on our northward course across the sea.

On the evening of 28 May Cairo received a signal on the 'Typical' wavelength that the party 'were all safe after a lucky drop in the dark'. This was followed by a message from 'Fungus' on the following day: 'Deakin party happy landing with stores.'

On 1 June Cairo cabled to S.O.E. London, who were as yet unaware of the dispatch of the 'Typical' mission: 'The party consisted of Captain Deakin with British W/T operator and one Croat from Canada. Also Captain Stuart with British W/T operator and British clerk. Independent W/T and ciphers. Party sent after initial official proposal sent by us to Partisan H.Q. Croatia through "Fungus". . . . The party has been sent to establish direct liaison with Partisan H.Q. whose commander-in-chief is Tito at present in Montenegro.'

This signal was presumably sent, on the same day, in answer to an urgent cable from S.O.E. London: 'The Foreign Office requested on 1 June the following details: Who is the head of all Partisans? Where is their G.H.Q.? Who has officially contacted the leader?'

* There is some evidence to this effect, but it does not belong to any responsible account of these events.

This elementary but essential information, hitherto unknown in London, had been established, in regard to the first two of these queries, just prior to our departure. A leader, under the name of Tito, was in command of a general central headquarters of the Partisan movement, now located in Montenegro.

The transmission of any further evidence as to the nature and structure of the 'Croat and Slovene guerrillas' would depend on the survival of this mission, and the ability of its W/T operators to maintain radio contact with their base.

At the beginning of June Mr. Richard Casey, the Resident Minister of State in Cairo as the personal representative of the British Cabinet, sent two confidential reports direct to the Prime Minister summarizing the intentions of S.O.E. Cairo in regard to operations in Yugoslavia which implied a clear departure from existing official policy of exclusive support of Mihailović. On 8 June the Prime Minister called for a report 'on these extraordinary series of documents', to the embarrassment of S.O.E. London and the Foreign Office. Apparently Casey's reports had been handed to him during a visit to North Africa a few days previously.

By chance I had written a personal note through our Embassy in Cairo to Mr. Churchill, with whom I had worked as his literary secretary before the war, merely telling him that I was about to leave on a mission to Yugoslavia. It must have been during his North Africa visit that this private letter reached him. It contained no hint of high politics, or that I was being sent to Tito. But its effect was unexpected and certainly unintended. Mr. Casey received a telegram instructing him to arrange that I should be sent from Cairo to report to the Prime Minister on the latest situation in Yugoslavia. A reply was sent that I was not available as I had been dropped into the country a few days earlier.

This episode seems to have prompted these reports on the development of British policy in Cairo, and by a minor footnote, the personal interest of the Prime Minister was directed at a critical moment of decision to the Yugoslav scene. His private office, with admirable tact, informed the Foreign Office that no particular political event seemed to have prompted Mr. Churchill's message. I had been a friend of his in peace time and helped him with his biography of Marlborough, and it was possible that this telegram had been prompted as much by a friendly desire to see me as by anything else.

On learning that I had already departed on this vaguely reported mission, Mr. Churchill asked for news of the operation. He was informed that the party had dropped safely, but no contact had been made since, and in view of the conditions briefly described in the first message it was possible that nothing further would be heard.

On 18 June Lord Selborne, the Minister of Economic Warfare, wrote to the Prime Minister that he feared that I was there. The present Axis offensive might alter the whole set-up. Nothing had been heard from the mission for a week.

On 8 June the Middle East Defence Committee reported to the Chiefs of Staff in London their plan for supporting Tito to the west and Mihailović to the east of the river Ibar. Maximum resistance to the Axis was the paramount consideration, and both the Yugoslav government and Mihailović must be induced to place operational considerations first. The Partisans were now the most effective resistance movement in Yugoslavia, and British assistance to them therefore was logical and necessary. If support were withheld from the Partisans in Western Serbia (namely to regard the whole of Serbia as exclusively Mihailović territory), one would not only jeopardize resistance to the Axis in that area, but also prejudice the position in Croatia and Slovenia.

The British Chiefs of Staff resisted the criticisms voiced at this reappraisal of policy. In a memorandum of 17 June they stated that, according to War Office sources, the Četniks were hopelessly compromised in their relations with the Axis in Hercegovina and Montenegro; during the recent fighting in the latter area it had been the well-organized Partisans who had been holding down the Axis forces. The Middle East Command put forward the view that the Partisans were the most formidable anti-Axis force in the country. The Chiefs of Staff supported Cairo in general, but felt that General Mihailović's sphere of influence should be in future considered as comprising Serbia and Macedonia only. Outside Serbia, the Partisans deserved the strongest support that S.O.E. were able to give them.

This recommendation was a central statement of military policy, strengthened by intercepted intelligence from German and Italian sources, but it contradicted the basic policies both of S.O.E. London and the Foreign Office. The former were disturbed by the basic implication of uncontrolled support to a rival guerrilla movement; the latter expressed alarm at the political implications of this statement of the Chiefs of Staff. British policy must be concerned with converting all resistance groups into one Yugoslav movement: any arbitrary lines of territorial demarcation must lead to the ultimate disintegration of Yugoslav unity, which the British were under formal obligation to preserve.

But any consideration at government level of the maintenance, or change of emphasis, in sending supplies to Yugoslav resistance groups had to be related to the bleak shortage of aircraft for such missions. The six Halifax bombers, based on Derna, still formed the only squadron available for special operations throughout the Balkans.

The Prime Minister had already shown a personal interest in this state of affairs on his way through Cairo at the end of January 1943 on his return from the Adana Conference with the Turks, when he received a report on this matter from British Headquarters, Middle East. It was unrealistic to plan to extend our operations to Croatia and Slovenia, which were now for the first time being studied in their technical aspects, and the trickle of supplies to Mihailović was essentially conditioned by this lack of aircraft; and both provided him with a reasonable pretext to avoid any activity against the Axis and offered a plausible excuse, which he stressed in his outburst to Bailey at the end of February, for collaborating with the Italians in return for supplies and equipment, which the British had shown themselves incapable of providing.*

On 18 June a summary of the British activities in Yugoslavia revealed the true position.

Since the middle of April twenty British officers and other ranks had been dropped to Mihailović † and twenty-three tons of material to districts under his control and where British liaison officers were present. No supplies had been sent to Mihailović himself pending his acceptance of the government's directive of 28 May.

During the same period five ‡ British officers had been sent to the Partisans, in Northern Bosnia and the Lika in Croatia, to-

* See p. 183.
† Subsequent to Hudson and Bailey's mission.
‡ Jones and Hunter had been parachuted to Croatia; Stuart and myself to Montenegro. The 'Northern Bosnian' party consisted of Canadian Croats. This summary of 18 June referring to 'five' British officers is not quite accurate.

gether with six and a half tons of supplies. These were the first missions to be sent to the Partisans.

As to other resistance groups, whoever they might be, no contact had been made or support given.

The Prime Minister minuted on this summary to General Ismay on 23 June: 'All this is of the highest importance. . . . I understood when I was last in Cairo that an additional number of aircraft were to be made available. I consider that . . . this demand should have priority even on the bombing of Germany.'

On the same day a Chiefs of Staff conference was held at Downing Street at which Mr. Churchill stressed the very great value, particularly at the present time, of giving 'all possible support to the Yugoslav anti-Axis movement, which was containing some 33 Axis divisions in the area'. This matter was of such importance that he considered 'the small number of additional aircraft required to increase our aid must be provided, if necessary at the expense of the bombing of Germany and of the anti-U Boat war.'

This would be a small price to pay for the diversion of Axis forces caused by resistance in Yugoslavia, and every effort must be made to increase the rate of delivering supplies, working up to 500 tons or so each month by September.[40]

The conference agreed to order the implementation of this new policy. If there was doubt remaining in government circles in London as to the Prime Minister's understanding of the composition of 'the Yugoslav anti-Axis movement' this was dispelled, some days later, by the decision to send Fitzroy Maclean, a former diplomat and Member of Parliament, and now an officer attached to the Special Air Service, 'to work with Tito'. As Mr. Churchill put it in a minute of 28 July to the Foreign Secretary: 'What we want is a daring Ambassador-leader with these hardy and hunted guerrillas.'[41]

These decisions, pressed through by the personal intervention of the Prime Minister, were to revolutionize and bedevil British attitudes to Yugoslav affairs, which had been frozen into a formal immobility of argument for the past critical months, but they were directly related to the turning point in the whole war in the Mediterranean, and were taken on the eve of the Anglo-American landings in Sicily. Unrecognized in their isolation, and barely observed by small British parties which had been dropped into these bleak and barren regions, the forces of Tito now emerged as

the leading movement of resistance in an area which was acquir-
ing an immediate strategic interest.

As Churchill expressed it, in a letter to General Alexander on
7 July:

I presume you have read about the recent heavy fighting in Yugoslavia and the widespread sabotage and guerrilla beginning in Greece.
Albania also should be a fertile field. All this has grown up with no more
aid from Britain than the dropping of a few bundles by parachute. If
we can get hold of the mouth of the Adriatic so as to be able to run
even a few ships into Dalmatian or Greek ports the whole of the
Western Balkans might flare up, with far-reaching results. All this is
however hunting in the next field.

And again on 22 July:

I am sending you by an officer a full account which I have had
prepared of the marvellous resistance put up by the so-called Partisan
followers of Tito in Bosnia and the powerful cold-blooded manoeuvres
of Mihailović in Serbia. The Germans have not only been reinforcing
the Balkan peninsula with divisions, but they have been continually
improving the quality and mobility of these divisions and have been
stiffening up the local Italians. The enemy cannot spare these forces,
and if Italy collapses the Germans could not bear the weight themselves. Great prizes lie in the Balkan direction.[42]

EPILOGUE

During the interview with Tito on 10 September at his head-quarters in the Turkish fortress in Jajce, following the Allied radio broadcast of the Italian surrender, he agreed that I should accompany General Koča Popović and units of the First Division in the race with the Germans for Split on the Dalmatian coast. The prize was the capture of the main Italian supplies concentrated in that city. Before setting out, I signalled to Cairo that, in the confused repercussions of the Italian armistice, it seemed urgent to witness the surrender of the nearest Italian Army Command. I confirmed that technical arrangements had been made for the reception of Brigadier Maclean and the new British mission who were due to arrive during the following days.

On the night of 11 September I left in a captured German staff car, together with Captain Benson, the American officer attached to our mission, for the headquarters of the Yugoslav First Division at Bugojno. Walter Wroughton, transporting with him our W/T set to maintain contact throughout the expedition with our mission base and, if need be, with Cairo, followed on the partisan train which now operated intermittently on the local line linking Jajce and Bugojno. Stoked with wood, the locomotive wheezed painfully across the river bridge and up the hillside track to the west of the town. The convoy then coasted through rolling country to the next and only stop.

As a symbolic mark of confidence, the train carried civilian mail, on its irregular journeys, franked with a National Liberation post mark.

Our task was to reach Split before the arrival of the main German forces, moving southwards along the Adriatic coast and bent on the same enterprise as ourselves. On paper they had the advantage of one day, according to the calculations which Tito had shown me on the map.

Our march was a model of speed and organization. The Yugo-slav units, with their long training in such expeditions, moved in ordered columns, day and night, pausing only at intervals for a few minutes' rest at a time. There were no camps or bivouacs and sleep was confined to such brief halts.

Within twenty-four hours we had covered the seventy kilo-metres which separated us from our Bosnian headquarters. Just before dawn on 14 September, General Popović and his staff, with forward patrols, emerged from the frontier of the Bosnian forest on to the white hillsides of the Dalmatian coast. We found ourselves on the edge of a deserted village. An open plain lay below, cut by a road leading due south. This was our route to the coast. No Italian posts or outlying garrisons lay in our path. These had been withdrawn into the perimeter of Split. But we were entering a region where small towns and villages were nominally under local Ustaša control.

We were about to pause at dawn in the empty houses of the village. Within minutes, bursts of rifle and machine-gun fire brought us running from our quarters. A few hundred yards below us on the road were two lorries moving northwards, headed by a motor cyclist. Through our field glasses we could discern the black uniforms of the Ustaša. The Yugoslav divisional staff, in a flash of recognition, identified the figure on the motor cycle as Colonel Boban, the notorious commander of the Black Legion.

Without any apparent orders, one of our companies, in open order with rifles and sub-machine guns at the hip, advanced briskly on the enemy column, which had halted abruptly, taken unawares. The action was over within minutes and the convoy overrun. Boban turned round, accelerating back down the road to the south pursued by a swarm of fire from which he emerged unscathed and vanished over a rise in the road.

The enemy lorries carried useful supplies of food and ammunition. We returned to our village headquarters for a meal, punctuated by the sharp bursts of rifle fire announcing the dispatch of the prisoners. Quick thinking by the leading troops had given us the initiative, but heavy shooting from the woods to the north of us revealed the presence of a considerable Ustaša force. We had by chance ambushed part of their supply column. They must have been aware of our southward move, and advancing on parallel lines in the night in opposite directions, we had both inadvertently missed a frontal clash.

The following hours were lost in beating off this enemy attack from the north, and disengaging ourselves for our onward march. At nightfall we moved again, at the same rhythm. In the early hours of 16 September, Popović and his staff, together with our party, had reached a point on the bare hills which dominated the main road leading down to Split and to the coast which we were now to see for the first time after many months of mountain

and forest warfare. We were in an exultant mood which matched
the sudden appearance, ludicrous and inadequate, of a small
Fiat car from the city. From the driver we learned that the
Italian garrison of Split had already been disarmed in their
barracks by the local underground Partisan committee and the
students of the high school.

General Popović, his political commissar Mijalko Todorović,
and myself squeezed into the small machine and set off to liberate
the city, leaving the main body of troops to follow, together with
Benson, Wroughton, and our radio set. As we passed in the bright
morning through the villages on the outskirts of Split, the peasants
constantly blocked our path, excited by our incongruous appearance, offering us at each halt wine and fruit. The city was in a
state of joyous confusion. We pressed our way to a hotel on the
port where a temporary headquarters had already been set up by
the local military and town command, which had now disclosed
its presence. The corridors and rooms of the building were
thronged with scurrying supporters.

During the course of the morning, troops of the Yugoslav First
Division entered the city and took up positions on the fringe of
heights dominating the town and in the villages immediately
beyond, awaiting the first clashes with the German units advancing down the coast from the north. The Italian transport,
arms, and equipment was already being assembled. Routes of
evacuation into the hills had already been prepared.

Benson and Wroughton joined me after a narrow escape from a
German air sweep on a column of captured Italian lorries descending into Split with the main body of the division. They had been
caught on the open road during the brief halt by a flight of
Fieseler Storchs. One lorry had overturned, and some of our
equipment was lost.

Benson and I, together with Wroughton and our radio set,
improvised a small headquarters in a villa at Kastela, a suburb
on the seafront of the bay of Split. As Wroughton recorded in his
diary: 'Very good wine here and lots of figs and grapes. Nice
place for a holiday.'

Our first reaction was to go for a swim. As we were splashing
naked in the water a squadron of German 'Stukas' arrived heading
straight for the Italian barracks across the bay. We watched them,
as with their sinister howling they dive-bombed the Italian hut-
ments and jolted us back to reality.

On our first arrival at the Palace Hotel a smart figure in uniform had accosted me. By his decorations and boots I recognized
him as an Italian general, and in spite of my dusty battledress he
had taken me to be a British officer. His manner was a little con-
descending. 'What are you doing with these bandits?' was his
first remark. He received the reply that perhaps he was two years
too late in using such a phrase. I declined an invitation to call on
him at his villa to discuss events, and made it clear that if he had
anything to say this would have to be arranged in the presence of
Yugoslav representatives. His position was unenviable. As commander of the Bergamo Division, with the elements of an Italian
Corps Headquarters based on Split,* General Becuzzi was responsible for the well-being of some 14,000 men, already disarmed, confined to barracks, and with some 100 of his own troops
armed with rifles to act as sentries and patrols within the perimeter
of the Italian barracks.

When, the next morning, the German Air Force bombed the
Italian barracks, killing more than several hundred Italian
soldiers in a few minutes and dropping leaflets to encourage them
not to join the Communists, General Becuzzi urgently sought me
out. His position and that of his forces must be regularized, and
the formalities arising from the present untidy state of affairs
could perhaps be discussed. Would I go with him in his staff car
to his villa to talk matters over? I repeated that as the British
liaison officer with the Yugoslav General Staff I would only meet
him in consultation with their Divisional Commander. I was prepared to act as an intermediary. In case General Becuzzi had not
listened to the radio, I reminded him that his duty was clear.
Marshal Badoglio had signed an armistice with the Anglo-
American Command in the Mediterranean and had ordered all
Italian units to join the Allied side. I was prepared to guarantee
personally the safety of General Becuzzi if he issued such orders to
his troops instructing them to evacuate Split and to join the Yugoslav forces in the hinterland. He knew as well as I did that the

* Split was the headquarters of the Italian Eighth Army Corps whose Commander, General Spigo, had departed to Zara, with most of his staff, on 8
September. After the fall of Mussolini in July, General Spigo had taken over
the civilian administration of the city, which he now handed over before
leaving to the 'revolutionary' committee formed by the underground
Partisan organization.

General Spigo was arrested later by the Germans in Zara, and interned in
Germany.

Yugoslavs had no intention, nor the means, of holding the city without artillery or heavy military equipment against the Germans, who would arrive within a matter of hours. The Yugoslav aim was to remove Italian military supplies. They were indifferent to the fate of the Italian troops, although, for propaganda purposes, they were prepared to discuss, with condescension, the rallying of Italian units to the Allied side. The matter seemed to have a certain urgency and I went to see the Yugoslav Divisional Commander.

General Popović accepted with a touch of irony my proposal that we should go through the motions of signing some armistice document with the Italians which would regularize the future position of General Becuzzi and might possibly bring over some of his troops against the Germans. It was agreed to hold a meeting in the presence of Captain Benson and myself as representatives of the American and British headquarters in the Mediterranean. Neither of us had of course any instructions. A brief radio contact by our W/T set had informed our immediate superiors in Italy of the position in Split and the plight of the Italian garrison.*

General Becuzzi was more concerned with his future reputation than the present dilemma with which his troops were faced. He made it clear that, in spite of any safe-conduct which might be extended to him, he was not prepared to follow the orders of Marshal Badoglio and lead his forces into the hills. He was anxious to regularize his position according to the conventional laws of war, which could not have been actively in his mind during the previous two years. He now sought to devise a formula to conceal that his men had been disarmed by the local population of Split without showing any resistance. The Yugoslavs were interested only in the cases of individuals whom they regarded as having committed crimes in recent months against Partisan prisoners.

Our discussions narrowed to two points: the mode of surrender, and the definition of war criminals. On the first, the Yugoslavs were contemptuously easy. It was agreed that the Italians had formally surrendered and voluntarily handed over their arms. The second matter broke up the first meeting. Becuzzi explained to me with some excitement that a draft document which the Yugoslavs had drawn up stated that all members of the Italian

---

* Some 3,000 Italian troops were evacuated by the arrival of destroyers of their own navy and by local fishing boats.

Armed Forces would be regarded as prisoners of war except those guilty of war crimes. Becuzzi pointed out to me that the latter phrase might apply to any of his men who might have stolen a chicken from a village; an all too frequent event. On occasions looted food supplies had filled the ammunition wagons of the Italian artillery instead of shells. On this issue of war criminals we reached a deadlock, but the unreality of these talks was sharply broken by the German air attack.

My offer to mediate with the Yugoslav Command on the interpretation of this draft clause was accepted and I asked Koča Popović how many Italians he intended to shoot. His prompt answer was eleven. These were police officials and intelligence agents who had been directly responsible for the deaths of captured local Partisans. This seemed to be a small proportion of the 14,000 men involved. Becuzzi complained that he could not sign any document condoning the death of any Italian citizen. He was not cheered by the retort that he had no choice and that his duty was to protect his troops.

At a second meeting, however, held that day, he signed the draft Yugoslav terms and the document was witnessed by Captain Benson and myself.* Its contents bore little resemblance to the confused situation. That night a soviet of young Italian officers sought a meeting with the Yugoslav Command in our presence. The discussion between us underlined the tragic reality of the Italian position. These self-appointed spokesmen of the Bergamo Division proclaimed their desire to fight the Germans and to reject the attitude of their general. But they were only prepared to do so if they could remain as independent units under the Italian flag and fight alongside the Yugoslavs as Allies on an equal footing. Such an offer the Yugoslavs were not prepared to accept. Italian officers and men would be dispersed as individuals under direct Yugoslav command in Partisan brigades.

Speaking in Italian, I attempted in vain to stress the brutal realities of the situation to this committee of officers whose desire to fight was patent, and whose anti-Fascist sentiments were clear. But the issue of their oath to the King of Italy and to the national flag, sadly out of context as it seemed that night, decided the issue. The meeting broke up without rancour but without any

---

* A copy is now on display in the Museum of the Yugoslav Army in Belgrade. The document was also signed by the British liaison officer with the Partisan Dalmatian headquarters, the late Lieutenant John Burke.

decision in spite of my plea that the Yugoslavs would leave Split
as soon as the Germans arrived in force and that the Italians had
no choice but to join us in the hills, or at best be interned by their
former allies. In the event, the young officers with whom we
had been talking, and many of their comrades whom they represented, were later shot by the Germans outside the city or sent to
camps.*

Separately from this overture, an Italian battalion of light
tanks came over to the Yugoslavs and was decimated in the final
skirmishes round the city upon the arrival of the main German
forces. About two thousand men of the military police – the
Carabinieri – marched gallantly into Bosnia. I was to meet their
colonel later, puzzled and bored in unfamiliar surroundings,
asking me whether I played bridge.

Just before we had reached the coast, a radio signal from Cairo
was picked up by Wroughton which instructed me to meet my
successor without delay. There was no immediate way back and I
was obliged at least to continue with the Yugoslav First Division
until we had taken over Split. Having witnessed the liberation of
the city I told Koča Popović of my orders to return to Bosnia
without waiting for the planned Yugoslav withdrawal northwards. There was no problem. An Italian aircraft had been
captured by the Partisans which could fly me back. This machine,
however, turned out to be a seaplane and the project was for-
tunately abandoned. It was agreed that I should set out on foot
with Walter Wroughton, leaving Benny Benson to act as Anglo-
American liaison officer with the Division and to return with
them.

On the previous evening a demonstration was held in the main
square of Split in the presence of the victorious notables: General
Popović, and his political commissar Miljako Todorović; Lola
Ribar who had arrived separately on 9 September as the representative of the Supreme Staff with the Dalmatian operational
zone; the commander of this territorial region, Vicko Krstulović
– an old friend and comrade from the Dalmatian units in the Fifth
offensive; and the local civil and military authorities who had
assumed control of the city. As we stood on the balcony of the

* The Germans shot two Italian generals and 55 officers. 300 officers and 9,000
men were sent to camps in Germany.

R

Venetian town hall, looking down on the assembly of citizens, I framed an appropriate impromptu speech, translated by Lola Ribar. The circumstances were unusual, and the bare presence of representatives of Great Britain and the United States seemed inadequate for the occasion. In a few impromptu phrases I attempted to convey the fateful consequences of the Italian surrender which had accelerated the Anglo-American occupation of continental Italy and had already led to the occupation of ports and air bases on the western Adriatic coast facing us across the sea, whence decisive aid to Yugoslavia would be soon on its way.*

It was only later that I was to read in the German newspapers published in Zagreb that a local Jew disguised as a British officer had made an unfortunate speech from the balcony of the town hall in Split.

On the night of 19 September Walter Wroughton and myself left Split by lorry on our return journey to Jajce with a small group of Partisans and couriers bound northwards on the tracks leading back into central Bosnia.

At the request of Lola Ribar, I took with me copies of *Free Dalmatia*, and a fountain pen – which had presumably been used to sign the 'armistice' with General Becuzzi – as a token of our achievement to present to Tito.

The improvised journey was a simple opportunity to observe the life and daily existence of local Partisan organizations in territories which were relatively quiet and between enemy expeditions. We travelled with small escorts, changing from place to place and drawn from local *odreds*. As soon as we reached the barren white rock formations of the Dinaric Alps, the road petered out into ancient tracks. Our first halting place was in the village of Sajkovići.

Here we lived for several days with the local Partisan *straža* (village guard), which was quartered in the school house. It consisted of an officer and about thirty men and youths, either under the age of 14 or over 70. The remaining inhabitants of this Serb village had either been massacred by the Ustaša in the summer of 1941, or were with Partisan brigades in other parts of the country.

---

* The text of this ephemeral but exultant exhortation was printed in the issue of *Free Dalmatia*, a Partisan paper which had begun to circulate in nearly twenty thousand daily copies before our arrival in Split.

The commander had been hit by a machine-gun bullet in the leg.
The wound was gangrenous. With only one first-aid bandage in
my pocket there was nothing I could do. But he seemed to derive
comfort from a pasty substance liberally applied to the wound by
a peasant woman.

The village lay on one of the main paths winding up from the
coast along which the Partisan soldiers and peasants were moving
in mule columns the Italian arms and munitions from Split.*
They went in silence past the compound of the school. During
the following three days we saw in miniature the typical elements
of local conditions prevailing in a 'free territory'. About a thousand yards to the east of us lay an Ustaša garrison of some eight
hundred men. We could observe their movements through field
glasses. This force could have liquidated the Partisan post at any
moment, and cut the supply tracks passing through the area. But
there was a kind of unwritten precarious stability which the commander explained to me. If his unit were overrun, the nearest
Partisan brigade or division would appear and liquidate the
enemy garrison. This threat was a standing discouragement to
any such isolated and local action.

In the hills to the west of us was a Četnik band, one of a group
under the command of an Orthodox priest, Pop Djuić, Mihailović's representative for the Dinaric region, until the previous
week a close collaborator with the Italians, and now with the
Germans. This band was drawn from the next village, about a
mile away, and at the time of our arrival its members were spend-
ing the weekend with their families. Their presence across our
path obliged us to stay with the Sajkovići village guard until the
Četniks returned to their mountain bases.

One evening Walter Wroughton and I were listening on our
radio set to the B.B.C. news, and he noted with fitting irony in his
diary: 'London today broadcast a few truths about Partisans and
Četniks. About time.'

This enforced idleness enabled us to pause in the simple world
of the daily life of an isolated Partisan post. During the daytime
we would sit about in the fenced compound round the school
observing our companions. They might have been any group of
peasant rebels, symbolizing previous revolts against other
occupiers. Indeed the old men were veterans of such historical

* A new Dalmatian Corps was formed by the Partisans out of the equipment of
the 'Bergamo' division.

actions and the youths would be later recruited into the present conflict. Their equipment was touching in its variety. Each man or boy possessed a rifle or pistol of different make with a few rounds apiece. As a military force they did not exist; as a symbolic presence they were all-powerful.

Our meals were cooked by a young girl who never spoke, neither to us nor to any of her companions. At first we thought that her silence was due to excessive timidity at the sight of strangers, but then I learned her story from the commandant. She was the sole survivor of the population of a nearby Serb village which had been massacred by the Ustaša two years previously. The men, women, and children had been flung over a cliff, and this girl had been the last victim. Her fall was broken by the bodies of her family and friends. She had lain there for several weeks, keeping alive by licking the moisture from the rock face until the Partisans had found her. She had been struck dumb with shock and so remained.

This tiny post was also a primitive intelligence centre. Peasants seemed to travel, particularly the women and shepherds, to and from both friendly and hostile villages and bases in the region bringing constant reports of enemy movements. One morning, a peasant woman stood outside the compound carding wool on a stick. She completed the silent operation, and handed to the commander a piece of paper wound round the wood. Thus we learned that the Četnik troops in the next village had returned to the hills. There were no menfolk in the houses which we could see on the tracks to the west. It was time to move. The commander drew up his tiny force, in ragged but spirited martial array, and made a stirring speech impressing upon them the honour of escorting on the next staging post of their journey members of an Allied mission to their Supreme Staff. Mounted on an emaciated horse with Walter Wroughton behind me and our radio set and kit loaded on a sullen mule, I headed the column. We passed in silence through the Četnik farms on our path. There was no sign of life except for an occasional hostile face peering through a half-closed door.

As we moved northward we were entering the region of Western Bosnia, the historic military frontier of Croatia against the Turks, and now a Partisan stronghold in the present fighting. The march carried us to a small hamlet to the north of the town of Grahovo, now the centre of a Partisan territorial military command. We had covered nearly fifty kilometres before resting in a small hamlet where we took leave of our motley escort.

The following day we moved, in a wide circle to avoid another Ustaša strongpoint, to reach the town of Drvar on the morning of 24 September. It was here that the Partisan rising in Bosnia had been organized in 1941. Drvar was the centre of a timber industry with its saw mills. The workers formed here the first local Partisan units, and the local Communist party had its underground head-quarters before the rebellion. We were now in firmly held 'free territory' and within the area of the First Bosnian Corps whose commander, Kosta Nadj, I had already met during the previous months in Eastern Bosnia.

Throughout our journey the local peasants received us with sustained curiosity. Our physical presence clearly had some primitive effect in creating at least an awareness of the existence of another Ally other than the Russians, news of whose exploits reached the smallest Partisan unit in roneoed wireless bulletins.

The area through which we were now passing was strongly held by regular units of the National Liberation Army. We spent one night at Corps Headquarters, sitting into the late hours in fierce argument with the political commissar about the course of the war in the world outside. The atmosphere was heated by his obsession that ultimate victory would be decided exclusively by the advance of the Soviet armies. In vain we tried to explain to him the existence of an Allied front in Italy and the looming invasion of western Europe. This was a summary of many such conversations with our companions of a day.

At Bosnian Corps Headquarters the British had already established a liaison mission whose radio operator, Corporal Small, we now met for the first time since Cairo. He had been parachuted into Bosnia in the previous April, and it was with a natural excitement that we exchanged news of our experiences.

On the afternoon of 26 September Walter Wroughton and I departed in a farm cart with one Partisan soldier as escort for the last stage of our trip. The surrounding country was now strongly held by Bosnian troops and we had no need of special protection. Our last stop before Jajce was to be the small town of Mrkonić-Grad where I had been told by peasants on the previous day that a conference of Partisan brigade commanders was being held, and that I should be expected to make a speech. On reaching the outskirts of the town a Partisan patrol reported that a senior Allied officer and his staff were being entertained that evening in the town hall. I realized that it was now, and in such circumstances, that I would be meeting Brigadier Fitzroy Maclean.

Our entry into Mrkonjić-Grad was unmilitary. We lumbered through the streets on our wagon, covered in hay. On arriving outside the municipal building Wroughton and I were ushered in. There were tables with rows of officers and notables sitting ceremoniously. At the top of the room, in the place of honour, were six British officers impeccably dressed and accoutred. In the centre of this high table was a tall, alert, and welcoming figure in the uniform of a Brigadier-General. Brushing the remaining wisps of straw from my battledress, I saluted smartly. We shook hands and joined the party.

This gesture completed the 'Typical' mission.

The arrival of the Maclean mission, on 17 September 1943, had placed the relations between Tito and the British on a more formal and senior level. Fitzroy Maclean was the personal representative of the Prime Minister, and his arrival marked implicitly the *de facto* recognition of the Yugoslav National Liberation Army as a military force fulfilling a significant rôle in South-Eastern Europe. With the Italian surrender, and the massive capture of their military equipment and stores, the striking power of the Partisan forces was increased to a point which gave them effective superiority throughout Yugoslav territory, with the exception of Serbia where Mihailović and the auxiliary troops of the Nedić government were still wedged.

The first task, however, of the new British mission still remained to press for an extensive programme of military supplies to Tito's forces to enable the latter both to carry out a series of sabotage operations against the main lines of communication in Croatia, Bosnia, and Slovenia to disrupt the whole structure of German military occupation, and to confront their divisions stationed in the country on technically more equal terms. Together with the organization of military supplies from Allied bases in Italy, the arrival of the Maclean mission also led Tito to seek, by cautious and expectant stages, for the official recognition by the British of the National Liberation Movement, as a formal military ally and as the provisional administration of the country.

After conversations with Tito beginning on the night of his

arrival, and in a series of long talks which we had together on brisk walks through the countryside round Jajce, Fitzroy Maclean left the town on 5 October, together with his Chief of Staff, Colonel Vivian Street, to travel overland to the coast now held in part by Partisan forces since the Italian surrender, and thence by sea to Italy. He carried with him both a detailed report on the military and political situation as seen from Jajce, and a list of requirements for military aid. The British mission and the Yugoslav staff were engaged on planning the reception of material from British and American bases in Italy to be brought in by sea and by air on a scale which hitherto had not been technically possible until Anglo-American armies had occupied the Adriatic coast of Italy, and, under the direct personal intervention of the Prime Minister, the necessary squadrons of transport aircraft for such operations in the Balkans and Central Europe had been provided, based on Italian airfields. The early experimental stage of small-scale sorties from North Africa now lay in the past.

For the moment, the underlying political considerations were left dormant. Efforts were concentrated on planning to receive the arms and equipment listed in the schedules to be presented by Fitzroy Maclean at the Allied headquarters in the Mediterranean. This required firm military control by the Partisans of the territory lying between central Bosnia and the Dalmatian coast, the protection of at least one small port of entry, and the means of ferrying supplies from certain of the Adriatic islands now cleared of their Italian garrisons. With improvised ingenuity a small Partisan fleet of armed fishing boats had been assembled after the Italian surrender and the elements of a ferry service precariously existed. It was intended that the Royal Navy would now detach special units to operate and control the sea routes between Bari, the Dalmatian Islands, and the coast.

It was also planned that, in addition to increased air sorties, an attempt should be made to hold an improvised air strip in Partisan territory where a shuttle service could be organized by the Royal Air Force to bring in a steady flow of material. These plans would also be a major test of the ability of the Yugoslav forces to hold, for a period of months, a territory strategically and centrally placed, from which this flow of military supplies could be distributed to the now strengthened divisions and brigades in Croatia and Slovenia and in the Bosnian regions, sufficiently protected and garrisoned to hold the inevitable

German counter-attacks and penetration. Such was the blue-print of the new plan of military aid.

The three main airfields constructed by the Royal Yugoslav Air Force before 1941, at Sarajevo and Banja Luka in Bosnia, and at Mostar in Hercegovina, were firmly in German-Croat hands and the strength and equipment of the Partisan divisions was not yet of such an order as to capture and hold these urban centres. It was therefore imperative that a secret landing ground must be chosen and laid out in an isolated mountain area, disguised from enemy reconnaissance and protected on the ground.

During the weeks after Fitzroy Maclean's departure such an enterprise was conceived. A broad plateau was selected near the town of Glamoč, embedded in the belt of territory on the edge of the Dinaric Alps, lying on the routes leading from Bosnia to the coast. It was arranged that an experienced British Air Force officer, to be attached to the Maclean mission, would be parachuted to this field to take over the technical responsibility for its construction as an improvised landing ground where it was hoped ultimately to bring in up to ninety air sorties a month. The remaining members of the Maclean mission in Jajce, whom I now joined, decided, according to a prearranged plan with its commander, to set up a sub-mission at the nearest Yugoslav Corps headquarters in the vicinity at Livno which now became the operational military base for the territory. A small party would be quartered in Glamoč itself to organize the arrival of the Royal Air Force group from Malta and to act as a forward radio communications base.

On 16 October the group left Jajce by lorry for Glamoč. It included the new American officer attached to the Maclean mission, Major Linn Farish,* Walter Wroughton, and myself, and took up residence in the market town of Glamoč within sight of the broad field, stretching for ten kilometres between the surrounding hills, which was to be the subject of our attention.

The town had been fought over many times during the previous two years and recently burned to the ground by the Italians. It lay not only on one of the main routes running from north to south, but also on the road running along the watershed of the hills northwards from Croatia towards the river line of the Neretva and the borders of Hercegovina.

* 'Slim' Farish, a good companion, was later killed in a plane crash on a mission into Greece.

We set up our headquarters in the only house left standing. A local town command maintained a military presence amid the ruins of the white stone houses with their blackened chimneys and burned roofs forming a broken and ghostly skyline. Some of the villagers had remained. It was harvest time. The semblance of normal life, in a slow and simple rhythm, continued around us. As we awaited news of the plane from Malta, we settled into the pattern of existence of our neighbours to whom we were a constant object of friendly curiosity. In front of our flimsy cottage, on the initiative of Linn Farish, we installed a bath which had been extricated from the ruins. Our daily ablutions became a highlight of local life. Farish insisted on this ritual being conducted in a military manner, and the sight of him sitting in the tub, naked except for his military cap, became a modest contribution to morale.

In the evening, after the peasants had brought in their ox wagons with the hay, the soldiers of the Partisan *odred*, with their rifles slung over their shoulders, and ourselves in our khaki uniforms, would dance the traditional *kolo*, moving rhythmically in multi-coloured circles.

The plane from Malta never came. The winter weather set in, and the seasonal movements of the German forces began to threaten the lines of communication throughout the territory surrounding us. News, however, reached us that a first consignment of stores had arrived on the coast and Lynn Farish departed to organize the movement of this convoy inland.

I returned to Jajce to await further instructions to the mission, and for information from Cairo where Fitzroy Maclean was negotiating with our General Headquarters, both on the scale of the supply programme and the formal military recognition of the National Liberation Army as an Allied force.

Lack of news from Cairo created an atmosphere of tension in Tito's Headquarters which was not at first clear to me, nor to my brother officers of the new mission. Fitzroy Maclean was making every effort to persuade the British Foreign Secretary, Anthony Eden, who was accompanying the Prime Minister and the British government delegation through Cairo on their way to the Teheran Conference, of the extent and importance of the Yugoslav Partisan movement.

The first promised supplies had arrived by sea, some of them as a result of a buccaneering enterprise by the Americans.* This episode, which was later the subject of a strong protest by Fitzroy Maclean to the American military authorities, merely confused the situation in Jajce which was clouding with suspicions at unexplained delays on the part of the British and Americans in proclaiming any form of recognition, military or political, of the National Liberation movement.

At the beginning of October 1943, just after Maclean's departure, I had a formal talk, as the commander of the previous British mission, with Colonel Velebit acting on instructions from Tito.† Tito wished to convey certain official views to us. The political programme of the National Liberation movement had not yet been considered, as all energies were bent on winning the war. 'But a meeting of inner leaders will in fact be held by the end of the month.' On the question of the King, Tito wished to point out that no official decision or declaration had been made on this subject, and no propaganda had been directed against the King as this was a matter to be decided by the people. Three considerations, however, should be emphasized: as the representative of the Pan-Serb tradition of the Karageorge dynasty, he commanded no support whatever among the Slovenes and Croats. The exploitation of his name by Mihailović had weakened the hold of the monarchy generally, and especially in Serbia. In general, the people had no loyalty towards him.

'The Partisan leadership has *no* plan or intention of immediate social revolution. The prime object is the reconstruction of the country after the war, and it is realized that a revolutionary programme would cause an internal struggle which would fatally weaken the country.' ‡

This conversation had taken place some days after my return from Glamoč. The Partisan leadership would now clearly press for some form of recognition. They had already proclaimed a provisional administration, or a 'war parliament' as one of its members had called it, at Bihać in November 1942. This move, whatever its internal implications, had met with no response either in Moscow or London, but, with a strengthening hold of the Partisan

* The episode of Major Huot, an O.S.S. officer, who later described his one-man operation in a book entitled *Guns for Tito*.
† The following summary is taken from notes made by me on this occasion, and dated 7 October 1943.
‡ From pencilled notes of the author at the time.

movement throughout the country, inevitably a second and more determined step in this direction would now be made.

At Tito's headquarters in the Turkish fortress in Jajce across the river from the British mission, there was much coming and going during these days. As Vlatko Velebit had put it, 'a meeting of inner leaders' was in fact taking place, but no details of their deliberations were revealed to us. On 26 October, however, Tito sent a message to the British mission requesting the acceptance of a Yugoslav delegation to be received by General Wilson in Cairo.

German forces had already occupied the whole Dalmation coastline and the routes to the sea were cut. Winter weather had reduced air sorties by the Royal Air Force to the various missions in Partisan territory to a minimum. Reports reached Jajce that Fitzroy Maclean was waiting in vain to fly back after his talks with Eden and to return to Bosnia. In his absence no one British officer was in formal command of the mission but we acted as a united and friendly committee. In this atmosphere of suspense and inaction our daily relations with the Yugoslav headquarters perceptibly lowered in temperature. The proposed Yugoslav delegation was now nominated by Tito. It was to be led by Lola Ribar as Tito's personal delegate and member of the inner circle of the Yugoslav Politburo; Colonel Miloje Milojević, the second-in-command of the First Division, and one of the leading war heroes of the Army; and Colonel Velebit as liaison officer to the British mission.

We were awaiting the return of Fitzroy Maclean with high level instructions, and had received messages that he intended to parachute back as soon as weather conditions permitted.

Some members of the British mission in Jajce moved back to Livno, with the Yugoslav delegates, and together with our outpost at Glamoč, we proceeded, on our own responsibility, aided by radio instructions from the Royal Air Force in Bari, to lay out an air strip. It was a simple affair, but constructed according to the technical specifications which had been transmitted to us in a series of radio messages. Work began in earnest on 31 October, and was mainly the responsibility of the young engineer officer attached to the Maclean mission, Captain Donald Knight, together with Major Robin Whetherley and myself. The creation of this air base became the centre of our attention, both for the reception of Fitzroy Maclean and, if and when sanctioned, the journey of the Yugoslav delegation to Allied headquarters. A heavy fall of snow complicated our work and increased the tension between us and our Yugoslav companions. A party had been sent to probe the routes to the coast, but the Germans were now in firm control of this belt of territory and our only possibility of establishing communications with the outside world was confined to the Glamoč air strip.

During these days of enforced inactivity, and deteriorating weather, a Dornier bomber with a Croat crew deserted from the German air base at Banja Luka and made a forced landing near Livno. In the joint task of constructing our air strip we had the co-operation of an optimistic Partisan group with the title of Air Force Headquarters under the command of a colonel. We now had an aircraft. Simultaneously with this novel event, reports came in of German concentrations in Sarajevo and Mostar and of advancing troops some twenty miles to the south-east of Livno.

Together with the German occupation of the coast, these reports were the familiar precursory signs of a new offensive most probably aimed at Tito's political and military headquarters at Jajce, and at Livno, and other nearby centres of the present 'free territory' on the Croat-Bosnian borders.

The British headquarters in Jajce across the river Vrbas was now installed in the house of the former German manager of the local chemical factory, and was visited one morning by three Yugoslav Staff colonels. The cold weather had set in and snow descended on the town. Politely I offered our visitors glasses of plum brandy. In the course of a desultory but friendly conversation, one of the Yugoslav officers announced that a German major had just been captured in an ambush, his staff car having been wrecked, his driver killed, and he himself wounded. The Yugoslav colonel added that orders had been given to shoot the prisoner. I suggested another drink, and asked if I could be shown the papers of the German officer. These were tossed upon the table and revealed that he was a member of the German Military Intelligence Headquarters in Belgrade and, in a sense, one of our opposite numbers. I urged that no action should be taken until the case could be raised with the Yugoslav Supreme Staff. A rough argument followed during which our visitors pointed out my unyielding attitude towards any acquiescence in the execution of German prisoners, implying that this had created a gap of understanding between us since the beginning of the first British mission. Tempers rose and further discussion among the brandy glasses was pointless. I sent an immediate message to the Chief of Staff, General Arso Jovanović, with whom I had never been on friendly or confidential terms, and requested an urgent meeting. He backed the attitude of his colonels, and refused my request to hand over the German officer to the British mission until we could evacuate him by air to Italy.

I took the final recourse of seeking a formal interview with Tito himself explaining, as tactfully as I could, that our Intelligence authorities were more experienced at interrogations, that the German officer now in Yugoslav hands might be of very special interest to us both, and that I would give my word of honour as a British officer that the complete report of any such interrogation which might be carried out in Italy would be passed to the Yugoslav command. Tito accepted my proposal without discussion but made one condition. The German must be returned to Yugoslavia after the war for military trial. Perhaps this was only characteristic of Tito's wry sense of humour, and his manner of teaching me a lesson because of my attitude to the whole question of prisoners of war which I had taken up on my own responsibility.

On returning to the headquarters of the British mission, I signalled to Cairo urgently with the details of the captured German officer and the result of my conversation with Tito. An immediate reply was received, instructing me to take charge of this man at all costs. That evening he was delivered to our head-quarters, in a curt and off-hand manner. The rest was now up to us. There was no exchange of dialogue between the prisoner and ourselves. I concealed the fact that I spoke German and there was no talk between us. We asked neither his name nor his identity. He had been stripped of his great-coat and tunic and had been wounded in the arm at the time of his capture. That night we were due to return to Livno for a conference with the Yugoslav delegation at their Corps Headquarters. Together with Colonel Velebit we took our prisoner in a captured German staff car. We put him in the front seat beside the Partisan driver and I sat behind him with a loaded revolver concealed under a raincoat on my lap. We could not afford to lose him in an enemy ambush, and such a precaution was elementary.

On our safe arrival at Livno the two British and Yugoslav groups dined together to discuss a proposal put forward by Lola Ribar that we should wait no longer for the return of Fitzroy Maclean or the arrival of British planes at Glamoč, but attempt a sortie on our own with the captured German Dornier, now painted with Yugoslav rondels, and somewhat inadequately camouflaged in an orchard near the town.

Such an operation presented unusual and obvious complications. We were subjected to a verbal barrage of criticism by our Yugoslav colleagues, eagerly led by Ribar himself, both as to the reluctance of the Royal Air Force to fly in winter and insinuating that the British had no real intention of either receiving a Yugoslav delegation at their General Headquarters in the Middle East or extending formal recognition to the National Liberation movement. A heated argument extended into the early hours. After a separate consultation among the members of the British mission present, I put forward the view that, although the suggested operation itself seemed unreal in its boyish defiance of the technical complications and risks involved, the simple truth was that the prestige of the whole mission was at stake in the eyes of our Yugoslav colleagues. Some wild gesture of this kind should be considered and an attempt made to work it out as far as possible on a professional basis. Indeed the impudent novelty of the plan came as a kind of exaltation after weeks of inactivity and loss of face for which no one, either in the mission or in our Headquarters across the Adriatic, could in any sense be held responsible.

We decided to try out this operation and signalled Bari for authority and technical instructions. Permission was granted. We were given a precise time and course on which to fly to limit the risks of being shot down by our own planes or anti-aircraft defences. Once the plane was airborne from Glamoč, we calculated that we could take on with its machine guns any local hostile aircraft. The peril of the operation was limited to the security of the airfield itself, and to a speedy takeoff to avoid ground attack from the air for a few defenceless moments.

A Dornier carries a crew of three, and there was no space intended for passengers in its thin, narrow fuselage. We agreed among ourselves, Yugoslav and British, to limit the first experiment to two delegates on each side. If the trip was successful, the plane could return to make a second journey.

Late that night the two Croat pilots and their radio operator were briefed by us on the instructions sent from Bari as to the course on which we were to navigate to Brindisi and the timing of our flight. In order to cut down to a minimum the chance of being caught on the ground on Glamoč field, the crew were instructed to fly the plane from its camouflaged hideout near Livno up to the air strip just before dawn on Saturday 27 November. We would travel by lorry an hour earlier and would be waiting for the aircraft to taxi towards us on the air strip, where a small Partisan escort were stationed and scouts posted in the surrounding hills. The pilot was ordered not to cut his engines, and we planned to take off almost immediately after he had touched down.

The group of us gathered, just before daylight, in the centre of the field. I had instructed Walter Wroughton to stand by his radio set in our cottage at Glamoč and to send off a signal as soon as we were airborne. The air strip was a flat path of grass which we had cleared according to specification, but as we had no means of marking adequately its limits, I stood somewhat apart from the others to mark the point of touchdown and to guide in the pilot. He flew in so low that I was obliged to fall flat on my face to avoid being run over, and then ran to join the waiting group which consisted of the party who were to fly to Italy and the other members of both missions. We walked briskly up to the Dornier, whose engines, according to our instructions, were still racing. At the last second, by some instinct, I looked over my shoulder, and saw two objects like small round footballs bouncing a few feet from us and a small German plane diving straight at us. As I flung myself to the ground there was an explosion and fragments flying in all directions. The only risk which we thought we had calculated had befallen us. The attacking Henschel caught us unprotected. We fanned out instinctively across the flat grass, hunted by the plane above us flying in narrowing circles a few feet above our heads and chasing each of us as a personal target while we sought in vain for cover on the vast billiard table of Glamoć field.

The Dornier blew up in a second low bombing run. The ammunition from its machine guns was exploding in aimless directions. One of the British officers was wearing a sheepskin coat. I had a clear picture in my mind of him running near me as we ran from the burning Dornier seeking some cover from which we might make some kind of defence. There was none. Each man was forced to run in short bursts and fall flat as the Henschel skimmed the field shooting at each of us as an individual target. Exhausting its ammunition, the aircraft flew off over the boundary of the hills.

I found myself in a shallow hollow of ground at the edge of the field with three Yugoslavs. We had remained stuck to the earth as the German plane flew back and forth over our heads attempting to train the trajectory of its guns low enough to hit us. The pilot was only able to wound one of the Yugoslavs. Another, the liaison officer from the Corps Headquarters at Livno, had been lying on his back coolly photographing the scene. As I stood up there was no one in sight and no sound except the engines of the stricken aircraft which were speeding up as the fire reached the controls. For a brief moment there was the macabre spectacle of an empty plane moving slowly and directly towards us. After a few seconds the tail fell off and the debris collapsed in a cloud of smoke and flame.

My first instinct was to find Robin Whetherley, the British officer whom I had seen in my mind running beside me. I called and there was no answer. A search revealed no one except the group with whom I had found frail cover. The rest of our party seemed to have vanished. I walked very slowly and alone towards the aircraft with a sudden thought that I had dropped my brief-case, containing secret documents, at the moment of explosion of the first two bombs. Round the smashed Dornier was a circle of bodies. All had been killed instantaneously. The dead included Robin Whetherley, who had never moved. His running had been a hallucination in my mind. Such happenings were not uncommon in war. I had been standing next to him at the moment of the attack and on the other side of me was Velebit, who like myself was unharmed.

With dragging movements, the survivors collected. Among the others missing and lying round the plane were the head of the Yugoslav delegation, Lola Ribar, Donald Knight our engineer officer, and most of our Yugoslav escort. Miloje Milojević was slightly wounded, for the seventh time. We felt impotent and cold. There was no dialogue between us.

At the sound of firing Walter Wroughton had run the mile from Glamoč to learn what was happening. With the help of the local *odred* stationed there we collected the bodies and bore them gently back to the village. The briefcase which had been in my hands at the moment of the attack was in pieces, riddled with bomb fragments. The two pilots had managed to extricate them-selves from their seats at the moment when the Dornier was hit, but the radio operator who had been standing at that second at the top of the narrow steel ladder attached to the plane had been flung headless to the ground.

It was only after the war that a Yugoslav inquiry stated that it was he who had been forced by the two pilots to desert from Banja Luka airfield, and throughout the whole of our operation he had been in radio contact with the German base, thus enabling the mounting of the surprise attack against us. If this is accurate, he must have learned the exact timing of this enterprise, and was a very brave man.*

On returning to our house in Glamoč I sent a personal signal to Maclean in Italy: '27 November. Deakin for Fitz. Plane attacked by Henschel just before take-off noon. Whetherley, Knight, Ribar killed outright by bomb. Miloje wounded. Aircraft destroyed. Am returning Jajce reporting details soonest.'

That afternoon we buried the dead in the village cemetery in a simple military ceremony. The party of survivors travelled by lorry to the Corps Headquarters at Livno where Major John Henniker was temporarily detached from the Maclean Mission. His gentle and perceptive understanding of the shock produced on us by the disaster was to me of incalculable support. The following morning we continued our journey to Jajce.

The death of Lola Ribar was for the Yugoslavs a major tragedy. As the organizer of the university students' movements during the pre-war years, he symbolized both the youth of the National Liberation movement and, as a close personal companion of Tito, he was destined for high office in the future administration of the new State now coming into being. His body had not been buried with the others at Glamoč but was brought back for a ceremonial tribute to Jajce. The British were not invited to the funeral. Bitter accusations were launched against us by certain senior members of the Yugoslav Supreme Staff, accusing the British of mishandling the operation and of failing to provide a fighter escort from Italy – a project which had never been requested and was at the extreme limit of range. I was too empty and cold to argue, but requested an immediate interview with Tito to report to him the details of the tragedy.

In the final planning of the operation, which Lola Ribar himself had pressed with such excited eloquence upon us, I had insisted that, just as I had sought instructions from Italy, he must

* Some considerable doubt has subsequently been cast upon this version.

S

assure me that he had obtained express authority from Tito to proceed with our plan. There was a telephone line working between Livno and Jajce. Ribar had given me such an undertaking. Those members of the Yugoslav Staff who now placed the exclusive blame on the British for the failure of the enterprise had also insinuated that Tito had never been informed in advance. It was for me to deny the word of a dead man and for Tito to accept or reject my interpretation of events. There was no hesitation in his manner. He confirmed that Ribar had informed him in advance and let this be known at once to his entourage. The hostile whispering against us was stilled, and we were left with the scars of failure.

The death of Lola Ribar was not only mourned by his Yugoslav and British companions. Throughout the last two years of long marches and savage clashes, Lola had seldom been without his horse. The animal had always shown strange signs of distress if separated for an instant from its master. It now became uncontrollable and no one could approach it. The instinct of loss drove the horse to frenzy. Some days later, with a wild deliberation, the animal dashed itself to death in a ravine.

During my report to Tito on the Glamoč incident, I had handed him a copy of a message of sympathy from General Maitland Wilson on the death of Lola Ribar and the other members of the Yugoslav party. In this signal the British Commander in Chief in the Mediterranean also expressed the hope that it would still be possible to arrange 'a very early meeting' between Tito's representatives and himself. Tito asked me to send an appropriate reply, which he dictated to a secretary: 'The victims who fell on the plain of Glamoč symbolize our brotherhood in arms. May their sacrifice create a still closer unity between us in our further struggle.'

The tragedy at the airfield was a human disaster, but also related to broad political decisions on the Yugoslav side. Since the end of October the inner political group of the Yugoslav Communist Party had taken the decision to hold at Jajce, as the symbolic capital of the whole movement, a session of delegates from all regional Central Committees of the Communist Party and personalities associated in a common front to proclaim both to the outside world, the internal rivals, the Četniks and the Ustaša, and the passive elements of the population, the forming of a new

provisional authority. A hint of this decision had been conveyed
to me by Velebit in early October and throughout the ensuing
days from all parts of the country columns of delegates were
converging upon the Bosnian capital.

Tito's request of 26 October 1943 that a Yugoslav delegation
should be received in Cairo was related directly to this political
decision, in an effort to force the ambivalent deadlock stemming
from the events of 1941. The British were now implicitly recog-
nizing the military contribution of the National Liberation Army
while still regarding Mihailović as the Minister of War in the
Royal Yugoslav government in London with whom Great
Britain, the Soviet Union, and the United States had formal
diplomatic relations.

The Jajce assembly was designed to set up an independent
national authority in calculated defiance of the international
situation. The mission headed by Lola Ribar had been set up in
the hope that it would be present at British General Headquarters
in Cairo at the moment when the Jajce gathering would proclaim
in formal and public terms the creation of a new political structure
in hostile competition with the King and the Royal Yugoslav
government. The delegation had been briefed for this purpose and
with the intention of seeking British support for this revolutionary
step.

The message of General Wilson contained a direct hint that he
would receive such a delegation in the near future. Unknown to
those of us who were at Tito's headquarters, and as the direct
result of Fitzroy Maclean's conversations with Eden, the Allied
powers at the Teheran Conference had formally recognized the
Yugoslav forces as a military ally, in spite of the patent reluctance
of the Russians to take this step. This was the news which Fitzroy
Maclean was hoping to bring with him, if favourable weather
conditions had permitted his return by air before the disaster.
But the reception of a Yugoslav delegation had now been admitted
on the British side as a result of the Teheran Conference. Its
political implications remained to be faced in negotiations
which would inevitably be initiated when the reconstructed
Yugoslav party ultimately reached Cairo.

In place of Ribar, Tito now instructed Colonel Velebit to head
the new mission, on the eve of the meeting of the delegates of the
whole National Liberation movement who were now gathering in
and around Jajce. The town had been bombed by German

aircraft on the same day as the attack at Glamoč airfield. Their air reconnaissance could not have failed to detect the movement of columns travelling from all regions of the country in the direction of the city. But neither they, nor those of us of the British mission present, were as yet aware of the import of this assembly.

The streets were thronged with eager clusters of delegates, many of whom I recognized from earlier gatherings at Tito's headquarters; the party leaders from Croatia and Slovenia, the members of the earlier political council which had been represented at Tito's headquarters during the previous months representing an embryo and parallel political authority which had been formed at Bihać in the previous November. There were also strange and unknown faces of men and women from other regions.

Next to the small peasant house which had been the headquarters of the first British mission, on the left bank of the river Vrbas cascading through the town, was the hall of the pre-war sports organization (the SOKOL) which had been destroyed by enemy bombing. Masons and carpenters were now feverishly at work to reconstruct this building in preparation for a fateful meeting.

On the evening of 29 November the British mission were informed that the assembly would meet that night. Three of us, accompanied by Vlatko Velebit, were seated in the balcony looking down on the gathering below and facing the platform where Tito and the inner group of leaders were seated. Behind were draped two Yugoslav flags with the red Partisan star in the centre, and between them a massive plaster cast of the emblem of the National Liberation movement.

Throughout the night, as we leaned on the balcony, a series of resolutions was passed and speeches made which proclaimed the setting up of a provisional administration and executive council, in formal rupture with the Royal Yugoslav government in exile, and banning the return of the King to the country at the close of hostilities.

The President of the proceedings, Dr. Ivan Ribar, a gentle and composed figure bearing no marked sign of his grief at the death of his elder son two days previously,* announced the symbolic nomination of Tito as Marshal of the Army. The series of political delegations which followed was embodied in formal resolutions. Those British officers present were aware that a unilateral revolu-

* His younger son had recently been killed by Četniks.

tionary act with wide-ranging historical consequences was being committed which marked the culmination of the Partisan struggle throughout the regions of Yugoslavia of which we had been the only foreign witnesses. We were the silent spectators of the birth of a regime. The implications of this night of enthusiastic and triumphant oratory must be conveyed by us to our superiors.

Typed copies of the formal resolutions passed at this assembly were given to me by Moša Pijade for communication to the British authorities. On the following morning the British mission sent a signal to Fitzroy Maclean, a fragment of which has survived: 'Waiting at Jajce for your instructions. Attended opening anti-Fascist council last night. Am obtaining text of speeches. Meeting sent telegram to Churchill.'

The Jajce decisions were an ultimatum to the Allies to recognize in formal terms the political authority of the National Liberation movement, and although the details would only be known if and when we reached Cairo with the documentary evidence, the significance of this challenge aroused surprised alarm on the receipt of our first signal at British General Headquarters. The following urgent reply came back: 'You should not leave for Cairo until you receive orders from us. Partisan delegation should also not leave until such orders received. Signal of explanation and questionnaire follow.'

We were also informed that a British plane would land at Glamoč at the first opportunity.

Our party set out again – Velebit, Milojević, certain members of the British mission, our bewildered German prisoner who had been bundled to and fro from Glamoč to Jajce. On previous occasions, for the benefit of our German officer, we even went through the sinister-seeming motions of lining up a firing squad. From Livno we moved on to our Glamoč base where Walter Wroughton was maintaining regular signal contact with our forward H.Q. in Italy.

The air strip had been cleared of the wreckage of the Dornier, and only blackened stains in the grass remained.

But we would not be caught again. Special security measures were taken: units of the Bosnian Corps quartered round Livno held strong positions beyond the range of the hills bordering the air strip; trenches were dug on the edge of the airfield and manned with anti-aircraft machine gunners.

The weather had suddenly cleared: cold but bright. A series of technical messages from Brindisi on 2 December instructed us to prepare for the landing of an aircraft on the following morning.

Just before noon we heard the hum of engines. In a single steady circle an unarmed Dakota made one sweep over the field and came in to land as if on a routine practice flight. Wheeling overhead, for a calculated twenty minutes and in covering flight, was a squadron of American Lightning fighter bombers operating on the edge of their range. Their reassuring presence broke the tension of those waiting on the ground. Amid shouts of excitement, as the whooping of an Indian tribe, our group ran towards the plane taxi-ing towards us across the grass. The first to emerge was Fitzroy Maclean. There was a brief exchange of greetings. Our protecting Lightnings were already heading for their base as the party clambered into the Dakota.

Our flight to Brindisi was without incident. The manner of my exit and the closing of my own mission to Yugoslavia seemed a tidy and relaxed counterpoise to its beginning. The 'Typical' mission had arrived alone and dropped into an unknown world; I was leaving in the company of my successor, now in command of a regular and senior mission attached to a recognized Allied force, together with Vlatko Velebit and Miloje Milojević, both proved comrades in arms in a conflict the style and nature of which had formed the familiar contours of our daily lives for the past months.

The German prisoner, Captain Meyer according to his military identity papers, was a more unexpected traveller. His alien presence among us in the aircraft seemed to me to symbolize the whole change in the climate of Partisan war since our arrival. We had at first been the hunted quarry of the Germans in the mountains and river gorges of Montenegro. During the ensuing months our more numerous enemies, the Italians, had capitulated. The Germans were now lumbering in confused strikes against our Yugoslav friends, having lost the initiative in the conflict, increasingly concerned with the shadowy menace of an Allied landing in the immediate future, and of British and American material support to their opponents. The presence of Captain Meyer in our hands represented these changes in the scene. His removal from Yugoslav bondage, the revolution in his status as a prisoner of war, and the realization that he had been propelled out of range of certain death, provoked an immediate and natural reaction.

Voluble and febrile, he sat next to me in the plane throughout our uneventful journey. It was comforting to learn from him, in jerky phrases, fragments of his experience as a military intelligence officer, revealing the frustrated shortcomings of the Abwehr (the German military intelligence) network based on Belgrade. Meyer had been on several missions in Partisan territory, and when captured in an ambush and brought to Jajce he had been on his way to organize German support to the Četniks in the Lika and northern Dalmatia under Pop Djuić – a character not unknown to us by repute – whose source of supply of food and weapons had collapsed with the Italian surrender. Meyer had been in Yugoslavia, as a member of the German community and an intelligence agent, at intervals since 1935. He was a specialist in the section of the Abwehr in Belgrade dealing with captured documents, and in particular of the Četnik movement, whose lines of communication to Turkey and the Middle East he had uncovered, and one mission had taken him to Istanbul working ostensibly as a commercial traveller for refrigerators. I was too tired to show much interest in the details of his story, which would be pieced together by our own counter-intelligence authorities in Italy, but his company on this flight added a note of cheerful incongruity.

Our plane landed at dusk at Brindisi, now one of the two bases from which the Royal Air Force was operating into Yugoslavia and Southern and Central Europe. The crew of young New Zealanders formed part of this special squadron and they must have been members of the same group who had piloted the Halifax bomber which had so neatly deposited us in Montenegro in the previous May.

Fitzroy Maclean was determined to override the local Royal Air Force authorities, whose instructions were limited to the pickup operation from our field at Glamoč to the squadron base in Italy, and to continue our flight non-stop to Egypt. We delivered Captain Meyer to the British security officer awaiting him, and began to talk our way to Cairo. Fitzroy was cheerfully persistent, and presided over our relaxed gaiety. Our first scheme, somewhat irregular in its conception, was to approach the commander of an Italian light bomber squadron, now stationed on their own airfield as Allies, and whose new rôle added a further brief touch of irony to our adventure. Until recently these very planes had been an active nuisance to us. In order to reach Cairo we would have to land and refuel, in Malta, and we urged the commander of this Italian flight to lend us an aircraft to take us on the second stage of our journey. He insisted that his crews were not trained in night flying, and in spite of our comments upon the deeds of the Italian Air Force in the operations against the island of Malta, we were unable to secure his co-operation in our present enterprise. Our young New Zealand crew, already elated by their incursion into occupied territory, had other ideas. Backed by Fitzroy's assurance that he would deal with any disciplinary consequences at a higher level, we took off the same evening and landed unannounced at Malta, where we looted bedding from a surprised British Headquarters and transformed our Dakota into a flying bedroom for the last lap of our journey.

We came in to land at Alexandria at dawn with the sun rising over the desert. Memories were too crowded and confused to form any clear or coherent shapes. Another British officer, Anthony Hunter, was in our party. It was he, together with Major Jones, who had been dropped into Croatia in the previous May to prepare the way for our mission to Tito. He had since been, as part of the Maclean mission, attached to the Yugoslav headquarters in Slovenia, and was coming out to report in detail on conditions in this region, now of increasing strategic importance. Hunter and I had shared the mysteries of early contacts with the Partisans. It was appropriate that we should be again together at the moment of our exit from the scene. He was later killed in the Normandy landings. A special tribute is due to him for his pioneer mission which had been vital to our Yugoslav operations.

At Alexandria we were abruptly integrated firmly and unconsciously into an ordered military society with whose ways we were not easily familiar. We were housed, together with our Yugoslav companions, in a luxurious villa where preliminary staff talks began and reports were made on the latest events at Jajce. Cautious moves were made by representatives of our General Headquarters to define the credentials of the Yugoslav delegation, whose formal mission had only been authorized to initiate talks on military aid.

The next day we travelled to Cairo and dispersed to our individual duties. I returned to my office in the Yugoslav section of the Special Operations Headquarters, to physically familiar surroundings but still detached and divorced from its routine, and in my imagination and thoughts I was still in Bosnia. There was a private mental gap to be bridged and the process was not immediate.

On the morning of 9 December, I received a visit in my office from a very regular staff officer who came with instructions that I should attend a dinner the same night at the British Embassy. I protested that I had no suitable uniform for a ceremonial occasion, and had hardly yet greeted my wife, who was a refugee from Roumania since the arrival of the Germans in her country in 1941, and was working at our military headquarters in Cairo. The officer replied that he had special orders which could not be questioned, but for security reasons he was unable to explain to me the purport of the occasion and that my wife would be included in the invitation. I had been the guest of the British Ambassador on previous occasions, but was surprised at the seemingly urgent haste of the invitation.

At the appropriate hour, and suitably fitted out, I presented myself at the Embassy together with my wife. On entering the spacious drawing-room I found myself not only in the presence of the Ambassador and his staff, but of the Prime Minister, the Foreign Secretary, the British Chiefs of Staff, General Maitland Wilson, and the senior officers of the British Headquarters, Mediterranean, and other gentlemen of formidable rank. The British delegation from the Teheran Conference was on its way back to London and it was suddenly apparent to me that orders had been issued by the Prime Minister himself to summon members of the British missions in Yugoslavia, Greece, and Albania, who might be in Cairo, and to interrogate them in person on the situation in these regions. I found George Jellicoe and Julian Amery among the gathering, both of whom had also arrived by chance from respectively Greece and Albania. We immediately formed a small group of the irregular colonels holding back with modesty from this imposing gathering.

When we passed into the dining-room I found myself for a moment standing next to a tall and distinguished bearded figure in the uniform of a Field Marshal. It was Smuts. 'And what do you do?' I was asked. I could only reply, 'I think that I am some sort of a bandit.' Smuts gave a wink. 'So was I once,' and we took our places at the dinner table.

Later that evening we returned into the Embassy drawing-room where staff officers had prepared operational maps of the

Balkans on the wall. To my trepidation I suddenly realized that this was a military occasion. Late into the night, and without time for reflection or ordered thoughts, George Jellicoe, Julian Amery, and myself were ordered by the Prime Minister, each in turn, to make a personal report on the situation in the territories whence we had come. To me this was the bridging of the gap, in the most unexpected of circumstances and surroundings, and I have no recollection of what I said.

The Prime Minister was staying at the villa of the resident Minister attached to the British Mediterranean Command, Mr. Casey. The following morning Fitzroy Maclean, Ralph Stevenson the Minister to the Royal Yugoslav government, and myself were summoned to Mr. Churchill's bedroom for a further examination of the whole Yugoslav situation, which had a special and acute political bearing. Fitzroy Maclean had already reported personally to Mr. Churchill on the state of relations with Tito and the Partisan movement, and the present meeting was designed to survey the whole delicate question of the position of Mihailović and the Royal Yugoslav government in view of our plans to increase substantial military support to Tito. A decision would have to be made at Cabinet level as to whether or not we should face the political implications of our recognition of the Yugoslav National Liberation Army, and to what extent, and to consider the consequences of such action on our formal diplomatic relations with the Royal Yugoslav government.

Mr. Churchill was concerned that the first-hand evidence of Četnik collaboration with the enemy was sufficiently strong for him to propose to his government that the whole position regarding British relations with the Yugoslav King and his administration in exile should be revised. They had now moved expectantly to Cairo in case the situation warranted their direct intervention in the affairs of their country. There was even talk that the King himself might be sent on a daring mission to Serbia.

For nearly two hours the Prime Minister interrogated me as the officer mainly concerned with interpreting the evidence derived from captured German and Četnik documents concerning the links between Mihailović and his commanders with the Italians and Germans. It was a miserable task.

The questions were pointed and searched out every detail within the range of my knowledge, and as I talked I knew that I was compiling the elements of a hostile brief which would play a decisive part in any future break between the British government and Mihailović. It was a formal occasion, and there was no personal or private dialogue.

The same evening Mr. Churchill invited me to dine at the villa of the Minister of State. The relentless questioning was resumed into the early hours.

On this occasion, the Prime Minister gave instructions that I should personally convey to King Peter of Yugoslavia the summary of the conclusions which the British had now reached in regard to the position and strength of Tito's movement and the degree of collaboration between Mihailović and our enemies. Mr. Stevenson gave a private lunch at which the King, his English aide-de-camp, and myself were alone present.* It was perhaps characteristic of Mr. Churchill that he would entrust to his subordinates such tasks for which they themselves bore a direct responsibility. It was an unpleasing form of testing evidence, but it was a simple and tidy manner of proving the point once he as Prime Minister had accepted it.

I was received by the King with a shy and dignified courtesy. Neither of us appreciated our lunch. I was not at my best, but conveyed without trace of misunderstanding that those of us who had been attached to Tito's headquarters were not only convinced that his forces were engaged in successful combat with the Germans, but that the followers of Mihailović and his subordinate commanders were, in varying forms of intimacy, in contact with the latter. I made it plain also that the substance of my remarks had already been conveyed to the British Prime Minister.

The young King permitted me to curtail our discussion, which was more a monologue on my part. He asked me politely to call on him again. The occasion never arose.

It had been agreed at the Teheran Conference that the Soviet government would now send a military mission to Yugoslavia as the result of a formal British proposal in this sense. At the beginning of January 1944 I was informed that such a mission was on its way by air through Teheran to Cairo and that it would be my responsibility as head of the Yugoslav section in our General Headquarters to receive the Soviet mission and arrange for its

* Fitzroy Maclean relates that he also was present for the same reasons, on a separate occasion. (*Eastern Approaches*, op. cit., p. 404.)

dispatch to Yugoslavia. Fitzroy Maclean had now returned to join Tito. The circumstances of this direct Soviet presence in Yugoslav affairs were intriguing. Although the detailed evidence was published much later, I was aware, from fragments of conversation with the Yugoslav leaders, that they had awaited in vain for several weeks in early 1942 the arrival of just such a Soviet delegation at the very spot near Žabljak where we ourselves had parachuted in May 1943. It was an ironic pleasure that it would now fall to me to be responsible for the safe dispatch of such a mission more than a year later.

While preparations were being made for an appropriate banquet to receive our Soviet guests, I went to the Royal Air Force airfield at Heliopolis to receive the mission. It was not a jovial meeting. The one-legged commander, General Korneev, had been very airsick on the journey and found the exchange of courtesies beyond him. The banquet which we had organized was cancelled, and the Soviet delegation were escorted to a villa placed at their disposal in the suburbs of Cairo.

It was our intention to send this mission by plane to land at Glamoč in the same manner as we ourselves had left the previous month, but by a strange quirk of fate the Germans had reoccupied the area almost at the same time as the arrival of the Soviet mission to Cairo. We were therefore obliged to inform our Russian colleagues that their departure would be delayed until the Yugoslavs had recaptured a suitable landing ground. General Korneev refused to believe my explanation, and treated me contemptuously as a colonel and therefore of subordinate rank. He insinuated that the British were dissembling and there was some sinister interpretation in the delay which I had announced to him. I repeated the simple fact that there was no airfield in Allied hands where his mission could land, but that I would take full personal responsibility to parachute his whole party without delay in the region of Tito's headquarters. General Korneev had lost a leg at Stalingrad. This ended our conversation, and it was some days before contact was renewed with our Soviet guests. Tempers in the meantime had cooled, and those of us of the Yugoslav section of the British General Staff organized a detailed briefing of the Soviet mission regarding the situation in Yugoslavia as interpreted by us in the light of the latest intelligence, not only from the Maclean mission and the outlying British liaison officers with the Partisan forces, but also, in general terms, the situation as we saw it from the British mission with Mihailović and our officers attached to his commanders in Serbia. Our briefing, which I conducted in a formal military manner, was a plain description based on our own operational map on the wall of our Head-quarters. The junior officers of the Soviet mission took busy notes while I was talking, and no questions followed the conclusion of my speech. But, in some strange way, I sensed that my inter-pretation of Yugoslav affairs had made little impression upon the Russians, and that they had the conviction, possibly as the result of their own instructions, that the British were playing a highly subtle game; that we had little confidence in the military value of the Partisans of Tito; that our support of his movement had some subtle and devious political design; and that the only resistance group of any military significance was in effect that of Mihailo-vić, whom we now affected to ignore as a decisive factor. I had no confirmation at the time of this intuition, but recently I had occasion to meet a member of this delegation, who admitted to me that I had not made the wrong general assumption.

In the event, the Soviet mission to Tito was dispatched without incident by glider to a new landing field and their adventures form part of another record.

'Typical' mission had been disbanded at the end of September 1943. Its members were absorbed into that of Fitzroy Maclean, and in the course of the ensuing months scattered to other duties.

Wroughton was eventually posted back to Cairo. 'Rose' re-turned to his farm settlement in Palestine. Campbell was sent to his unit. Starčević joined the Yugoslav Communist Party, but at the end of the war returned to Canada. I was appointed head of the S.O.E. Yugoslav section in Cairo, and, on the transfer of British General Headquarters to Italy, was seconded to the staff of Mr Harold Macmillan, the Cabinet representative for the Medi-terranean theatre, and attached as adviser to a newly formed command, Balkan Air Force, under (then) Air Vice Marshal William Elliot, with headquarters at Bari. This body assumed responsibility for all operations by land, sea, and air into Central and South-Eastern Europe.

Personal memories of an isolated parachute operation to the mountains of Montenegro were overlaid by daily concern with the general pattern of the war in these regions.

Twenty years later I made a journey back in place and time, with the baggage of confused and fragmented recollections. In the stillness of the woods and upland slopes surrounding the peaks of Mount Durmitor the ghosts of a battle and of the past deeds and fate of men among whom a small band of outsiders had been tossed abruptly from another world, appeared in fragile silhouettes.

They were not at once apparent, in the still grandeur of the scene. No visible signs of the terrors and the exultation of a distant conflict. The trees had grown and their dark green patches hid the scars of fierce encounters, and the eternal snows of the mountain crests obliterated the traces of our marching.

The mental effort to recall a shared encounter was diverted by images of the present. Distant memories were at first blocked by the imposing weight of the landscape.

One May morning my wife and I left the small town of Žabljak, now re-built, and bustling on market days. The only sign of war was the memorial to the dead of the Durmitor partisan detachment erected in the shape of a stone peasant house, the walls lined with the names of the fallen and close to the onion cupola of the Orthodox chapel, built in a previous century to mark a Montenegrin victory over an invading Turkish column.

The events of twenty years before were submerged in vestiges of endured history. Peasants told us that the Greeks had come in distant past to this barren land, and left their tombs in the neighbourhood.

We found these monuments grouped in a mound, a bare vantage point on the vast grazing lands stretching southwards from the base of Durmitor. Here we halted for a space of hours, seeking to decipher the inscriptions.

These showed that the dead who lay here were of Bogomil origin, medieval Christian heretics eschewing both Catholic and Orthodox creeds, who had founded an independent kingdom in Bosnia, the last Balkan stronghold to fall to the Turks. Their capital at Jajce had been our own headquarters twenty years earlier, and the Bogomil chapel with its graffiti beneath the Turkish fortress our refuge from enemy bombardment.

The Embattled Mountain, rising above the horizon, had been also their refuge from the Turkish invasions of the lowlands to the west.

Behind the burial ground, falling away to the south, were the dark waters of a lake where local legends tell that, on one night in the year, devils with wings rise and dance in weaving circles: the Manichaean servants of the Antichrist of Bogomil eschatology.

In the western distance lay the scattered houses of a settlement, as all Montenegrin hamlets not grouped in close clusters but each standing aloof from its neighbour with steep sloping roofs reaching towards the ground.

Behind the buildings a grove of trees surrounding a well marked, according to lore, the spot where a Turkish aga had been slain in his tent by a Montenegrin girl dragged to share his couch during one night of bivouac.

As we lay among the tombs, in the warm summer air, convoys of laden carts, drawn by oxen, halted to rest briefly at this point, by the habit of centuries on a track linking the scattered settlements. The peasants seemed barely aware of our alien and incongruous presence, exchanging short ceremonious greetings of their kind; at times asking with quiet courtesy whence we came, and gently taunted by us into guessing. One veteran of Salonika informed his companions with the authority of one who knew that we could only be French. England was to them an unknown land, some submerged Atlantis beyond their horizon.

Our identity was soon to be revealed in an unexpected manner. There appeared at our vantage point a family group: the father walking in front, a small boy on a horse, and the wife following behind. They were on their way to school in Žabljak. The party halted at our side. The man stared in a minute of silence and then in one Serbian phrase thus addressed me. 'You are the man who came out of the wood.' Further talk revealed that as a boy of eighteen he had been a member of the partisan patrol sent to find us at the moment of our landing. Recollection came in an instant.

After excited and tumbling talk, we were invited to his house the following night. Our comrade was a member of the local Žugić clan, about seventy souls grouped in settlements strewn around us. A pre-war member of the Montenegrin Communist Party, Tomo Zugić and his family had been marked down by the Italian occupying authorities in 1941. His house had been used in the previous year as the secret meeting place of the party committee for Montenegro which Tito had attended. The farm and the surrounding buildings had been burnt by an enemy patrol and reconstructed after the war by the local authorities with a plaque to commemorate the party session.

The family feast in our honour, lasting till dawn, was the epitome of a private world: the women folk in black and standing; the men grouped at rough wooden tables; the roasted sheep borne in from hidden kitchens, glasses quickly filled with wine and brandy, the mournful gusla, the single stringed harp of the mountaineers, plucking in the corner the epics of the past and improvised songs of the partisan war. The low-ceilinged room was ornamented by three tapestry portraits: Czar Alexander of Russia, King Nikola of Montenegro, and Marshal Tito, an interweaving of unbroken traditions in a simple logic of history, which were represented by the fate of one mountain family.

When the Italians burnt this house, a rebel hideout for generations, Tomo and members of his family escaped. There remained the patriarch, a hundred years old and blind, and one daughter-in-law, who was tied up and taken to Žabljak.

Peasants rescued the old man from the burning ruins, and carried him to the left bank of the Tara gorges to the east. Here lay the historic frontier of Old Montenegro facing the Turkish pashaliks of the Sandžak and Albania, where for centuries the men of the mountain stood guard against their incursions. Tomo's father had kept many watches above the sheer plunging precipice. He died on reaching this place.

Our meeting with Tomo was the first of such encounters in the region of the Embattled Mountain half a generation in time since a British party had landed there. The sum of these recollections provoked the creation of this record.

NOTE ON SOURCES

(a) BRITISH

The nature of this study does not permit of a formal bibliographical list.

The only relevant printed sources, which contain certain material, are those papers written by the author.

(i) 'Britain and European Resistance' delivered at an international historical conference held in Milan in March 1961 under the auspices of the Italian National Institute for the History of the Movement of Liberation in Italy (published in their proceedings Lerici editori, Milan 1961).

(ii) 'Britain and Yugoslav Resistance' read at a seminar on Britain and European Resistance 1939–45 held at St. Antony's College, Oxford, in December 1962. (A limited edition was published in roneoed form.)

(iii) 'The First British Mission to Tito' (May to September 1943): a paper read at an international conference held at Sarajevo, by the Historical Institute of the Yugoslav People's Army in June 1968 on 'Neretva-Sutjeska 1943' – the two major Axis operations against the main operational group of the Yugoslav National Liberation Army. (This paper is published in Serbo-Croat in the collective proceedings of this conference.)

The general reader will find little profit in consulting these papers, which are not only difficult of access, but largely incorporated in the present work.

Unpublished sources relating to these events in the official British government records are not yet available to scholars, and I have, with some hesitation, not awaited their expected release in 1972, for reasons outlined in the Preface.

(b) YUGOSLAV

The main printed source of official Yugoslav documents relating to the Second World War is the series (still to be completed) of reports and telegrams to and from Tito, the Supreme Staff and its delegates on missions, the material which has survived from the records of all military units from Corps to local detachments. Much valuable Axis documentation (in Serbo-Croat translation) is contained in this invaluable collection at present consisting of some one hundred and

T

twenty volumes. It is published by the Historical Institute of the Yugoslav People's Army in Belgrade under the title *Zbornik Dokumenata i Podataka o Narodnooslobodlačkom ratu Jugoslovenskih Naroda* (collection of documents and facts relating to the National Liberation War of Liberation of the Yugoslav People).

I have noted below references only to the essential documents relating to this account, and, on the same principle, from other printed Yugoslav sources.

NOTES

PROLOGUE

1. The above, and subsequent, messages from Yugoslav printed sources quoted in this section relating to the first contacts between the British and the Partisan movement are to be found in *Zbornik*, op. cit., vol. II, 9 (Belgrade 1960).

2. Article in *Sutjeska* vol. II, p. 486. This work, in six volumes, contains articles and extracts from diaries by Yugoslav participants in the battle on their reminiscences. The contributors range from Tito himself and senior members of the Partisan leadership to the rank and file. It contains invaluable historical material, and has been widely used by the author, bearing in mind that the evidence which these volumes contain is presented charged with the emotions of a national epic, and written to mark the celebrations held on the spot in 1958.

3. ibid., vol. V, p. 553.

4. Vladimir Dedijer, *Diary* (in Serbo-Croat), vol. II, p. 296. Written in notebooks at the time and a prime historical source.

5. National Archives, Washington. Records of the German First Mountain Division. The author has consulted these files for incorporation in a future study in detail of the war in Yugoslavia, in which precise references will be noted.

6. ibid.

7. Pero Krstajić *Durmitor in the National Liberation War and Revolution* (in Serbo-Croat), (Titograd, 1966), p. 279 ff. An indispensable account of local events by one of the political leaders in the Durmitor district.

PART I

1. See the quotation from Marko Miljanov 'Primjeri Čojstva i Junastva' in General Nikoliš's remarkable paper 'The Wounded as a moral and operational factor in the Fourth and Fifth Enemy Offensive'. (Sarajevo Symposium July 1968, published in Neretva-Sutjeska 1943 (Belgrade, 1969).)

2. Dr. Djordje Dragić, *Partisan Hospitals in Yugoslavia*, pp. 43 ff. and *passim* (English edition, Belgrade, 1965).

3. Lindsay Rogers, *Guerrilla Surgeon* (London, Collins, 1957), pp. 157–8.

4. Paper by General Nikoliš, op. cit., p. 12.

5. See the paper by Colonel Eliezer Katan, 'The supply of medical

stores to the Central Hospital and operational units during the Fourth and Fifth Offensives', Neretva-Sutjeska, 1943 (Belgrade, 1969).

6. Report in *Zbornik*, special volume of medical documents, Book One, Document No. 82.

7. V. Dedijer, op. cit., vol. II, pp. 358–9.

8. Tito, *Selected Military Works*, p. 168 (Belgrade, in English translation, 1966).

9. Tito, *Vojna Dela*, vol. VI, p. 290 ff.

PART II

1. Vojmir Kljaković, 'Great Britain, the Soviet Union and the rising in Yugoslavia in 1941' (in Serbo-Croat), Vojno Istoriski Glasnik, May-August 1970, No. 2, p. 72, Note 7.

2. Tito, *Vojna Dela*, I, p. 105.

3. ibid., p. 231.

4. Quoted by Kljaković, op. cit. There are several drafts of the telegram. 'Against the others' is obscure. One text reads 'against the one and the other', i.e. Germans *and* Partisans.

5. V. Dedijer, *Tito* (Serbo-Croat edition), pp. 308–9.

6. For details of these talks see Jovan Marjanović, 'Četnik-German Talks at Divci Village' (in Serbo-Croat). Extract from the proceedings of the Faculty of Philosophy, vol. X, 1, Belgrade, 1968.

7. Kljaković article, op. cit., p. 98, Note 126.

8. E. Wisshaupt. 'The Rebel Movement in the South-East' (unpublished manuscript in German Nuremberg Trial Documents No. NOKW 1898). The author was the archivist attached to the Headquarters of the German Army Group South-East at Salonika.

9. *Zbornik*, vol. III, 4, p. 150.

10. ibid., vol. II, 2, p. 377.

11. ibid., p. 432.

12. ibid., p. 441 ff.

13. ibid., 3, p. 76.

14. ibid., pp. 104–5.

15. ibid., pp. 66–8.

16. ibid., p. 42.

17. ibid., p. 114.

18. ibid., p. 131 ff.

19. ibid.

20. M. Pijade, *The Fable of Soviet Aid to the Yugoslav National Rising* (French edition, 1950), p. 37.

21. V. Dedijer, *Tito* (Serbo-Croat edition), pp. 106–7.

22. This message is dated 5 March, which cannot be correct as printed. Atherton reached Foča on 20 March. It is also possible that

'Supreme Staff' could be interpreted in the sense that Atherton had met Pijade, a member of the Supreme Staff, on 14 March at Žabljak. A series of radio messages, of which this is one, are quoted in an article by Pero Morača, 'Relations between the Communist Party of Yugoslavia and the Comintern, 1941–1943' in the Jugoslovenksi Istoriski Časopis, 1969, No. 1.

23. Morača, ibid., p. 106.

24. *Zbornik*, vol. II, 3, pp. 345–6.

25. ibid., p. 390.

26. V. Dedijer, *Dvevnik*, vol. I, p. 122.

27. *Zbornik*, vol. II, 3, p. 366.

28. V. Dedijer, op. cit., vol. II, p. 97, under the date '10 February 1943'.

29. *The Trial of Draža Dragoljub Mihailović*, op. cit., p. 387.

30. *Zbornik*, vol. II, 9, p. 159.

31. Pavle Pavić, 'From Canada to the Partisans' (in Serbo-Croat), Četrdeset Godina, vol. VI, pp. 281 ff. A collective work of articles commemorating the twentieth anniversary of the 1941 Rising.

32. *Zbornik*, vol. II, 9, p. 162.

33. ibid., vol. X, 9, p. 264 note.

34. ibid.

35. ibid., vol. II, 9, p. 283.

36. ibid., p. 287

37. ibid., p. 291

38. ibid., p. 287 note (quoting the signal).

39. ibid., 10, p. 293.

40. W. S. Churchill, *The Second World War*, vol. V, p. 410.

41. ibid., p. 411.

42. ibid.

INDEX